Security at the Borders

Borders are not just lines in the sand but increasingly globalized spaces of practice. This is the case in West Africa, where a growing range of local and international officials are brought together by ambitious security projects around common anxieties. These projects include efforts to stop irregular migration by sea through international police cooperation, reinforcing infrastructures at border posts, and applying new digital tools to identify and track increasingly mobile citizens. These interventions are driven by global and local security agendas and by biometric passport rules as much as by competition between local security agencies. This book draws on the author's multi-sited ethnography in Mauritania and Senegal, showing how border security practices and technologies operate to build state security capacity, transform how state agencies work, and produce new forms of authority and expertise.

PHILIPPE M. FROWD is Assistant Professor in the School of Political Studies at the University of Ottawa. His primary research interest is in the transnational governance of security in West Africa's Sahel region, with an emphasis on interventions around irregular migration and border control. His research draws on ongoing fieldwork in West Africa, with his current work focusing on transit migration in Niger. Dr Frowd is a past winner of the Northedge Prize (2013), and his writing has appeared in *Security Dialogue* (2014), *Millennium* (2014), *International Political Sociology* (2017), and the *Journal of Ethnic and Migration Studies* (2017).

Security at the Borders

Transnational Practices and Technologies in West Africa

PHILIPPE M. FROWD
University of Ottawa

CAMBRIDGE
UNIVERSITY PRESS

CAMBRIDGE
UNIVERSITY PRESS

University Printing House, Cambridge CB2 8BS, United Kingdom

One Liberty Plaza, 20th Floor, New York, NY 10006, USA

477 Williamstown Road, Port Melbourne, VIC 3207, Australia

314-321, 3rd Floor, Plot 3, Splendor Forum, Jasola District Centre, New Delhi - 110025, India

79 Anson Road, #06-04/06, Singapore 079906

Cambridge University Press is part of the University of Cambridge.

It furthers the University's mission by disseminating knowledge in the pursuit of education, learning and research at the highest international levels of excellence.

www.cambridge.org
Information on this title: www.cambridge.org/9781108455213
DOI: 10.1017/9781108556095

First published 2018
First paperback edition 2020

A catalogue record for this publication is available from the British Library

ISBN 978-1-108-47010-0 Hardback
ISBN 978-1-108-45521-3 Paperback

Cambridge University Press has no responsibility for the persistence or accuracy of URLs for external or third-party internet websites referred to in this publication, and does not guarantee that any content on such websites is, or will remain, accurate or appropriate.

Contents

Figures

Acknowledgements

This work would not have been possible without the belief, encouragement, investment, and sacrifice of colleagues, friends, and family.

I would not have had the peace of mind, travel funding and free research time that enabled this book to become a reality without the financial support of the Social Sciences and Humanities Research Council of Canada, the Government of Ontario, Privacy International, and McMaster University's Institute on Globalization and the Human Condition. The fieldwork I carried out for this book also depended on the goodwill and patience of key contacts. For my fieldwork in Mauritania, I would like to thank Ahmedou Ould-Abdallah, Saleh Cheikh, Amadou Sall, Cheikh Saad Bouh Camara, Mohamedou Moktar, and Martin Ewi. In Senegal, the help of Ababacar Diop, Abdoulaye Niang, Koli Ndiaye Cisse, and Fallou Kebe was essential. I am also greatly indebted to all of my interlocutors for having shared their stories with me.

I am particularly thankful for the immense intellectual and personal support I have received from academic mentors and colleagues. Peter Nyers's composed assurance and belief in my project from the very start helped me to confidently develop the ideas that underpin this book. It was a privilege to count on the advice and support of J. Marshall Beier and Diane Enns during my time at McMaster University, where I was lucky to count Mike Di Gregorio, Liam Stockdale, Jennifer Mustapha-Vanderkooy, Mark Busser, Katie Winstanley, and Jessica Merolli as colleagues. It is a great privilege to have had the tireless support of friends, colleagues, and advocates like Can Mutlu, Christopher Leite, Adam Sandor, Cédric Jourde, Mark Salter, Miguel de Larrinaga, Debbie Lisle, Heather Johnson, Vicki Squire, Ben Muller, and Paul Saurette. Thanks also go to the countless discussants, panel chairs, and audiences who helped challenge and refine the ideas developed in this book at numerous conferences, workshops, and invited talks.

Thanks are due to the outstanding editorial team at Cambridge University Press and to the two anonymous reviewers. Maria Marsh's enthusiasm for this project was contagious, and Abigail Walkington's logistical support smoothed the process of turning a manuscript into a book. Their efforts meant that my sweat and tears were limited to the process of writing and rewriting. All errors remaining herein are mine and mine alone.

I am also grateful to SAGE and to Oxford University Press. Portions of Chapters 1 and 5 appear in 'The Field of Border Control in Mauritania', which was published in *Security Dialogue* (2014), and Chapter 6 is a heavily expanded version of 'The Promises and Pitfalls of Biometric Security Practices in Senegal', which was published in *International Political Sociology* (2018).

Finally, I am thankful to my parents, Andrew and Yacine. This book is dedicated to them as well as to my wife, Rabya, and daughter, Lena, who both missed me on too many evenings and weekends. This book simply would not exist without their love and patience.

1 | *Introduction*

[Sahel] states have insufficient operational and strategic capacities in the wider security, law enforcement and judicial sectors (military, police, justice, border management, customs) to control the territory, to ensure human security, to prevent and to respond to the various security threats, and to enforce the law (conduct investigations, trials, etc.) with due respect to human rights. This is notably reflected in the insufficiency of legal frameworks and law enforcement capacity at all levels, ineffective border management, lack of modern investigation techniques and methods of gathering, transmitting, and exchanging information, as well as obsolete or inexistent equipment and infrastructure.

– European External Action Service, Strategy for Security and Development in the Sahel

Combating irregular migration and establishing comprehensive migration management systems can contribute to enhancing national and international security and stability.

– African Union, African Common Position on Migration and Development

[The biometric identification system] will enable us to build a biometric database of all inhabitants in Mauritania, which will enhance national security and establish key statistics needed to take decisions about targeted and effective developmental policies.

– Mohamed Ould Boilil, Minister of Interior (2011–2013), Mauritania

A Study of Borderwork and Security in West Africa

Borders are anxious places. In West Africa, and particularly in the Sahel, these anxieties crystallize around supposedly weak states with

porous borders, factors which we are told provide safe haven for terrorism, facilitate migrant smuggling and trafficking, and lead to weak
governments that neither know nor control their mobile populations.
As global fears around these cross-border threats increasingly shape
West African security agendas, a variety of corollary security practices
have gained prominence. Transnational forms of intervention, involving global as well as local actors, have sought to reinforce security provision in the Sahel zone – traditionally one of various flows of goods
and people – and make it better legible to the security imperatives
of Western states and also of post-colonial states in the region. The
former seek assurances about migration and fear the mobility of terrorism and drugs from the south, while the latter prioritize the reinforcement of their security apparatus and welcome external investment in it. This book looks beyond costly and headline-grabbing military interventions to examine the raft of practices such as hardened
migration control, biometric citizen identification, reinforced airport
security, capacity-building and training of police forces, and a greater
emphasis on migration management policy. These security practices
have been extensively documented and debated in their European and
North American contexts, particularly since 9/11. Yet there is a dearth
of analysis of African cases and histories despite the rapid and unique
proliferation of such security practices around borders, migration, and
identification. In Mauritania and Senegal, the focal countries for this
book, practices of border security take the form of police cooperation
around irregular migration, the reinforcement of infrastructures such
as border posts, and the deployment of new digital forms of identification and border screening. As post-colonial states continually seeking better knowledge of and authority over their territory and population, they are increasingly turning towards new security technologies and transnational relationships that blur the lines among policing,
border security, diplomacy, and development. Contemporary border
security in West Africa is so much more than patrolling a line in the
sand.

What is at stake when Spain decides to help Senegal patrol its maritime borders? What effects do new identification technologies have on
the role of the state's various security agencies? How does European
Union (EU)-funded construction of border posts tie in to the development of state sovereignty in Mauritania? Answering these questions
requires us to pay close attention to the increasingly transnational

governance of security in West Africa. This book builds on the critique made by Hameiri and Jones (2013) that security studies has not taken trans-boundary threats seriously, noting that 'as the identified range of threats and risks has widened, so have the actors and instruments tasked with managing them' (3). This book investigates a wide range of actors and tools, from beyond the world of security in many cases, who pursue security with the broad aim of assuring what Scott (1998) calls legibility – the idea of better knowing, seeing, mapping, and controlling nature and society. In what ways do West African states pursue this legibility? What kinds of actors, practices, knowledges, discourses, and objects are implicated in this pursuit? Tackling these questions and more, this book investigates the everyday practices behind new border security practices and relations adopted by states in West Africa. Its main argument is that we should understand border security in West Africa as a social and technical practice underpinned by the pursuit of state capacity. The book argues that the technocratic practices of African and international security professionals, often working together, show the role of knowledge and technology transmission in the reshaping of state structures in West Africa.

Examining border security in West Africa more closely is significant for four key reasons. First, it highlights the nature of borders as heterogeneous spaces that are policed well within and beyond the territorial line. Controlling borders therefore brings together a diversity of actors, practices, and knowledges across space. A major contribution of this research is therefore to shift the emphasis to border*work* as a practice that includes migrant interception patrols at the territorial border as much as the biometric enrolment of populations elsewhere. Focusing on borderwork in West Africa pushes us to think about practices of inclusion and exclusion throughout territory, and contests the view of African borders as simple lines that are poorly drawn colonial holdovers, hampering the continent's development. Second, these practices of border security create new relationships and linkages between security actors. Investigating these can tell us about the functioning of international organizations, how actors work together on the ground, how policies are implemented in practice, and how practices of border control in sub-Saharan Africa have stimulated the formation of new transnational military and police relations. The research avoids attributing excessive smoothness to security and showcases the material underpinnings of security, contesting the idea of security as a 'finished article' anchored in discourse alone. By investigating the level of practices through an ethnographic approach, the research shows the complexity of state formation in Africa and the divergent desires and outcomes of the multiple agencies that operate around African borders. The research is therefore instructive about new modes of global governance, since it probes the multi-scalar forms of practices of legibility and the work that goes into maintaining them. Third, border security in West Africa incarnates and sometimes transmits particular culturally situated ways of doing border control. Where there is no direct intervention, there is emulation or adaptation of global standards. This shows us the pedagogical underpinnings of security. Security practices are transmitted through the circulation of best practices: the adoption of biometric technology, for example, draws on a desire for integration (at a regulatory level) and emulation (at a normative level). Fourth, relationships in border security point to a broader rapprochement between security and the re-articulation of state authority. Capacities to enact surveillance are intricately associated with the consolidation of state power and the security that flows from it. Security is therefore a technique (of justification) and a technology (that enacts the border and produces identities). The research deepens our understanding of the security politics of a region that has so far been under-researched from this standpoint, where border security practices lead to new clusters of authority and expertise. This focus on the interface of security and technical forms of statebuilding also points us to a renewed focus more on the technical, small-scale, and bureaucratic forms of security in Africa that go beyond conflict yet remain within the realm of security: advising, training, piloting, equipping, and reforming in the security sector.

This book is focused around three cases developed in Part II. None of these cases is a rigidly bounded case study, as each of them tackles a cluster of projects and forms of cooperation that are truly transnational and interlinked. The first case relates to one of the least studied European border security interventions in Africa, off the coasts of Senegal and Mauritania. While this case is commonly seen as part of the 'externalization' of the EU's frontiers in the name of deterrence, the chapter emphasizes the new and often enduring security institutions and relations that emerged in response to the spike in migration to the Canary Islands in the late 2000s. While numbers of migrants wax and wane, a primarily Spanish-led police cooperation effort has intensified and produced new technologies and practices. The second case captures an ongoing trend in the construction of new border infrastructures across West Africa and the Sahel, focusing on EU-funded efforts to rebuild Mauritania's border post infrastructures. With border security cooperation in the region focused on bringing states up to international standards, this case is focused on how such interventions align a multitude of external actors, shape the technological practices of local partners, and actively promote new forms of understanding borders and security. The third case in this book is focused on how seemingly peripheral technologies such as identification tools operate as border security tools through practices of airport security and registration systems. With a focus on visas, screening systems, passports, and national ID, this case focuses on the ways that technologies bear visions of modern and efficient bordering yet in doing so actively shape inclusion and exclusion.

The prompt to which each chapter in this book responds to is: 'What are the everyday security practices around borders in West Africa, and what underpins them?' This project is concerned with the governance of borders in practice but also the logics and technologies that underlie it. As such, it asks questions about actors (human and non-human), their practices (discursive and material), and the subject and state formations that result from this politics of security and surveillance. This brings forward two more specific questions, which are tackled in the two sections that follow this one.

Border Security Assemblages

A quick glance at the myriad border security projects in West Africa shows a wide range of actors involved, often with convoluted and conflicting mandates and priorities. Projects intended to curb migration may also include public sector financial management objectives, while development actors can find themselves as uneasy bedfellows with local police forces. My first major concern in this book is therefore to map out what actors enact border control in West Africa, and how we can theorize their relations, roles, and arrangements. The overarching question is 'Who are the actors involved in the transnational governance of borders in West Africa?' This question probes who does what, but first demands a definition of what the governance of borders actually is. While it is (relatively) easy to find out what agencies are involved in border control in West Africa, it is much harder to identify who does what, with who else, why, and under what logics. This book's conceptual approach therefore begins with an institutional topography exercise, focused on the spatial and organizational arrangement of actors and their practices. Examining this governance necessarily implicates contemporary debates about what borders are, who governs them, and what borders are made of. The linkages between border security, migration management, and national identification come into clearer focus. Once this analytical scope is established, the question of 'who' can be better answered, through mapping and a critical analysis of relevant actors. First of all, we have to ask 'what are borders', and what practices are associated with them. Second, we have to theorize the actors themselves.

This book is founded on a view that borders are not simply 'lines in the sand' – this much is clear to the traveller confronted with a checkpoint, to the migrant intercepted at sea, and to the bureaucrat organizing a border management workshop. Borders are not simply territorial demarcations, but sites of governance oriented around inclusion and exclusion, which are necessarily of selective permeability. In this book, I use the issues of mobility and migration to critically examine the emergence and dynamics of security arrangements in West Africa. To speak of borders means defining them, and to speak of governance is to mean talking about a particular type of practice. What is a border? The contemporary consensus on borders in social science points out the proliferation, multiplication, hardening, and displacement of borders. This is in opposition to the 'geopolitical trajectory' (Walters 2002) of thinking about borders, which would see them as geographical barriers along which inside and outside or justice and anarchy rest. The consensus in question emerges from a shift from thinking about borders to a more social constructivist view concerned with border-*ing* as a process. The primary question, once we establish the nature of borders, is to understand what the process of bordering is. This is where the concept of 'borderwork', from Chris Rumford (2008) is particularly useful. Rumford uses 'borderwork' to refer to practices, by states as much as by citizens, that build and maintain borders: these can be control-oriented practices like patrolling the sea and training border guards but also include practices that undermine control like police corruption or the agency of irregular migrants. Borderwork is a broadening move that highlights the *practices* – routinized actions – of actors. Borderwork, then, helps us to appreciate the very making and unmaking of borders.

The heterogeneous and disaggregated empirical terrain of border control in West Africa demands a re-articulation of how we theorize the organization and agency of border control actors. How can we understand a space in which the actors and technologies combine in such unexpected ways? To do so, this book draws on the concept of *assemblage*, which has emerged across the social sciences as a means of understanding the complexity of social and material relationships. There is a vast range of approaches to assemblage, each driven by specific philosophical assumptions and methodological commitments. This book holds that *assemblages emerge from the assembly and disassembly of social and technical components without a single dominant point of organization or direction. These forms of assembly are potentially transnational, can be durable, and can contain stronger sets of connections and alliances between particular elements.* This view of assemblage is drawn from and informed by a range of social science visions of this blending of the social and technical. It is influenced in part by work on actor-network theory (ANT) as well as perspectives on 'agencement' from Gilles Deleuze and Félix Guattari. ANT is not – as the name might suggest – a theory in the sense of a coherent explanatory set of propositions. Rather, it is a methodological approach and conceptual toolbox. Its origins lie in the sociology of scientific knowledge and in science and technology studies (STS), in work on the social construction of technology and more generally in the post-structuralist trend towards emphasizing social construction. STS, according to John Law, argues that 'science is a set of practices that are shaped by their historical, organisational and social context [and] scientific knowledge is something that is constructed within those practices' (Law 2004: 8). The thrust of social studies of technology writ large is that knowledge is the product of a social-technical system that involves human – and most strikingly, non-human – actors. Michel Callon (1986) draws our attention to the dynamic and continually fluid nature of networks, and he rejects the narrow view of the social as a discrete scene independent of the material, tangible world. ANT's understanding of assemblage is itself unfixed, but most definitions stress heterogeneity, dispersed agency, and an emphasis on materiality.

Looking beyond the lab, we see that ideas of assemblage hold considerable promise for the analysis of international politics. In particular, this sensibility has been helpful to point out the variable disassembly of the state and its multiple engagements with the international space (Sassen 2006). Drawing heavily from Sassen's view, Abrahamsen and Williams (2016) define assemblages as 'diverse hybrid structures that inhabit national settings but are stretched across national boundaries in terms of actors, knowledge, technologies, norms, and values' (251). The analytical focus on the politics of scale, heterogeneity, and practices of (dis)assembly helps to better understand the social and technical elements that make up the international. When applied to border control actors, the idea of assemblage pushes us to think about their organization as a *socio-technical* one. This means that human and non-human actors are considered equal in their capacity to make things happen (the ANT principle of 'generalized symmetry') and that the 'social' is only as durable as the consistently bundled and unbundled sets of associations that make it possible. These kinds of associations – assemblages – are the main lens through which the organization of border control actors is articulated here. More specifically, this enables a specific focus on the often decisive role of technologies of border control that one encounters, from expanding police databases all way to faulty night-vision goggles. Each of these tells a story, and assemblage helps to link it to broader concerns about agency in the field of security. This project's approach to the *socio*-technical generates a concern with the mapping of actors' self-understandings, knowledges, perceptions, histories, and relations.

Security Culture and State Transformation

In addition to thinking of the place of border control actors in the international space, this book focuses on the knowledges that underpin their work and the ways they succeed and fail in transforming governance in African states. The second question on which this book centres are 'What are the logics through which borders have become sites of security intervention in Africa, and what impacts do these interventions have?' The question of 'logics' is fraught: it raises a further question about the relationship between ideology, practices, and norms. In this book the idea of logics works to tackle the way that discursive as well as material factors are involved in shaping the meaning of security, and to highlight the way that 'security' justifies and is subtended by corollary practices of care and control such as surveillance, development, and capacity-building. The question also seeks to get at the underpinnings of border control and to shine light on what makes border control practices seem self-evident.

The book therefore builds on the discursive view of security articulated by securitization theory and practice-oriented approaches to theorize the emergence of security knowledges. Both of these approaches see security as something that is enacted socially through an intersubjective process of construction. However, more sociological approaches drawing on Foucault's and Bourdieu's sociologies embed the context of securitization better. If we think of security as emerging from the struggles of security professionals rather the elite discourses alone (Bigo 2012) we necessarily draw attention to what Bourdieu (1977) calls the 'doxa' of a field. The term doxa refers to practical, tacit knowledges inherent in particular actors' perceptions of a field. But security knowledge is more than this – it is also the standards, norms, best practices and objects that transmit understandings of how security (and by extension border control) should be done. These 'cultures of border control' (Zaiotti 2011) not only force us to examine the sociological questions of *who* controls borders, but also the question of how 'security' as a concept is constructed. Border control normativities are reflected in policy documents and official pronouncements (Schengen Borders Code, Frontex Risk Assessments, ICAO Doc 9303) but also in actors' practices and relations.

Establishing contending knowledges as a key element of security practice, this book turns to the question of how they move, given that transnational security practice brings together actors who may have radically different understandings of how border security should look. This book therefore thinks through the movement of security knowledge, emphasizing the fact that knowledges – usually moving from north to south – are durable and able to act at a distance to dictate specific ways of doing border control. To do so, it draws on the concept of the (im)mutable mobile from ANT, which describes 'convenient packages that hold together and maintain their coherence even when they are moved, enabling them to be effective in a variety of settings' (Kendall 2004: 65). This focus on the mobility of knowledge relies on an understanding of the international space as a collection of transnational spaces between which objects and ideas can move with varying degrees of success. This mobility of security knowledge is in turn underpinned by practices of intervention that focus on statebuilding, which often targets very specific parts of the state whilst excluding others. Global and local actors associate security to state capacity, which means the ability of states to enact sovereignty through surveillance of territory and population. This refers us back to Scott's concept of legibility, which ties in to long-standing techniques inherent to modernity such as surveillance, development, and bureaucracy. The desire for legibility, Scott argues, stems from a 'high-modernist' worldview that predominates in states' grand projects: it thrives in the joining together of Enlightenment will to order and a weak civil society. Legibility is essential as it points us to the issue of *capacity*: the technological ability, willingness, and sensory capability of a state. This process of intervention makes security about modernization, which is a mode of reinforcing the state (through knowledge practices and equipment) as well as a mode of risk management (Hameiri 2010) that depends on the prevention of state failure and ties security intervention to a whole domain of administrative rationalization and state effectiveness. In the context of the Sahel region, where state power is often sporadic, intervention is intimately tied to improving the state's ability to act and see comprehensively.

Assessing the effects of border security intervention requires an attentiveness to state transformation. A major objective running through this book is to show the extent and limits of the state transformations achieved by border security interventions. With border security programmes continually associated with state capacity – by African and European actors alike – one might consider the reinforcement of borders to be a fundamentally political project of realigning state sovereignty towards a more complete Westphalian model. However, this book seeks a more granular approach to state transformation that questions whether international intervention is as influential as it seems in achieving wholesale reform of the state. Although the book finds that some programmes are very effective in terms of transmitting methods and approaches to security, many others are purely symbolic. Rather than focusing on spectacular or violent forms of intervention, this book focuses on the cultivation of new forms of governance within and beyond the state.

International Political Sociology as Research Method

The research underpinning this book is guided by an interdisciplinary international political sociology (IPS) approach, which draws on critical social theory and embraces the empirically minded insights of sociology and anthropology. The research is multi-sited, and uses multiple research sites in two countries to provide a variety of forms of evidence to sustain the broad theses of the book. The IPS approach, favouring an emphasis on the interlinking of macro and micro, encourages me to identify global security norms as much as minutely local practices, and how webs of meaning and practice link the two together. To achieve this goal, I use a combination of policy analysis and an ethnographic approach combining semi-structured interviews and participant observation. Using an IPS approach, I am seeking a precise empirical application of the broad conceptual underpinnings in 'assemblage'.

What is international political sociology? It is not a discipline, but rather an attempt to bring together streams of thought from IR and sociology as well as social and political theory. Didier Bigo and R. B. J. Walker (2007: 4) argue, in their editorial for the initial issue of *International Political Sociology* in 2007, that the project is 'a political sociology of problems that are identified by the overloaded term international'. Careful to insert many caveats and considerations into this argument, they call for an approach that privileges disciplinary openness, a rethinking of the scope of analysis away from the states system and an orientation to *practices* (broadly defined). Mark Salter (2007: 49–50) summarizes the approach clearly in the same issue of the new journal, stating that

International political sociology balances theoretical analysis and empirical material, with an overtly political but not prescriptive frame. By focusing on the system of policies, practices, and discourses that govern particular intersections of the local, national, and global, international political sociology explores the intersections of power and authority that shape the governance of these specific institutions. By eschewing a strict linguistic turn, international political sociology examines not simply the language of politics but also a wider notion of discourse including practices, institutions, and authorities.

IPS therefore makes use of methodological tools from sociology and conceptual tools from modern social theory to critically bring to light practices not confined to any scale of global or local. By drawing on ANT, this book also keeps an inductive orientation to the social world it examines. An IPS sensibility, by this attention to the non-discursive elements of power and authority, is open to the role of materiality emphasized in assemblage approaches.

This book takes up the task of being political without being prescriptive, finding critical energy in the task of mapping actors, practices, and knowledges. Bruno Latour's (2004: 246) view of the critic as 'not the one who lifts the rugs from under the feet of the naïve believers, but the one who offers the participants arenas in which to gather' is key to the sensibility of this project. In this project, that idea has been put in motion by a method of criticality through exposition. In other words, this project's criticality comes from the exposition of everyday practice and its conditions of emergence.

Putting an IPS approach into practice means examining particular sites of the international at which global and local forms of authority combine in interesting and unexpected ways. My selection of Senegal and Mauritania as sites of fieldwork is driven by the fact that both countries display the kinds of security relationships that triggered my interest: they maintain close cooperation with the EU on the management of irregular migration, their security agencies have border security and anti-terrorism high on their agendas, and they have both launched initiatives to better 'file' citizens and foreigners using biometrics. These countries are also part of a dynamic geographical context in the Sahel region has seen its strategic importance (and integration into security arrangements) growing. While Senegal and Mauritania are not unknown quantities in the migration literature (Choplin 2008; Kunz, Lavenex, and Panizzon 2011; Anderson 2014a, 2014b), the security angle on their border control and identification policies merits deeper exploration given the growth of security cooperation in the Sahel region. For example, in very few academic publications (e.g. Brachet, Choplin, and Pliez 2011) can any mention of Mauritania's emerging biometric security apparatus be found, even though this technology is rapidly gaining ground in Africa.

Although this book uses the terminology and shorthand of statehood, my main research approach in this project is to undertake what George E. Marcus (1995) calls 'multi-sited ethnography', which emphasizes the possibilities of drawing global conclusions from in-depth studies of multiple and diverse research sites. Marcus establishes a six-point typology of types of multi-sited ethnography: follow the people, follow the thing, follow the metaphor, follow the plot/story/allegory, follow the life/biography, or follow the conflict.

This book sets out as an attempt to 'follow the people', but the princi-ple of generalized symmetry – between human and non-human actors – of my methodological approach has meant that focusing on people alone was not a viable strategy. Following the 'actors' or the 'life', in my case, means to trace how they interact with each other, and how they understand their (border)work and relations with other actors. Following the 'thing' means taking into account the agency of objects (i.e. their effects). Following the 'story' and the 'metaphor' means to uncover the webs of meaning (in text, in interviews) that make partic-ular concepts such as 'border management' be used in particular ways.

The IPS approach relies on an analysis of the social dimensions of international politics and lends itself neatly to methods that reveal the sociological realities of different sites of the 'international'. That being said, this project does not rely on a gruelling twenty-four months of participant observation in one site, as might be the convention in the anthropological studies in which ethnography is the prevalent method. Rather, it draws on five months of research across multiple sites. This book is not so much ethnographic as much as it is a project driven by an ethnographic sensibility (Wedeen 2009) to an ongoing and reciprocal engagement with the subjects of research. This is also a multi-*scalar* project: it examines the global and local and their complex imbrica-tions: by studying similar actors in multiple sites, it does not seek to recreate the coherence of just one set of actors, or make generaliz-able conclusions. The use of an ethnographic sensibility in this project reflects its purpose – to provide a view of a patchwork of actors – and as such the contours of the sites of study come into relief as much from the breadth of participants in the study as from the depth of interaction with them.

This project is built on my ongoing engagement with professionals of migration management and border security in West Africa, notably in Senegal, Mauritania, and Niger. The empirical content of this book builds on fieldwork carried out over five months in Senegal and Mau-ritania during 2013. During this time I undertook fifty-seven semi-structured interviews with personnel involved in border management, from policymakers to officers trained by various capacity-building activities. I also spoke to migrants, smugglers, embassy security liaisons, staff in border management organizations, EU diplomats, think-tank leaders, development workers, police officers, customs directors, soldiers, and gendarmes. While most of these interviews are

cited throughout the book, others not directly cited inform my conclusions. In order to procure the critical mass of interviews required, I
used a snowball method based on existing contacts. This methodology
was particularly revelatory about *relations* between actors as it tapped
into pre-existing relationships between research subjects, and gave me
crucial insights into the formal and informal perceptions actors had of
each other. At times, I sought out and obtained multiple interviews with
the same interlocutors to re-examine existing material or to compare
perspectives of different actors. Throughout, I tried to remain aware
that research subjects wear multiple 'hats' (and straddle public and
private), and should not be pigeonholed by the role in which they are
formally interviewed. In some cases, providing information to interviewees about (non-secret) activities that other interviewees and organizations were doing was a productive strategy. This enabled me to
establish some form of credibility and expertise to integrate more easily into the security field. The research process of focusing on different
'sites' of the international was particularly fruitful. In both Senegal and
Mauritania, I was able to visit the main international airports and was
also lucky enough to be invited to workshops on counter-terrorism in
Mauritania and on privacy in Senegal. These specific spaces, and many
more, shaped my thinking about the importance of spaces where fields
of practice 'meet'.

The IPS approach is not only an analytical approach, but also one
that draws on the commitments to researcher self-reflexivity of the
thinkers (such as Bourdieu) whose research methods have given it intellectual coherence. To consider the practicalities of the research underpinning this book, and my own place within them, is itself instructive
as to the nature of the object of study and the nature of *field*-work
itself. Indeed, a self-reflexive approach dictates that the nature of the
social world I accessed be considered in order to better understand the
relations of power, race, economics, and more that enabled and con-
strained the research. Most importantly, the question of accessing relatively closed research contexts is crucial as it fraught with relations of
power in which the researcher sometimes – not always – has the upper
hand (Koch 2013). In order to gain access in my case, I used a variety of
formal and informal contact methods and forms of expertise. Formal
means were most useful when approaching expatriate security professionals. Emails, LinkedIn messages, formal appointment requests,
and phone calls to office numbers worked best. I used formal scripts

from my then-university's research ethics office out of diligence but also because they bore a university logo that might confer some credibility to my requests. Reaching Senegalese and Mauritanian security actors, who tended to use formality as a deflection mechanism, meant using more informal and sometimes fortuitous means. In Mauritania, I drew on contacts of the families with whom I stayed, taxi drivers who happened to be gendarmes seeking extra income, and even stumbled upon security professionals' relatives in the small Mauritanian diaspora in Canada. A chance encounter at a development NGO in Nouakchott also yielded a major breakthrough: I was put in touch with an in-house finance professional who had been invited to speak at a training workshop on counter-terrorism destined for Mauritanian security forces. This person showed me a list of attendees – which included senior state security actors – and put me in touch with the workshop organizer with a view to letting me in to the workshop. Once I established my credibility (university business cards came in handy) with the workshop's organizer, I was invited to sit in for the two weeks. This guaranteed me face time – rather than the endless wait for an authorization through formal channels – with key Mauritanian border security actors. In Senegal, similar chance encounters were instrumental in ensuring my access to senior police officials. A casual conversation with another customer in a passport photo studio gave me the chance to carry out in-depth ethnographic fieldwork at Dakar airport: the person happened to be a close friend of the director-general of the national police, who authorized my research.

The research process is necessarily shaped by the level of financial and temporal resources available to the researcher. It is also determined by the patience and generosity of potential research subjects. In many cases, those I sought out throughout the research process effectively had very little reason to cooperate. Stonewalling is a frustrating experience but it is also quite revelatory for the research process. Instead of dismissing interviewees' reticence as a lack of a data point, or as an inferior research outcome, I preferred to see it as being equally valid and revealing as an interview. In Western cases, the dynamics of state openness/closure can be understood as responses to differing mandates and types of organizational accountability (Belcher and Martin 2013). In the African context, stonewalling is particularly indicative with regards to the fragmentation of the state: so much about obtaining access is down to the individual nature of the person being sought, and in the

absence of formal codes about how to handle requests for information, there is considerable administrative discretion. The key point is
that there is no central logic dictating access, and that access is highly
personalized which in turn makes the encounter with the respectable
(or threatening) researcher essential.

The research process is therefore dependent on framings of
researcher subjectivity. Gaining interviews meant straddling a delicate
researcher identity balance between 'fitting in' and 'fitting out'. As a
mixed-race person with origins in West Africa, my cultural knowledge was crucial to gaining interviewees' interest. In Mauritania, my
appearance meant I was often mistaken for a local, which initiated
countless small conversations that later became valuable networking
encounters yielding interviews. My own 'tacit knowledge' of social
graces and cultural rhythms was also essential in gaining trust, even
though I remained a relative outsider to the fields of practice I was
studying. That being said, demonstrating expertise of border security
issues and terminology was essential, and the number and nature of
interviews changed when I was able to demonstrate expertise in border management: interviews came thick and fast, and were no longer
terse and official, becoming candid, relaxed, and often brutally honest. However, 'fitting out' was also strategic: in some cases, stressing a
'Western researcher' identity afforded me more patience and the benefit of the doubt (such as easier access to secure buildings) on countless
occasions when a local researcher would have been rebuffed.

I have used a discourse analysis methodology to dissect actors' self-
understandings and institutional contexts, what kinds of cooperation
activities they undertake, as well as how they understand borders and
the security-development nexus. My interviews used throughout this
book have leveraged the 'hearsay' knowledge of my interlocutors based
on interactions I observed (Watkins, Swindler, and Biruk 2009), which
ensured that interlocutors also served as rapporteurs for their own
social contexts – spaces of interaction outside the interview that were
hard for me as a researcher to directly access. The multi-sited ethnographic method helped me be attuned to how actors often unknown to
each other share a common policy outlook (Shore and Wright 1997).
The aim of this project is to chart broader understandings and motivations that actors have, and I place particular emphasis on disjunc-
tures, tensions, and disagreements between the policy analysis and the
interviews I undertook. While I eschewed a formal qualitative coding

method, I have remained consistently aware of the metaphors, social conflicts, stories, and objects arising within and across texts.

Précis of the Book

Part I of this book lays out the conceptual framework with empirical context. Chapter 2, following this one, begins sketching the theoretical framework in relation to borders, developing the idea of 'borderwork assemblages'. The chapter advances four 'theses' about borderwork as a practice: it is abstracted from territory, networked and cultural, constructed and performed, and creative of order. The chapter then traces the 'who' of borderwork in West Africa, providing a tentative mapping of some of the actors who shape the region's borders. The chapter builds on actor-network theory to argue that we must think of the topography of border control actors as akin to *assemblages*. This allows us to grasp the heterogeneity of the social and the emergent forms of association – involving human and non-human actors – that make borders the way they are. Chapter 3 describes the epistemic and cognitive logics that undergird borderwork. Drawing on work on the discursive and professional construction of security issues, it argues that security and its knowledges are produced sociologically through the interactions of security professionals but also through the influence of the objects that mediate these relations, stand in for them, or act to shape security itself. The chapter goes on to theorize that knowledge moves between 'sites' of the international space, and argues that these knowledges move, with varying degrees of success, through exemplars, emulation, and pedagogical intervention. The chapter concludes that the interventions that move security cultures draw on a worldview that privileges state capacity and modernization but have limited effects in terms of the scope of state transformation.

Part II of the book allies the conceptual frame to three empirical cases. Each chapter is true to a socio-technical sensibility and uses objects, sites, forms of knowledge, or discursive tropes as devices to show competition or claims to expertise, to illustrate the practical movement of security knowledge, and to compare policy goals and documents to actual practices and routines. These factors (such as boats, tropes, landscapes, visa systems, and more) are used as narrative devices to illustrate the webs of social relationships that they represent, mediate, or bring about. Chapter 4 opens with a view of the 'crisis' of

irregular migration from Africa to Spain, this chapter examines the
ongoing legacy of the Spanish and EU response, in partnership with
Senegal and Mauritania, to the spike of migrant arrivals to the Canary
Islands between 2004 and 2007. The chapter pushes beyond the literature on EU borders, which focuses on their 'externalization'. Rather, it
draws on the everyday practices of Spanish-African police cooperation
to show the limits of European knowledge and technology, the shift in
cooperation beyond migration questions alone, and the effects of intervention on the internal politics and struggles of Senegalese and Mauritanian security professionals. The chapter focuses on key human and
non-human elements such as Spanish security attachés in its embassies
in West Africa, the vehicles used for joint patrols between Guardia
Civil officers and the Senegalese security services, a regional communications platform for real-time coastal surveillance, and the symbolic
role of police decorations and certificates. Each of these tells us about
the competing cultures that flow from everyday practices, and more
generally about the growth of 'border control' as a category broader
than only the management of migration. Chapter 5 looks at an EU-
funded project, administered in part by the International Organization
for Migration (IOM), to build new border posts in Mauritania. This
project reflects concerns that emerge late in the previous chapter: a
growing amalgamation of migration with other national security concerns such as terrorism. The chapter reiterates the utility of a socio-
technical lens on border control, stressing the assemblage-like nature
of the competing actors involved in the project but also importance
of materials in the transmission of approaches to border control. The
chapter maps out the project's effects through key objects and practices: for instance, the border posts are considered as infrastructural
technologies that serve to enhance the state's capacity for legibility in
remote areas, while the IOM's entry–exit tracking system incarnates
the successful transmission of a technicalized, risk-based border screening culture. The chapter also focuses on the use of workshops and training as tools for generating consensus and routinizing security practice.
Chapter 6 builds on the focus on databases and registration tools in
earlier chapters, and argues that biometric technologies – which use the
body for identification – have become increasingly popular amongst
security professionals in both Senegal and Mauritania due to their
promise of swift, modern, and traceable border controls. Challenging
the existing literature on biometrics, which sees them through the lens

of privacy violation or risk profiling, this chapter focuses instead on the ideational and practical elements of biometrics in the African context. The chapter argues that key to biometrics' success has been their potential to make populations in the global south legible and traceable for the first time. The chapter argues that a 'biometric ideal' about their effectiveness has emerged through a set of images, discourses, and best practices produced by international organizations and emulated by African states. The chapter draws on participant observation at the Dakar airport and interviews with security actors in Senegal and Mauritania as well as citizens and activists excluded from biometric enrolment. The chapter concludes that while the biometric ideal may propose certain truths about the functioning of biometrics, resistances from security actors and beyond often foil these deployments and undercut their claims to improve state capacity.

The book's conclusion serves as a summation of the main conceptual and empirical arguments. Beyond this, it addresses the questions of power and inequality that arise from the research, arguing that although the relations at play in borderwork practices are not neo-colonial they remain riven with relations of inequality and domination. It also recapitulates the argument about state transformation: that border security intervention is not so much about a remaking of the state as it is an activity reinforcing Western-style sovereignty. At the heart of this pursuit, the chapter argues, lies a negation of politics: first because interveners frame their activities as technical and managerial, and second because interventions depoliticize border security through a focus on humanitarianism. The chapter reaffirms the importance of critically interrogating the sources of authority for state-making in the global south, and notes that local agency should complicate claims about the neo-colonialism of intervention.

PART I

2 | Borderwork Assemblages in West Africa

At the most general level of abstraction, a border is the space in and through which an inside relates to an outside. Borders are ubiquitous, and the concept – as it is used in the social sciences and humanities – applies to myriad phenomena from cultural frontiers to the territorial border of the nation-state. Over the past century or so, borders as well as frontiers, borderlands, barriers, and demarcations have become a primary object of study across a range of disciplines. International borders, the focus of my present study, should not be seen only as lines drawn in the sand (or on a map): they have become complex spaces of governance. However, there are some unresolved lacunae in the study of borders. First of all, there is a solid range of work in critical border studies that speaks of the proliferation of borders and of various forms of bordering. However, there is correspondingly little work that tackles the various practices that stretch the border – whether biometric ID or internal immigration controls – with the same conceptual vocabulary. Secondly, there has only recently been concerted attention given to the global governance of borders, particularly beyond the West, and to how the 'who makes them' question of borders can be addressed. In particular, this question is largely not applied in the context of the global south, and there is a general dearth of work on borders and bordering in sub-Saharan Africa in critical border studies.

In three moves, this chapter theorizes the 'what' of borders and the practice of bordering, highlights the 'who' of borders by looking at the diverse set of actors around borders in West Africa, and proposes a conceptual lens – assemblage – attuned to the complexity of the making and unmaking of borders. First, we can understand a range of border-related security practices in West Africa to be forms of *borderwork*. I establish that there is a virtual consensus in the literature that borders are not simply 'lines in the sand' but rather complex and socially constructed functions that encompass diverse practices well away – spatially and temporally – from the territorial line. Critically assessing the literature on African borders, I move on to argue that the concept of borderwork is a way of capturing these diverse enactments of the border. I propose four 'theses' on borderwork: it is usually referential of the traditional geopolitical border but can be exercised well away from it; the control it implies is carried out by networked actors who bring particular normative understandings of how borders should be controlled; borderwork is a construction as well as a performance of the border; and finally, borderwork is an order-making activity. In the second major section of this chapter, I ask 'who does the borderwork?' and identify an indicative range of actors involved in borderwork practices in West Africa. These include United Nations agencies, development actors, police forces, embassies, and criminal networks, amongst others. Although the mapping is organized by actor for clarity, it points us further: to the range of strategies, ideas, funding arrangements, and projects that go into making borders work. Faced with the complexity of the landscape highlighted there, the third section of this chapter goes on to suggest that the idea of 'assemblage' best captures the arrangements at hand. Drawing from actor-network theory ideas of assemblage, I conclude that this approach provides us with several analytical payoffs: an attention to the heterogeneity of the social, avoiding rigid views of global organization; an account of power relations; a sensitivity to non-human agency; and a more nuanced view of space and scale. Although 'assemblage' is intended to capture complexity and is potentially infinite, the book's three more deeply empirical chapters in Part II (Chapters 4, 5, and 6) show the contours and limits of assemblages too. The chapter concludes by recapping the argument and tracing a preliminary link between borderwork and security knowledge that is developed further in Chapter 3.

What Is Borderwork?

African borders tend to conjure up visions of artifice: colonial lines drawn on a map, dividing populations, imposed from outside by colonial powers. While this is an incomplete story of the demarcation of today's African states, we should extend the premise of the question, which border *isn't* artificial? This book examines a vast range of practices that have precisely the artifice that makes borders in West Africa. These do not always take place at the border line as conventionally understood but help to enact the border or shape and extend its effects.

The IOM's construction of border posts in Mauritania, the Spanish patrol missions in Senegal or the uptake of biometric ID in both countries relates to some degree to territorial demarcations and national sovereignty, but each also calls into play much broader phenomena and much more complex decisions about inclusion/exclusion and security/insecurity. By thinking about these practices as *borderwork* activities, we foreground the ongoing labour of policing the border that is performed by an international consultant, an ID card database system, or a national census project. In this section, I answer the 'what' question about the practices and policies with which this book is concerned: can we identify and name a practice that is common to the types of border construction, migration management tactics, and national identification we see across West Africa?

The concept of *borderwork* provides a set of useful conceptual tools with which to understand the actors and practices around borders today. In using this term, I am drawing on Chris Rumford's (2008: 1) description of borderwork, which originates in 'a concern with the ways in which borders are becoming generalised throughout society' as opposed to sitting at the edge of territory. Rumford's view of borders echoes an assumption that is central to recent work in critical border studies: that the border is socially constructed, multi-faceted, and not fixed either spatially or temporally. It also stresses the seemingly obvious but crucial point that borders require various forms of *work* to be put into place. Borders are nothing without the work of security professionals but also the labour (physical, emotional, or otherwise) of migrants and citizens. They are complex, networked spaces in that their governance and effects are enacted and often felt far from the site of territorial demarcation. Think of the ways that European visa policy is assembled in Brussels but also felt at the Italian embassy in Dakar (see Zampagni 2016) or the use of British-designed risk-analysis methods for the analysis of border crossers' data in Mauritania. I use this idea of borderwork, with its connotations of ongoing labour, in much the same way Madeleine Reeves (2014: 6) does in her work on the spatial extent of the state. Reeves uses the term to describe how the Central Asian state comes to make territory not just known but also 'integral' to itself. This argument is applicable beyond the Central Asian context in which Reeves's work is grounded, particularly as West African states use border security as a means of knowing their territory and population but also harnessing and managing them better.

These conceptions of 'borderwork' I draw upon fundamentally challenge the idea of borders as linear, strictly territorial markers of inside and outside. This more traditional view is epitomized by my somewhat caricatured view of African borders above, but also in places such as the earnest vision of space in the 1907 Romanes lecture given by Lord Curzon of Kedleston (once Viceroy of India). Discussing the theme of *frontiers*, Curzon spoke of borders as a 'razor's edge on which hang suspended the modern issues of war or peace, of life or death to nations' (Curzon 1908). In doing so, Curzon assumed not only the border's nature as an outward looking defence mechanism but also the centrality of the state and its security as the border's central corollary factors. Curzon's view of the border typifies what William Walters (2002) calls the 'geopolitical trajectory' of thinking about borders, the hallmark of which is a focus on state power and its projection. Later interventions in the nascent research area of border studies, such as J. R. V. Prescott's (1965) *The Geography of Frontiers and Boundaries*, maintained this 'positivist epistemology' about borders (Vaughan-Williams 2009). This positivist epistemology is most importantly reflected in the essentially Westphalian assumptions about sovereignty made in this literature, most important of all being the role of borders as limits of the national ambit. This geopolitical view of borders is certainly not irrelevant, as testified by the militarized nature of Mauritania's eastern border with Mali, but it does not give a complete picture.

This 'geopolitical' view of borders as fixed lines, demarcating tracts of sovereign political territory, is increasingly challenged by developments in the academy and beyond. In response to a growing complexity of borders, and owing to the influence of post-structuralist thought, the primary source of evolution in border studies since has been a focus on modes of bordering. To focus on *modes*, and on *bordering*, is to assume that borders are produced in a complex way, i.e. that they are socially constructed, and to understand this process of making borders as one of many performed strategies of power. R. B. J. Walker's (1993) seminal intervention highlights the embeddedness of the inside/outside dichotomy in political thought – highlighting the linkage between inherited political imagination and the empirical reality of a world in which concrete practices starkly reflect binaries of statism/cosmopolitanism. John Agnew's (1994) caution against a 'territorial trap' similarly questions the neat alignment of state and territory, contesting the reification of the state as a hermetic container preceding society. With this 'critical geopolitics' came an attention to the various practices – modes of bordering – that sustain geographic representations: cartography, mapping, discourse, culture, and more. With a growing concern for transnational flows and the speed and connection brought about by global interconnection, calls for borders – theorized as social processes – to be decoupled from territory (Paasi 1998) abound. In sum, a renewed ontological emphasis on social construction has increasingly animated border studies.

The perspective on borders developed for this book brings together the insights of both European and African border studies. This book emerges from a dissatisfaction with some of the foci of each bundle of literature and seeks to draw on their relative strengths. Much work on African borders has tended to focus too heavily on the literal frontiers, borderlands, boundaries, and peripheries of African states (e.g. Kopytoff 1987; Asiwaju and Adeniyi 1989; Herbst 1989; Nugent and Asiwaju 1996; Khadiagala 2010). These contributions are often heavily drawn from anthropological approaches that centre on the effects of the territorial fixity of borders and build on an early normative concern with African borders' artificiality and the forms of social and political life they cut through. More recent work on African borders has continued to focus on similar issues, such as border disputes (Kornprobst 2002) or boundary maintenance (Seymour 2013). Yet, in more recent contributions to this field, there has been what Coplan (2010) denotes a theoretical turn, with a focus on the impacts of globalization (Mbembe and Rendall 2000) and the consideration of the potential mismatch of territory and political authority. Recent work on borders and borderlands has pointed to emerging forms of statehood such as 'non-state orders' (Hüsken and Klute 2010), 'margins' (Raeymakers 2012), and sovereignty entrepreneurs (Hollstegge and Doevenspeck 2017). Conceptual innovation has not jeopardized the empirical rigour of studies of borders in Africa, with anthropological approaches to sites of borderwork in Ghana (Chalfin 2010) and border security as practice in South Sudan (Schomerus and De Vries 2014) leading the way.

Borders are proliferating, multiplying, hardening, and displaced. For instance, the persistence of extra-judicial enclaves such as Guantánamo Bay has provoked reflection on the lack of alignment among territory, political rights, and sovereign power. Work on the 'securitization of migration' (e.g. Bourbeau 2011) has shown that the experience of borders is also abstracted from the territorial line, and the use of biometrics and other information technologies for citizenship and border control (Torpey 2000; Amoore 2006; Epstein 2007; Lyon 2009; Muller 2010; Ajana 2013) means that the actual border is digital and technical and operates temporally well before the moment of crossing into national territory. A prominent example of this is the EU's Schengen zone, in which digital surveillance has compensated for the lack of formal internal controls. The idea that the border is rapidly spreading throughout society finds its most prominent recent expression in the work of Étienne Balibar (1998), but the idea of the multiplication and proliferation of borders has gained wide currency. Didier Bigo (2001), for example, sees the fusion of internal and external security apparatuses as akin to a Möbius ribbon, where inside and outside transition into one another. This fusion of inside and outside can be understood as the fusion between, on one side, the state security implied by 'geopolitical' boundaries, and 'societal' security (see Buzan et al. 1998) on the other. Work in border studies has increasingly drawn on Foucault's concept of biopolitics (e.g. Walters 2002) and therefore considered the border not only as a function that is exercised throughout society but also as part of a broader strategy of governance. Walters speaks of a 'biopolitical border' that is productive of a population governed with attention to the traits, risks, and histories of its biological bodies. Those drawing on Foucault's account of 'biopolitics' and on Agamben's (1998) Schmittian reformulation have tended to explicitly link the border function to sovereign power more generally. Vaughan-Williams (2009: 117) argues in this vein that speaking of a biopolitical border 'points to the way in which bordering practices are rather more diffused throughout society than the modern geopolitical imaginary implies'. Much of this literature emphasizing the dislocation of borders has a distinct European genesis, but it yields helpful conceptual tools for studying African borders.

This book's approach draws on the empirical emphasis on borderlands from African border studies and the theoretical emphasis on the border as a space of transnational governance practices found in Eurocentric border studies. This is a particularly important theoretical stance as more attention is paid to the interaction between Western efforts at border control in African contexts, with concepts such as 'Euro-African borderlands' (Andersson 2014a) and 'EurAfrican' borders (Gaibazzi, Bellagamba, and Dünnwald 2017) emerging to refer to these thickening transnational relationships. African border studies, despite empirical rigour, has not tended to study the transnational governance of African borders, particularly in relation to global interventions and local security politics. European border studies, for its part, has produced concepts whose impressive theoretical foundations have often come at the expense of close empirical work and draw too heavily from Western cases and experience, notably of EU integration and post-9/11 security practice. Below, I propose four theses on borderwork which capture how to understand and describe transnational practices of making and unmaking borders in West Africa.

Four Theses on Borderwork

Travelling by minibus from Nouakchott to Nouadhibou entails a half-dozen stops at customs and police checkpoints. These are every bit as much of a border as Mauritania's actual borders, which we were not crossing when I made this journey. Where officers profiled passengers at a glance, I could 'pass' as Mauritanian. Where documents were requested, my Burkinabè passport meant a trip out of the bus for registration and a delay to everyone else's journey. The first thesis on borderwork underpinning this book echoes this experience: *borders may be referential of geopolitical lines, but they can be exercised across territory.* Practices such as delimiting a territorial border or registering citizens' biometric profiles are both similarly referential of the traditional border line. This is the case even though these do not always take place at or in the name of the territorial border, and even if it is not always clear *whose* border is being drawn or enforced. As William Walters (2002: 563) suggests, 'there is a whole apparatus connected with the geopolitical border – not just a police and military system, but cartographic, diplomatic, legal, geological, and geographical knowledges and practices'. This is visible in practices such as integrated border management (IBM) which are explicitly about making the border mobile, flexible, multi-national, cooperative, and resilient, but still refer to a spatial border of some form. Switzerland's IBM strategy is a great example of this, as that country's border control relies on four 'filters': activities in third countries, cooperation within the EU's Schengen area, measures at the Swiss border itself, and measures within territory (Swiss Federal Office for Migration 2012). This emphasis on the integration of borders is visible in the practices aiming to secure

West African borders: in Chapter 5 I show how Mauritania seeks
out integrated solutions bringing together civil registry, border control, and identity documents. Indeed, this is a form of border security
that Western partners are also keen to see implemented in West African
states under the rubric of global interoperability. This is also reflected
in forms of cooperation between the EU and West African states on
irregular migration, which are a main focus on Chapter 4: agenda-
setting takes place in Brussels, patrols occur off the coasts of Senegal
and Mauritania, and formal detachments of Spanish police operate to
train and equip security forces in both countries. These practices are
referential of territorial borders, even if it is not clear whose border
is being controlled (Spain's? Europe's? Senegal's?) or where the border
is being enforced (does Europe's border stretch all the way into the
mid-Atlantic?). In my interactions with security professionals in West
Africa, I am consistently struck by how much of their work of ensuring security at the borders happens in air conditioned offices, through
remote technologies, or in coordination with colleagues even farther
afield. Their work is not fully abstracted from territory, but certainly
criss-crosses it. What this shows is that the practices associated to an
ostensibly fixed territorial boundary are largely independent of it in
territorial terms.

The weekly agenda of Western embassies' security attachés in
African capitals often includes coordination meetings with other
diplomats and donor representatives. Here, officials share tips (such
as visa applicants' latest ruse) as well as coordinate approaches to key
security issues such as drug interdiction. Despite frequently divergent
missions and viewpoints, there is often agreement and a common
culture about how to coordinate pressure on the host state to improve
airport security or drug searches. The second thesis on borderwork
is that it is just such a *networked and cultural practice*. Borderwork
practices are not simply discrete or isolated forms of action, but rather
focal points in diffuse networks that pull together myriad policy actors,
territorial locations, forms of expertise, and institutional competition.
Crucially, all of these elements are focused on the fundamental purpose
of borderwork which is to make determinations about inclusion and
exclusion. My case for calling borders networked builds on observations like Rumford's that 'the agencies responsible for constructing
and maintaining [borders] have also become more diverse' (Rumford
2008: 6), and argues that we must take into account the role of diverse

actors at various scales of governance and with various degrees of interconnection. The International Civil Aviation Organization's (ICAO) global biometric standards, EU bilateral assistance to gendarmes in Niger and Senegal, and biometrics manufacturer Gemalto's promotional materials all make borderwork actors of these organizations. Borderwork spans public and private and global and local, as illustrated by how an International Organization for Migration (IOM) project can involve private sector actors, be funded by the EU, and requested by a local government. In such forms of governance of borders, which are increasingly common in to stem illicit cross-border flows from West African states, it is the networked nature of actors that makes borderwork actually work. This echoes Kevin Haggerty and Richard Ericson's (2000: 610) observation that surveillance is increasingly 'driven by the desire to bring systems together, to combine practices and technologies and integrate them into a larger whole'. It is important, however, to note that considering practices to be part of a network does not impute overarching strategic objectives to networks, but rather serves to situate them in broader context. This is a point to which I return in the final section of this chapter on assemblages. This caveat is important to bear in mind when turning to the 'cultural' element of borderwork, which refers to the ideas underpinning the ways decisions about inclusion and exclusion are determined. Securing borders is always cultural in this way, and reflective of an ideological or cultural worldview. The proliferation of best practices and standards about borders, often diffused through technical assistance, are imbued with such assumptions. Contemporary border security practices in Senegal and Mauritania are reflective of this, as external interveners work in concert to inculcate specific approaches to security.

The third thesis is that *borderwork is both constructed and performative*. That is to say that the making of borders is at once material and semiotic, and that the associations formed by borderwork need to be continually enacted in order to retain their form. In material terms, the border is 'made' of physical artefacts ranging from the most obvious – walls and barriers – to the less visible such as databases and ID cards. Most importantly, the infrastructure of the border, the tools of migration control, and the tangible nature of identity systems all shape the functioning of the border. In the West African context, these physical elements of borderwork are visible in police fingerprinting systems as much as in patrol provided by external partners. In discursive terms, borderwork is constructed through the securitization of migration, and through the identification and framing of particular policy problems such as 'outdated paper documents' or 'porous borders'. To call borderwork constructed is also, therefore, to refer to the representation of its areas of application. In addition to being constructed, borderwork is performed and repeated – it depends on repetition and habit. The reason this book relies on the conception of borderwork, rather than the more common 'bordering', is to foreground its labour intensive nature. The Mauritanian gendarmerie commander's decision about who to send on Guardia Civil training course is very much about the literal control of border security labour. It is also the performed nature of *authority* that counts, and borderwork is a mode of reproduction for the authority to enact the border (or claims to it) and it is the way that the various networks of border actors are held together. Continual performance of the border is precisely what imbues the material and semiotic aspects of borderwork with meaning. Borderwork necessitates actors to continually make decisions about inclusion and exclusion, whether this is interpreted territorially or in terms of citizenship or status. The trained hunch of the customs I met in Rosso, on the Senegalese side of the country's river border with Mauritania, was one constant performance of determining what belonged and what did not – made in the absence of digital technology in what is a bustling melting pot of a border town. These decisions about inclusion and exclusion are the essential labour of borders, even though the realities of migration or identity are not so clear-cut. In short, sovereignty must have a material and ideological basis but it is the performative action of whoever is exercising it (a state or other actor) that constitutes the borderwork (see Figure 2.1).

Taken as a whole, most of the officials I spoke to about border security evinced a general vision of their work as taming uncertainty. This is a common bureaucratic imperative but its expression in the world of border security takes on a messianic zeal at times. One Abidjan-based law enforcement official I met found it unacceptable that African states' identity infrastructures allowed people to simply 'disappear' off the grid. In Mauritania, one official's workshop presentation I attended cited borders as spaces of anxiety and stressed the etymological link between *frontière* and the *front* of battle. All of this leads me to the fourth thesis on borderwork: that it is all about *order-making*. We can understand it as operating under a broader security rationale, in which

Figure 2.1 A border post in southern Mauritania, inaugurated in 2016. These structures were built by an EU-funded and IOM-implemented border management project. © IOM/Bechir Malum 2016. Image used with permission.

the continual pursuit of order and stability and the management of contingency and risk are paramount. Part of bordering necessarily involves *ordering*. As Gavin Kendall (2004: 64) argues, we must think of 'successfully governed space, not as a self-evident object, but as the result of the associations of networks, which are composed of humans and non-humans, and which are painstakingly built from the ground up'. This emphasis on what could be called 'ordering', and on associations between networks, is what allows me to draw similarities between border control, migration management and identification/biometric practices. Senegal's ultimately ill-fated biometric visa system was one such mode of ordering, through the attempts to interlink immigration and national ID infrastructures. Another example of the linkage between border technology and security is the statement by the International Air Transport Association president, in 2011, that 'for terrorists, travel documents are as important as weapons' (Canada Newswire 2011). This suggests that the insecurity of document systems is linked to dangerous types of mobility, which in turn directly threatens – by transgressing borders – the norm of order expected within states. By aiming for order across space, borderwork suggests that an analysis of borders cannot be limited to the territorial site of the border but must account for the dispersed practices of border control aiming at stable order. This analysis also presupposes the question 'whose order?', which points us to the ambiguity of borderwork as an order-making activity. Borderwork enacted by smugglers, migrants, or non-citizens can enact alternative orders based on activity that defies practices of security and control. Borderwork is therefore not only about state forms of order but also includes counter-ordering techniques.

Who Does West Africa's Borderwork?

If borders have to be produced, we must then answer the question 'who makes borders?' (Parker and Vaughan-Williams 2009) and be clearer about their ontology and epistemology. We must therefore be attentive to cross-section of the organizations, agencies, authorities, and people involved in borderwork in West Africa. All spaces of policy-making are obviously complex, but the all-encompassing nature of 'border security' and its associated practices in countries such as Mauritania or Niger is particularly amorphous. Tracing who 'does the border-work' in the region brings into relief the essentially interlinked nature of efforts to shape inclusion and exclusion: multiple and overlapping strategies and projects, agencies with varying degrees of coordination, or actors working to undermine borders. The institutional topography below highlights the complexity of actors that carry out borderwork in West Africa and shows why new conceptual tools best account for this diverse range of actors. Each of these actors brings forth knowledges, forms of expertise, supply chains, IT systems, imaginaries of the border, identities, and institutional cultures. The practices they undertake include border demarcation, databases, conferences and professional networking, policy harmonization, intergovernmental dialogue, pedagogy and training, direct financial aid, document security training, maritime patrols, standard-setting, advertising, biometric enrolment, and many more.

African Union (AU)

In 1964, the then Organization for African Unity members made the significant step of recognizing Africa's existing colonial boundaries, guaranteeing the status quo of African states' Westphalian sovereignty. More recently, the AU has committed to projects such as the African Union Border Programme (AUBP), which aimed to demarcate all of Africa's borders by 2017. The AUBP has enlisted the help of the German overseas development agency (GIZ) to demarcate borders in southern and western Africa, and uses the African Union Border Information System to collect geographical and boundary data. The AU has become an important peace and security actor on the African continent, through intergovernmental agreements such as the Nouakchott Process that is intended to facilitate the African Peace and Security Architecture in the Sahel region. This complements the AU's strategy for the Sahel, adopted in 2014, which calls for increased 'security cooperation', including the strengthening of border security through measures such as joint patrols (African Union 2014). The African Union's role as a borderwork actor therefore includes the promotion of 'rescaling' some elements of the governance of security to the regional and continental level. The AU is not as influential in shaping border procedures as regional economic groupings (such as the Economic Community of West African States [ECOWAS], below) but generates symbolic visions of frictionless border crossing in Africa such as the pan-African passport launched in 2016.

European Union (EU)

The European Union is a multi-faceted player in borderwork in West Africa. The European Commission (EC), the European Parliament, and the Council of the EU work together to pass border-related legislation (like the Schengen Borders Code) whose effects set the agenda on migration issues well beyond the Union's borders. EU institutions provide direct assistance for border management to third countries, under the Global Approach to Migration and Mobility (2005) which promotes new transnational linkages on issues such as deportations, travel documents, and 'root causes' of migration. The EU also makes its borderwork 'networked' through its participation in various dialogues, forums, and communities of practice involving West African countries. These include the EU-Africa Dialogue, the Rabat Process, the Dakar Strategy, the 2015 Valletta summit, and communities of practice such as the Migration for Development project. Indeed, it is often the primary funder or a key partner in swathes of projects run through the development agencies of its own member states and of organizations like the United Nations (UN) Office on Drugs and Crime. The EU's global diplomatic presence is assured by the European External Action Service (EEAS), which is the largely autonomous EU foreign service under which its embassy-like 'delegations' are managed. These delegations administer security and development projects – many funded by the EU Trust Fund for Africa adopted after the Valletta summit – with partners like the IOM, national security forces, and UN agencies. In Nouakchott (Mauritania) and Dakar (Senegal), local EU delegations administer millions of euros of such funding. These delegations have become outposts for borderwork in their own right, hosting the European Migration Liaison Officers under the Migration Partnership Framework announced in June 2016 (European Commission 2016a). Their work supplements the work of the European Union Capacity Building Missions (EUCAP) in Mali and Niger, which focus on counter-terrorism and anti-trafficking (under the banner of policebuilding), but who increasingly focus on irregular migration and countering organized crime. Beyond this, the EU has a digital footprint in West African states through the deployment of its Visa Information System (VIS) in member state embassies. The VIS records visa applicants' biometric data in order to prevent 'visa shopping' – the practice whereby migrants apply to multiple Schengen member countries' embassies to boost their chances of gaining a visa. Frontex, the EU agency tasked with coordinating the control of the Union's borders with non-EU countries, has coordinated joint patrols between member states and Senegal and Mauritania to prevent irregular migration by sea. It is also taking on an increasingly important role in the prevention of cross-border crime more generally, through an emerging risk-analysis and intelligence-sharing community with twenty-one African states (with nine observer members). The EU and its member states are amongst the most influential international borderwork actors in Senegal and Mauritania, as Chapters 4 and 5 in particular demonstrate.

International Organization for Migration (IOM)

After the European Union, the IOM is perhaps the most prominent international actor in border security in West Africa. The agency helps to design border control strategies and legislation and strongly advocates the use of biometrics and border management databases. The IOM's range of activities truly typifies the fusion of practices characteristic of borderwork: it provides regional document fraud training for West African police forces, sets border security norms through its publications and training manuals circulated via the African Capacity Building Centre (ACBC) in Tanzania, and literally 'builds' borders through programmes like the construction and equipping of border posts in Mauritania and Niger. The IOM has, through its focus on the European migration 'crisis', increasingly publicized its search and rescue activities (in northern Niger, for example) and adopted a stronger humanitarian discourse. While the IOM is an intergovernmental agency that draws on the symbols and practices of the UN system – to which it was formally affiliated in 2016 – and the broader development world, it is an entrepreneurial agency that must constantly seek out funding and partnerships. This makes the IOM one of the more 'networked' borderwork actors. The IOM works closely with, and receives generous funding from, the European Union and member governments. As Chapter 5 on Mauritania demonstrates, the IOM's role in the pedagogical nature of border control is particularly striking.

United Nations (UN) Agencies

United Nations agencies play a varied role in West Africa's borderwork. A key part of the UN's own Integrated Strategy for The Sahel specifically addresses the countering of cross-border threats through the promotion of better coordination, cooperation, and integration between states' security agencies (United Nations 2013). While the UN Counter-Terrorism Implementation Task Force supports global customs and border data information-sharing linkages, and endorses the formation of border management strategies, other agencies such as the United Nations High Commissioner for Refugees (UNHCR) intervene more directly and locally. UNHCR is particularly involved in managing the cross-border humanitarian fallout from the Malian conflict, managing camps in Mauritania and Niger for the hundreds of thousands of displaced. The UNHCR has also been an enthusiastic user of biometrics – usually more common in border control – for identification of displaced and stateless persons. A recent programme, for example, gave out biometric ID to Mauritanian refugees living in Senegal

(UNHCR 2012) as a means of ensuring them access to limited citizenship rights. The UN Office on Drugs and Crime (UNODC) proposes legislation templates on trafficking and smuggling, and coordinates projects (funded by the EU and Canada amongst others) to train customs and anti-drug officers in West Africa's coastal countries. Its Sahel Programme, administered from Dakar, covers a wide gamut of border issues through the prism of countering organized crime, such as training of West African police and customs officials on document fraud and drug smuggling. The UN Development Programme is particularly active in border areas such as the Liptako–Gourma region straddling Mali, Burkina Faso, and Niger, in which it funds projects to improve relationships between border communities and the security sector. The International Civil Aviation Organization (ICAO), which is discussed at greater length in Chapter 6 of this book, has used its role in regulating civil aviation to regulate travel documents. Its role is mainly one of setting standards, and it helps to foster the professional networks that bring diverse border control actors together. The ICAO set a deadline of 2015 for the worldwide adoption of machine-readable travel documents (MRTDs), and Document 9303 is the ICAO publication that sets the biometric standard according to which e-passports and other biometric documents are designed and issued. Mauritania's e-passport system, for example, is a system that is funded in part by the IOM but run according to ICAO standards and put in place by Morpho, a private manufacturer. Although the name of the organization suggests a focus on civil aviation alone, its regional MRTD meetings – like those run from the ICAO's regional office in Dakar – tackle a plethora of border management issues. These meetings, and the quarterly MRTD Report the ICAO publishes, are instrumental in enabling the professional networking on which border management cooperation thrives, and in setting the global normative agenda of how borders should be managed.

International Centre for Migration Policy Development (ICMPD)

The ICMPD, based in Brussels, plays a key role in mediating EU relationships with third countries and administering project funding. The ICMPD operates as a de facto implementation arm of mainly EU-funded border management projects, considering itself a clearinghouse for international expertise in the area of borders and migration. The agency works with the EU on projects like MIEUX-II, which provides 'expertise' to developing countries on asylum, migration and development, and border management. The agency's normative stance – advocating integrated border management and 'open yet secure' borders – echoes the cultural understanding of border security found in the discourses and practices of others such as the IOM and ICAO.

Interpol

Interpol's mandate covers the policing of cross-border crime and terrorism, and it has used this position to advocate for the worldwide adoption of e-passports. It also plays an important role in coordinating border management activities through its regional and national offices in West Africa. Not only has it coordinated police actions against human trafficking in West Africa, but it also maintains a global database of 'stolen and lost' travel documents, which holds information on about 68 million documents (Interpol 2016). Many West African states, including Senegal and Mauritania, have at least one border post equipped with computers that verify traveller documents against Interpol watch lists. Given the impetus towards integration, computerization, and data collection in contemporary border security practice, Interpol is in a crucial position in bringing together both border systems and police agencies. Its West Africa Police Information System (WAPIS) seeks to push states in the region to more institutionalized forms of data-sharing.

Economic Community of West African States (ECOWAS)

ECOWAS is the guarantor of the regional free movement protocol for West Africa, which gives citizens ninety days' visa-free access to other states in the region. This protocol ostensibly guarantees smooth cross-border mobility for citizens of the region (which excludes Mauritania) as long as they are in possession of a valid travel document or national ID card. This guarantee of free movement is a legal but also a practical question, with multiple projects – including one by ICMPD – in operation to remove obstacles to free movement of people in the region. ECOWAS also maintains a relationship with the EU on migration management questions and has been the recipient of capacity-building assistance from the Spanish government to implement the ECOWAS Common Approach to Migration. ECOWAS also plays an important normative role and is developing a common visa for the region, based on the European Schengen visa. This proposal is similar to plans put in place by other Regional Economic Communities in Africa, such as the East African Community which is implementing a common tourist visa (which is, incidentally, aided by the IOM). In the institutional topography of borderwork in West Africa, ECOWAS is often only weakly aligned with other international actors who tend to favour more security-focused approaches to borders.

National Police and Gendarmeries

Most Francophone countries in West Africa have a policing apparatus that divides the police, which tend to fall under interior ministries, from gendarmeries which commonly are the responsibility of defence ministries. Practically, both are involved in the 'policing' of borders, though gendarmeries tend to be more involved in rural border security and the more militarized aspects of internal policing. National police forces tend to be the institutional homes for the 'border police' including border agents from Police de l'Air et des Frontières which fall under or complement a Direction de la Surveillance du Territoire in charge or registering foreigners and have a limited intelligence-gathering role. Police and gendarmeries are key borderwork actors and recipients of most external capacity-building assistance in the border management sector. Under the Guardia Civil's Project West Sahel, for instance, the gendarmeries of Senegal and Mauritania benefited from assistance through transfers of equipment but also of legal and technical knowledge from the Guardia Civil, their Spanish counterparts. There is often a differential in prestige and capacity between police forces and gendarmeries which is consequential for the control of the border and the types of relationships they build with each other and with external interveners. The issues of law enforcement and national security are also often fused in part due to the organizational structures in which policing agencies are placed: in Senegal and Mauritania the upper echelons of the police are represented in broader national security directorates (Direction Générale de la Sécurité Nationale). This setup sets the agenda for how border security actually happens, with prevailing institutional cultures and forms of competition (with better-financed customs agencies, for example) shaping the borderwork.

Regional Military and Intelligence Cooperation Structures

The proliferation of security- or development-focused strategies for the Sahel space and the promotion of cooperation at new international scales has led to the formation of new cooperation structures that perform the borderwork in West Africa. One of these is the G5 Sahel (composed of Senegal, Mali, Mauritania, Burkina Faso, Niger, and Chad) whose object is to contribute to 'security and development' in the region. Headquartered in Mauritania's capital Nouakchott, the G5 Sahel counts France and the European Union as key patrons and its activities are oriented towards building up capacity for the training of members' security forces. While such a collaboration platform has long been favoured by foreign donors as a means of having a single interlocutor for security issues in the Sahel, its mission is hard to pin down: donors such as France prefer the G5 to have a security-first vocation expressed through a joint military force launched in 2017, while its communications and incentives have taken on a considerable development element. Looking to older institutions, the joint Comité d'État-major Opérationnel Conjoint (CEMOC) is a joint military staff created in 2010 and based in southern Algeria as a means of coordinating military actions and intelligence in the Sahara-Sahel. One of the elements of the CEMOC is an intelligence-sharing platform called the Unité de Fusion et de Liaison (UFL), which is charged with the collection and sharing of intelligence between member states Mauritania, Mali, Algeria, and Niger. The UFL shares intelligence on cross-border threats as well as emerging threats such as religious radicalization. These regional platforms not only put border security on the agenda and work to rescale the ways decisions are made about it, but also perform the cultural forms of borderwork that frame the threats such as terrorism and organized crime to which border security becomes the response.

Corporate Actors

In addition to intergovernmental actors, the for-profit sector – mainly border technology and ID manufacturers – have been prominent borderwork actors in West Africa. Companies such as Gemalto have sought to improve their positioning in key African markets by portraying themselves as reliable experts and by marketing their products as necessary and as desirable features of statehood. Morpho's identity solutions, for example, assume the public-private provision of identity services, and the company in many cases (such as Mauritania) stresses its ability to manage the entire 'life cycle' of document issuance – operating as a private authority within the state. Companies such as Zetes, a Belgian ID manufacturer, compete for BOT (build, operate, and transfer) contracts with West African states like Senegal, resulting in transfers of both technology and approaches to border management. Corporate and government officials mingle at security industry fairs and trade shows like the Nigeria Security Forum. The presence of private actors in West African borderwork brings in different dynamics of competition and cooperation, with points of differentiation such as biometric algorithms facilitating cooperation but undermining the integration sought by the public sector (see Chapter 6 on biometrics).

Embassies and Consulates

Embassies and consulates – specifically those of European countries in West Africa – are essential actors in border control cooperation. These diplomatic missions host police cooperation offices alongside the more visible political and cultural forms of representation. Police cooperation based in embassies provides diplomatic contacts to police liaisons and provides privileged access to the host country's security services. This helps information flows between embassy and host country, and also – due to cooperation between embassies – consolidates security relationships horizontally as well. As far as an 'international security community' exists in places like Niger or Senegal, it is performed through frequent meetings of security attachés, typically attended by representatives of other organizations such as the IOM and security missions like EUCAP Sahel. Embassies are key sites for the constructed and performative nature of borderwork, with such meetings ensuring actors speak from a similar standpoint or security culture in relation to the 'local'.

Development and Relief Agencies

One of the most striking trends in borderwork in West Africa – and one that I discuss at length in the next chapter – is the role development agencies play in what is ostensibly a security practice. The World Bank has mainly played an agenda-setting role from a distance, by putting out a *Border Management Modernization Handbook* in which it suggests a type of border knowledge as to how to better leverage the trading potential of more efficient border management. Like other actors discussed here, the emphasis is borders that effectively *manage* their openness and closure. Some agencies, like the German government's development agency (GIZ), relish the implementation challenge: it provides project management and training expertise to police capacity-building projects in Niger and Mauritania. The Danish Demining Group, a humanitarian agency which is part of the Danish Refugee Council, has undertaken work in the Liptako-Gourma region straddling Burkina Faso, Niger, and Mali with the goal of enhancing trust between local populations and security forces. This zone typifies international concerns about ungoverned border spaces, particularly as violent extremist organizations compete with the state for the loyalties of people living in the area. The Red Cross played a key role in operating the refugee 'welcome centre' in Nouadhibou, Mauritania, which came to be known by its residents and the local community as 'Guantanamito' (i.e. little Guantánamo) until its closure in 2012. As Andersson (2014b: 146–148) shows, Spanish Red Cross workers were frequently mistrusted and mistaken for police by Senegalese migrants during the Canaries crisis, and the controversial refugee 'welcome centre' in Nouadhibou took on the Red Cross 'brand' despite its efforts to distance itself. The continual emphasis on 'security and development' in the discourse of organizations such as the G5 Sahel but also the EU's Sahel strategy has produced an opening for questions of border security to be resolved through development and statebuilding interventions. It is notable that some of the EU's work on borders and migration in West Africa is channelled through EuropeAid and EU Emergency Trust Fund for Africa money.

Criminal Networks

Borderwork is not the exclusive preserve of control-oriented actors. In many ways, border control measures are *reactive* to the practices of non-state actors such as criminal networks of smugglers and traffickers. In West Africa, smugglers provide falsified identification papers or facilitate irregular migration flows. Smugglers, evading controls, shape the border by interacting with control-oriented actors. For instance, migrant smuggling routes from West Africa to Spain shifted in response to controls in Ceuta and Melilla in the early 2000s, in the same way that desert routes through Niger have been shaped by the collapse of the Libyan state in the 2010s. Smuggling networks, which are heavily disaggregated and lacking a central point of control over a whole route, are also ways of distributing work. Senegalese fishermen carrying irregular migrants to the Canary Islands are inseparable from a political economy of declining fish stocks but also of fixers and middlemen. In turn, police and gendarmerie forces refer to the threat of trafficking (real or exaggerated) in the pursuit of funding and recognition for their projects and practices.

Migrants and Non-citizens

The agency of irregular migrants undermines state controls, while activists reframe narratives about citizenship. Activists like Migreurop – whose 'Frontexit' campaign targeted the externalization of EU migration controls to Senegal and Mauritania – reframe the everyday ways border control is spoken about (see Chapter 4). Touche Pas à Ma Nationalité in Mauritania advocates for black Mauritanians who have failed to be registered by the state's biometric enrolment due to racial discrimination. Associations like the Association Mauritanienne des Droits de l'Homme in Mauritania work with European NGOs to document border control practices and defend migrants' rights.

Academics, Consultants, and Issue Experts

Given the 'cultural' nature of borderwork, the role of ideas about how border security should be done and how it must adapt to local context is frequently in the hands of academics, consultants, and local notables. Academics and consultants also play a crucial role in shaping border norms, by providing their expertise for programme design or suggesting policy paths. The IOM uses local sociologists to adapt its training programmes in West Africa, while the security situation in the Sahel has resulted in the proliferation of think tanks and regional meetings about counter-terrorism and border control. The African Centre for the Study & Research on Terrorism (CAERT), based in Algiers, is part of the African Union and seeks to 'conduct research and study on Terrorism and develop strategic policy, operational and training mechanisms' (CAERT 2016) within broader AU efforts. Attempts to think through and advocate on border security issues are visible in the West African context, which has witnessed a growth of strategic studies centres like the Mauritanian Institute for Strategic Studies (IMES), the Centre for Security Strategies in the Sahel-Sahara (Centre 4S), led by former diplomats, use their agenda-setting power to push for approaches to border security and bring together global and local actors in this area. This is something Senegal's Centre for Advanced Study of Defence and Security (CHEDS) has done through the annual Dakar Forum which brings together policymakers, professors, journalists, diplomats, and high-ranking security officials.

A Socio-technical Approach to Borderwork: Thinking with Assemblage

One of the key challenges of researching security practices in West Africa and the Sahel is contending with the fact that complexity – policymakers' divergent views, with competing funding mandates, corrupt informal practices, and lack of coordination – still produces governance effects with all their attendant forms of authority. A glance at who does the borderwork in West Africa shows a range of knowledges, institutional cultures, and practices. These actors are not only diverse but also combine together in complex and often unexpected ways. They cluster around specific issues, they operate simultaneously without necessarily coordinating, and they transcend the global and the local in their practices. The very distinctions between global and local actors collapse: some Guardia Civil officers I spoke to may have a more 'local' outlook than the smuggler they are working to put out of business. How can we theorize the relations and positions of actors while remaining conscious of the heterogeneous and disaggregated nature of the sites of practice we look at? How can we describe their arrangement and understand these structures, in order to better understand the ways authority is wielded?

One approach to thinking through relations, positions, and arrangements is based on Bourdieu's concepts of field, habitus, and symbolic capital. He defines field as a 'network, or a configuration, of objective relations between positions' held by actors (Bourdieu and Wacquant 1992: 97), which exists in constant interrelation with the habitus which is 'systems of dispositions [actors in a field] have acquired by internalizing a determinate type of economic and social condition' (105). This interrelation of structure and agency is mediated in part by symbolic capital which refers to the resources at stake within these fields, and is 'any property (any form of capital whether physical, economic, cultural or social) when it is perceived by social agents endowed with categories of perception which cause them to know it and recognize it to give it value' (Bourdieu 1994: 8). These concepts tell us about how people interrelate, what motivates them, and how we can account for their mentalities and lived experiences. They provide a helpful vocabulary, yet the broader theoretical edifice in which they are implanted is not always well attuned to the nature of border control in West Africa. The concept of 'field' provides an overly rigid and structuralist answer to the question of social organization. Beyond this, actors may not perceive themselves as part of 'one' field, or may not even recognize the 'field' in question at all, which then becomes the creation of the analyst. For instance, the IOM and the Union Économique et Monétaire Ouest Africaine (the economic grouping of francophone West African states) both build border posts but their respective staffs are not competing with each other for the same institutional prestige. While they certainly shape the projection of state authority in their *area* of policy activity, they are not necessarily in a same *field*. Finally, relations between actors are not only social but are also *material*, and the object of analysis should extend beyond security professionals to include the agency of other human actors (like migrants) and non-human actors (like databases).

Assemblage is a more persuasive approach to understanding the effects of social practice but also, crucially, the role of material objects in shaping and producing governance in their own right. It shows the connections between relatively self-contained areas of security practice, and the transmission of knowledge and practice *across* them in contexts of 'cooperation' that are such important sites of analysis in this book. Assemblage is a widely used lens within the social sciences with which to account for heterogeneous, nonlinear, and complex systems. In sociology, Haggerty and Ericson (2000) use it to point to the flattening and decentralization of contemporary surveillance. Sassen (2006) uses the term to describe the bundling and unbundling of territory, authority, and rights at the national and global scales. In international relations, Abrahamsen and Williams (2011) use the concept to show the interrelationship of public and private security provision, describing what they call 'global security assemblages' as 'transnational structures and networks in which a range of different actors and normativities interact, cooperate and compete to produce new institutions, practices and forms of deterritorialized security governance' (90). Salter (2013) refers to the aviation security sector as rhizomatic, disaggregated, and heterogeneous, while Doucet (2016) describes assemblages of intervention with reference to the different objects, knowledges, and actors at play in them. Even though each use relies on slightly different theorizations of 'assemblage', they all emerge in response to the complexity of causality and the broad distribution of agency across public and private, human, and non-human, global, and local. Broadly, it helps us think through the analytical potential of concepts like field, habitus, and capital without their attendant rigidity.

My vision of assemblage deployed throughout this book is aligned with those above and draws in particular from actor-network theory. ANT is sensitive to the heterogeneous and networked nature of society, the dispersal of agency across human and non-human actors, the simplification or obfuscation of networks, the performed and contested nature of durable social order, and the precarity of all social ordering (Law 1992). This is not dissimilar to other approaches to social organization. For instance, Latour (1999) has called ANT 'actant-rhizome ontology', which echoes Gilles Deleuze's idea of *agencement*, which is often translated as 'assemblage' and 'rhizome'. Law for his part writes that '"actor-networks" can be seen as scaled-down versions of Michel Foucault's discourses or epistemes' but that an actor-network sensibility 'asks us to explore the strategic, relational, and productive character of particular, smaller-scale, heterogeneous actor-networks' rather than the 'epochal epistemes' (Law 2007: 6) with which Foucault was concerned. This conception of ANT aligns with this book's project of allying the contingent and local empirical focus of African border studies with the conceptual innovations of its more Eurocentric iteration. Why is assemblage better? How does it help us understand borderwork in West Africa more effectively?

First, assemblage accounts for the socio-technical – adding in a crucial consideration for the role of materiality. This evidenced by the growing role of technological systems in West African border security, such as the Seahorse inter-agency communications system featured in Chapter 4. While an institutional topography like the one earlier in this chapter might draw our attention to large organizations or make methodological nationalists of us, we should remember that it is discrete technical systems that keep them humming: think of information-sharing systems and donated vehicles, which in turn carry assumptions about expected forms of social behaviour. Yes, humans are part of the social, but so are concepts, forms of knowledge, lab equipment, and so on. This is ANT's most radical claim: that the social is, ontologically, a diverse set of networks composed of human and non-human agents. ANT, in short, 'does not celebrate the idea that there is a difference in kind between people on the one hand, and objects on the other' (Law 1992: 383). Latour (2005) builds on this and uses the term 'actant' to refer to these sources of agency. Although this is a controversial claim of ANT's, it does not – unlike the 'new materialisms' literature (e.g. Bennett 2010) – ascribe intentionality to inorganic matter. This fundamental flattening of the social is the basis of ANT's claim that the social is necessarily *socio-technical*. Rather than limit ourselves beforehand to study of human actors and their interactions, we expand our frame of analysis to include other 'actants' that make the border what it is. Thinking with the term 'socio-technical' helps us to pose certain questions differently: rather than look only at the material as an effect of human agency (i.e. an biometric ID card *caused* by security actors' policies) we can look at materials as key actors in borderwork (security practices *shaped* by the functioning of these ID cards). By also emphasizing the agency of the material, we can consider a border post, a training manual, or a malfunctioning airport e-gate as objects with agency that shape the meaning and infrastructure of the border itself.

Second, assemblage is open to complex and distributed causality. This allows us to examine the effects of associations, and (un)bundling of socio-technical arrangements, without ascribing direct intentionality to all practices. That actors coalesce around particular policy problems such as 'irregular migration' might not necessarily imply there is a single hand guiding them to it. Drawing from Hannah Arendt's distinction between causes and origins, Jane Bennett argues that 'if agency is distributive or confederate, then instances of efficient causality, with its chain of simple bodies acting as the sole impetus for the next effect, will be impossibly rare' (Bennett 2010: 32). Not assuming linear causality is also a means of ensuring that we maintain the heterogeneity of the social as a starting assumption. The term 'actor-network' captures the complexity of objects and the relations that bring them into being. Objects therefore draw into play a huge set of relations, and John Law defines an actor as 'always a network of elements that it does not fully recognise or know' (Law 2007: 8). For instance, passport issuance appears to be a straightforward practice on its own, but it is through discursive and professional practices inextricably linked to a range of other elements: the power grid, electronic readers at border posts, technical standards, and so on. This vision of distributed agency might suggest that assemblage's envisioning of the socio-technical is prone to be ever-expanding (where does an assemblage truly *end*?), yet we gain more than we lose: we see how actors can therefore be part of an assemblage not by virtue of consciously taking part in a particular field (à la Bourdieu), but rather by virtue of being included through *relations* of (dis)assembly and (un)bundling. This pushes us to think of border security beyond a singular focus on 'professionals', including actors who may not identify as part of a field of struggles around security – such as development workers or citizens – but who are nevertheless imbricated (often not by choice) in border control. A good example of this is the activist struggle of Touche Pas à Ma Nationalité (TPMN) in Mauritania (see Chapter 6), who have challenged the government's biometric census on the basis of ethnic exclusion. TPMN's activists are part of the bundle of actors whose agency *shapes* how this security technology is implemented, but their struggle does not come from within a 'field' of security.

Third, the concept of assemblage helps us to visualize border security cooperation differently by focusing on (dis)association, (un)bundling, and (dis)assembly. These describe not just different coalitions of actors involved in borderwork, but also some of their effects on states and societies: as Chapter 3 shows, border security interventions often produce or target thin slices of recipient states (e.g. joint command centres) and profoundly reshape their outlook and purpose. The term *agencement* as used by Deleuze and Guattari to mean 'either "arrangement", "fitting" or "fixing"' (Phillips 2006: 108) helps us envision how new authorities and forms of expertise are fitted together in this way. This concern with connections calls for what Jeandesboz (2016) names as 'associational enquiry', which is geared towards understanding 'how certain sociotechnical settings become durable' (5) or not. This is precisely the goal of this book: to show how social relations underpinning border security bundle and unbundle, and how security practices are underpinned by shifting connections between actors and the forms of security knowledge they bring with them. This is particularly relevant in a context of international cooperation, in which actors operating in diverse sectors are brought together: for instance, the IOM border posts project in Mauritania (see Chapter 5) operates at the intersection of a primarily European set of border security professionals and the Mauritanian security establishment, to name but two. The assemblage lens can allow us to, amongst other things, see the state as an uneven association of disparate and often competing elements that maintain varying relationships with each other and outside actors. Being attentive to what (dis)association, (un)bundling, and (dis)assembly actually *do* means we also sidestep concerns about assemblage approaches' relationship to power relations. For instance, Mitchell Dean's (1996: 56) critique of the term 'network' in 'actor-network' suggests that it 'risks a certain flattening-out of the relation between the members and elements of the network and may result in a kind of realist reductionism'. Yet we can still account for power, authority, and inequality: think of the centrality EU delegation staff in cities like Niamey and Bamako take on by virtue of their central role in *assembling* forms of funding, local actors, and international partners.

Finally, the vision of space that assemblage entails is sensitive to the questions of scale that inevitably emerge when considering global and local border governance in West Africa. The EU's Visa Information System (VIS), for instance, registers visa applicants' biometric information at, say, the Italian embassy in Dakar. These data are then transmitted and stored in the EU, but also used to later police the border in a third country. They are part of an assemblage composed of bodily information, computer servers, embassy staff, and application forms, which collapses the distance between the migrant and the EU's space of control. Assemblage thinking does not fetishize flat territorial space, and helps us to understand how the *work* of bordering can defy conventional views of territoriality, of global and local. This question of scale is also reflected in the disassembly of the state which is precipitated by forms of cooperation: police forces building international relationships, different parts of the state competing with each other, or the governance of identification documents being simultaneously moved from the national to the global and the local. Thinking with assemblage is also crucial to envisioning how border security in West Africa is globalized, beyond the confines of national-territorial sovereignty.

Borders, Order, and Security

Borders are complex spaces of governance. Thinking with the concept of 'borderwork' urges us to think through contemporary border security practices as uniting diverse practices that take place at the border but also beyond it. The idea of 'borderwork' retains the primacy of the international border, but recognizes that its control is undertaken across territory, networked and sustained by cultures of security, constructed and performative, and driven by a desire for order. The concept of borderwork is not only a snapshot of a contemporary reality, but also provides an entry point into the nature of contemporary practices of control. This chapter has also argued for a view of the governance of borders that emphasizes borderwork is done by a range of international organizations, agencies, local security actors, and individuals in West Africa. Mapping out the global and local actors involved in doing the borderwork is, in the West African context, an important exercise in lifting the curtain on a highly technicalized and frequently opaque world of security practice. Rather than relying on concepts like regimes, fields, or hierarchies, I have here preferred the figure of the assemblage to describe the often tenuous patchwork of agencies that *do* the borderwork. Assemblage as a concept provides more openness to the heterogeneity of the social – including non-human agency, and provides a way of accounting for the uncoordinated nature of borderwork in West Africa, which is undertaken as much by the international organizations and NGOs as by gendarmeries and informal regional dialogues. The emphasis throughout this chapter has been on the role of borders as *making* the world, rather than simply dividing it. Borders – as defined here – take work to build and sustain, and should therefore be seen as modes of building and maintaining order. When borderwork is control oriented, its nature as an order-making activity bears striking resemblance to the way that security has tended to be spoken about in critical security studies: as a practice of inclusion/exclusion, a means of drawing a limit, a practice driven by anxiety and unease. In short, borderwork and security rely on some kind of common grounding that provides their condition of possibility. In West Africa, borderwork has focused on a transmission of security knowledges and technologies, underpinned by ideas about state capacity and the need to reshape the scale and mode of governance. It is to this question that the next chapter turns.

3 | Security Knowledge and the Politics of Intervention

Borders are not simply 'lines in the sand'. Rather, they are dense institutional spaces that are enacted across territory, which are constructed and performed as well as networked and cultural. The preceding chapter made this argument with particular reference to the multitude of actors who construct international borders in West Africa – those who 'do the borderwork'. That chapter argued for a socio-technical view of borders: in other words, the work of enacting borders is done by human as well as non-human actors, by security professionals as much as by surveillance technologies. Here the argument turns to the cognitive or epistemic work that goes into building and maintaining borders – in short, border security *knowledges* – and what how they move tells us about governance. Assemblages were described in the previous chapter are socio-technical formations, here they figure as the mechanisms of knowledge generation and transmission. The question of knowledge is inherent to practice, to be sure, but its centrality to border security in the global south is instructive about the social formations that put the border into action. In West African states such as Senegal and Mauritania, border control practices are inextricable from bilateral and multilateral forms of cooperation and capacity-building, partly due to the emergence of irregular migration, terrorism, and narcotics as key threats deemed as emanating from or transiting through this zone. The emphasis on transmitting knowhow and expertise to combat these threats, often through statebuilding interventions, is one of the defining features of border security practices in the global south. The importance of knowledge to borderwork is reflected in myriad instances in West African states: the Spanish Guardia Civil officers who put in place capacity-building programmes in Senegal have specific assumptions about how border control should work, which are transmitted in the course of their work, and these are shaped by institutional and personal histories. Similarly, IOM-run training courses for Mauritanian border guards facilitate a cognitive – and material – transfer of knowledge about border control drawn from global standards. To better understand the cultural element of border security practices, we must come to terms with the sites from which security knowledges emerge, and how this knowledge is used or moves. A better understanding of borderwork knowledge opens up a window into global-local security relationships and helps us theorize the impetus behind security provision in the global south.

This chapter thinks about security through the lens of the international political sociology (IPS) defined in this book's introduction (Chapter 1). This method is attuned to the interplay of global and local, to the complexity of transnational spaces, and to a sociological method that examines global factors beyond interstate interactions only: policing, migration, surveillance technologies, and more. IPS is not a singular view of international relations. This built-in diversity is a key asset as it draws from a range of approaches from international relations (notably constructivism and post-structuralism) and from sociology and anthropology. Driven by 'the sense that sociology might be able to add something that is currently missing from the analysis of international relations' (Bigo and Walker 2007: 2) IPS is not primarily bound up with the stakes specific to discipline of IR that pitted realism, liberalism, and constructivism as competing approaches to how states interact. Rather, the focus is on examining the conditions of possibility of global politics and, through the emphasis on sociology, the very concrete and micro-level practices (often in unexpected or neglected spaces) that make international politics what it is. An IPS approach is therefore sensitive to practices, broadly defined, whether they are discursive, institutional, or material. IPS places emphasis on process and practice, rather than on the given-ness or objectivity of social phenomena. This is partly why 'critical security studies' has become a particularly vibrant contributor to the IPS tendency.

Building on this sensibility, this chapter is structured around five key claims. The first is that security (at the borders and beyond) is a knowledge-driven process and practice. It is therefore the result of practices – routines and quotidian professional interactions – which are productive of knowledge about how to respond to fears and anxieties. The chapter's second claim is that the relationship between the framing of security problems and their solutions depends on context-specific forms of knowledge. This 'cultural' element of borderwork, akin to Zaiotti's (2011) framing of 'cultures of border control', is found in security professionals' everyday activities and practices but also shaped by the ways they are bundled and associated (e.g. in institutions or joint projects). Taking knowledge to be both agential and structural, tacit and explicit, the section concludes by calling for an attention to the everyday knowledge, rules, expertise, best practices, standards, norms, and procedures that dictate ways of *doing* security – all of which are found in and circulated by assemblages. In short, we must look the diverse 'people' and 'things' that create and bear security knowledge. The chapter's third claim is that the diffusion of security knowledge across international spaces is the defining feature of transnational border control practices in the global south. The section describes security knowledge as a mobile and mutable foundation for these practices, Knowledge bundles can be moved and exert control at a distance whilst retaining their shape (or not) to varying degrees. Drawing on the thesis on borderwork (see Chapter 2) that see it as networked and cultural, I go on to argue that knowledges tend to move through three modes: exemplars such as best practices, emulation of global norms, and pedagogical interventions. The chapter's fourth key claim is that the *content* of border security knowledge in West Africa tends to draw on a worldview oriented towards capability, modernity, and control. Given that the security elements of borderwork in West Africa are so tightly linked to external intervention (and its attendant pedagogical practices), it is best to think of intervention as underpinned by a view of control emphasizing statebuilding and the reinforcement of state security capacity, and a view of state modernity as improving capacity to control borders, territory, and population. The chapter's fifth major claim is that, in light of recent work on security and state transformation, we should think of borderwork interventions in West Africa as attempting to reassemble new forms of authority but also in ways that are often limited in scope. Interventions can be transformative, catalytic, or symbolic, a conceptual clarification that gives us a more granular view of how African states are shaped by assemblages of intervention in the area of border control.

The Production of Security

Borders, as spaces connecting inside and outside, safe and unsafe, are sites around which tremendous fear and anxiety crystallize. For instance, Spanish and EU authorities are anxious about irregular migration from West African states, the same way that the Mauritanian government is fearful of terrorist infiltration and undocumented migrants from the sub-region. William Walters (2008: 174–175) refers to such anxiety when arguing that 'border' is a 'sort of meta-concept that condenses a whole set of negative meanings, including illegal immigration, the threat of terrorism, dysfunctional globalization, loss of sovereignty, narcotic smuggling and insecurity'. The border is a dense space where security (and insecurity) is created, known, assuaged, and modulated. If security is not a given, and is rather given meaning by practices such as borderwork, the problems and solutions of security become questions of *knowledge* production, reflected in framings of threat, forms of expertise, types of common sense about policing, social rules and norms, standards, and bureaucratic practices. Recent constructivist approaches help us to build towards a view of security problems and their solutions as the products and objects of routinized practices. Building on this book's IPS method, which foregrounds process and practice, provides one entry point into conceptualizing security as a knowledge practice.

The last two decades have seen work in 'critical security studies' broaden and deepen the meaning of the term 'security' while fundamentally politicizing the concept (see Krause and Williams 1997). The meaning of security has evolved from a state-centric notion assuming the existence of objective, material threats, towards one emphasizing the constitutive role of identity (Campbell 1998; Hansen 2006), the discursive and performative construction of security issues (Buzan, Waever, and De Wilde 1998), and the importance of emancipation (Booth 2007). In CSS, security is seen as the result of an intersubjective process of construction. CSS has a complex heritage – drawing as much from the speech act theory of Austin as the social theory of Bourdieu and Foucault – but there is a consensus that, to varying degrees, its constitution implicates discourses as much as material and institutional practices. My discussion below starts from one of the seminal views on the discursive construction of security – securitization theory – later moving to a view of security as a more thoroughly sociological process.

The border as a space of anxiety is continually played up in the discourse of African security officials, who – in the same breath – tend to conflate terrorism, migration, organized crime, and other mobile threats. This emphasis on West Africa and the Sahel as threatened by the porosity of its international borders makes concerns about frontiers into questions of survival. Securitization theory (ST) emphasizes this form of naming of existential threats and the deployment of exceptional measures to stop these threats (Buzan, Waever, and De Wilde 1998). ST starts from the basis that there is no real definition of security 'out there', but rather it is a question of understanding how particular issues come to be seen in the frame of security, what security (its invocation or otherwise) *does* to particular issues or settings, and what responses it demands. The genesis of this informally named 'Copenhagen school' approach – formulated at the Copenhagen Peace Research Institute – lies in Waever's (1988) unpublished manuscript 'Security, the Speech Act'. However, its clearest published iteration came in 'Securitization and Desecuritization', a chapter Waever contributed to Ronnie Lipschutz's (1995) *On Security*. Here, Waever claims that 'we can regard "security" as a *speech act* [. . .] In this usage, security is not of interest as a sign that refers to something more real; the utterance itself is the act', adding that by this very utterance the actor who performs it 'moves a particular development into a specific area, and thereby claims a special right to use whatever means are necessary to block it' (Waever 1995: 55). This conception of 'security' is taken up by Buzan, Waever, and De Wilde (1998), who define the process of securitization as 'the move that takes politics beyond the established rules of the game and frames the issue either as a special kind of politics or as above politics' (23). This zone outside of politics specifies what Waever (1995) had earlier called simply the 'specific area' where exceptional actions are justified.

Securitization is therefore a *process* of moving issues outside of political or democratic contestation (Buzan, Waever, and De Wilde 1998: 23–24), and this process or 'move' is a discursive one – a *securitizing* move where the performance of speech itself is the act. A securitizing move is therefore a 'discourse that takes the form of presenting something as an existential threat to a referent object' (25). The central elements of securitization are actors who make the discursive acts in question, an audience on whose acceptance the success of a securitization move rests, and a referent object that is presented by the discourse of security as being under existential threat (Buzan, Waever, and De Wilde 1998). This framework, which is relatively parsimonious, has been subject to critiques and improvements adding an attention to gender (Hansen 2000), an expansion of the idea of speech acts to include images (Williams 2003), and an attention to audiences' 'psycho-social disposition' (Balzacq 2005) or professional character (Salter 2008a). These additions to the ST framework provide a greater degree of embeddedness to the question of how security comes into being, and bring us towards a view of security as the result of professional interplay. This view is the one I turn to next.

Securitization is reliant on a logical trinity – an actor with authority to speak, a referent object to securitize, and an audience to accept the securitizing move – to allow exceptional measures. However, security can also be thought of as an ongoing, routinized process with wider links to various forms of knowledge. It does not take grand pronouncements or press releases to train a team of sniffer dogs, to install a new passenger screening system in an airport, or to place a French migration expert into an African interior ministry. Yet there is an assembly of previously disparate technologies, forms of knowledge, and individual histories. This is what Huysmans (2007) points to when linking the emergence of security issues to 'domains of practice' and 'insecurity domains'. Huysmans acts to bridge ST with a body of literature, largely driven by Foucault's and Bourdieu's sociologies, that sees security as a routinized form of governance with linkages to broader fields of knowledge, emerging from the interactions of professionals. This approach, informally named the 'Paris school' (PS) by the CASE collective (2006), developed around 'an agenda focusing on security professionals, the governmental rationality of security, and the political structuring effects of security technology and knowledge' (449). The PS is therefore concerned with the *sociological* aspects of security and its nature as an ongoing political practice. The ST approach, by emphasizing discourse and audience, implicitly favours the analysis of the speech of influential actors. For the PS approach, a focus on the oft-invisible 'backstage' actors of security, and specifically to their social games and competition, is central to understanding the contemporary logics of security.

Work from the PS approach stresses the influence of security professionals in particular. Bigo's (2001) work on the trans-nationalization of security attributes this to 'interpenetration' of the police and the military. The assumption underlying his work is that security is the product of competition and struggles between professionals of (in)security (see Bigo and Tsoukala 2008). He succinctly encapsulates the sociological approach to security by defining it as 'certainly not a speech act, but the result of struggles of a configuration of professionals in competition for the categorisation of threats and the priorities and forms of the struggles against them' (Bigo 2012: 118). The Paris school approach does not reject securitization theory wholesale, but echoes or refines perspectives held by proponents of the original ST framework – notably the term 'securitization' itself. For example, Jef Huysmans (2007) conserves the idea of the securitization process as a prioritization of threats. However, the major contribution of the 'security as norm' approach is to see security as an ongoing governing strategy. While ST sees security as an exceptional condition, Huysmans (2006: 9) argues for a view of security as 'embedded in training, routine, and technical knowledge and skills, as well as technological artefacts'. Bigo (2009: 113), similarly, draws on 'the Foucaultian approach to security, territory and population which places the emphasis on security as norm'. In each case, security is a governing technology that emerges from the work of socially embedded actors, whose interactions, histories and interests (rather than discourse alone) shapes what security is.

It is important to look at practices of securitization because most borderwork practices in the global south are enacted almost completely outside deliberative politics in the first place, often through transnational expert networks. This was very obvious throughout my fieldwork in Mauritania and Senegal. One of my main concerns was to find out more about the Guardia Civil's Project West Sahel, for which only a very short description existed on the European Commission's website. Given the multi-million Euro funding, very little was accessible to the average European citizen about the project. The excision of border security from public deliberation is also visible in the persistence of public rumours about how and where police cooperation even happens (which leads to discursive tropes such as 'Le Frontex', see Chapter 4). In some cases, the 'assembly' of border security actors is not even institutional but highly personalized, and dependent on personal relations between, say Spanish police commanders (Chapter 4) or gendarmerie superiors and offices (Chapter 5). As a result, although policy documents may sometimes provide insight into the broad contours of various programmes, public-facing discourse is of limited analytic utility compared to an in-depth examination of the mix of professionals who put security into practice. To understand the transmission of knowledge, we must theorize how this knowledge emerges and circulates in their networks.

Security Professionals: Cultures and Knowledges

Investigating security in the global south entails being attentive to the practices of the diverse professionals who frame security threats and shape responses to them. Behind every practice lies a cognitive logic. For instance, a securitization move relies on claiming knowledge of a threat, of the target, of ways to 'block' it, and of how to persuade the audience to accept the securitizing discourse (or images), regardless of the move's success. This makes the expertise of the speaker and the assumed knowledge of the audience into essential elements of the security equation. Similarly, the 'security as norm' approach identified with the Paris school assumes knowledge to be produced in social fields of practice, in which securitization may not always be an identifiable or public-facing move. Border control, similarly, is a set of contingent practices that are reflections of societal experiences and priorities, which are mediated and put into practice by particular communities of practitioners. Many scholars have tackled these intellectual schemes by which borders are governed. For example, Louise Amoore's (2006) and Benjamin Muller's (2010) analyses of biometric governance have both identified a turn to risk-based modes of border governance, while Walters (2002) has identified a 'biopolitical' turn in bordering. These all suggest that there are broader 'normativities' behind border control, but they are not primarily concerned with *how* these border control norms come to be created, assembled, displaced, and adopted. If border security is embedded in social and historical context, those who 'do' it bring into play particular assumptions, histories, interests, and dispositions. These are of considerable importance to any discussion of border security in West Africa precisely because this space represents a meeting of a diverse range of actors. A range of norms, rules, best practices, tacit and unspoken assumptions, and procedures sustains border control practices in this region. Kaldor and Selchow account for some of this through the concept of 'security culture' to capture 'the set of actions taken to secure whatever is taken to be secured, together with the set of institutions that are designed to authorise, imagine, plan, and implement these actions' (Kaldor and Selchow 2015: 6). Similarly, but only within the realm of securitization theory, Klüfers (2014: 278) refers to 'security repertoires' to account for the 'sociocultural settings' of security. Social practices such as these depend on some cognitive work (see Adler and Pouliot 2011). How is this knowledge created? From where does it emerge?

One place knowledge comes from is from the personal backgrounds and hunches of borderwork actors. If we think of security problems and solutions as framed by ongoing routines of security, security knowledge reflects the experiences and interactions of the actors who construct them. One approach to thinking of this is emergence of knowledge in practices is through Bourdieu's concept of 'doxa' (Villumsen 2012) which links it in turn to the 'field'. The pithiest explanation for doxa – given by Bourdieu (1977: 167) himself – describes it as something that *'goes without saying because it comes without saying'* (emphasis in original). Doxa is therefore intimately tied to the practical knowledge that animates the actions of agents in different fields. Bourdieu and Wacquant (1992: 73–74) define doxa as 'uncontested acceptance of the daily lifeworld', which is in turn tied to social positions in a 'field'. As a result, doxa is partly derived from the habitus of actors – the set of learned dispositions that shape their subjective interrelation to the objective set of relations in which they act. Bourdieu's definition of doxa sees it as a largely 'prereflexive' and 'infrapolitical' (74). Actors are not automatons and do have strategies, according to Bourdieu, but these are conditioned by the position they occupy rather than a rational-actor calculus.

While I eschew a strict Bourdieusian analysis in favour of assemblage, this idea of 'doxa' helps to describe where security expertise comes from and is called upon. What we could simply call 'security knowledge' is inherent in the assembly of diverse border security actors, while *expertise* is a more self-aware and strategic form of this knowledge. Actors are aware of their expertise and of the fact that they derive symbolic and cultural benefits from its deployment. Expertise also confers credibility, and as Abrahamsen and Williams (2011: 93) argue, it is tied to 'ideational capacities' that function as 'socially recognized forms of legitimation and recognized expertise'. Expertise is a mode of professional advancement, highlighting the strategic (i.e. not only cognitive) applications of security knowledge. Take, for example, the work of police attachés in European embassies in countries such as Senegal. The idea that borders should be selectively permeable and buttressed by a strong policing capacity is part of their received knowledge as police officers or as security attachés fluent in EU border control standards and living in migrant-sending countries. Their expertise, on the other hand, is more reflexive and strategic, and may be used to design training practices or dispense advice, which in turn reinforces their claims to expertise. This is something that is also instructive about the divergence between global and local politics of border security, as disagreements within assemblages of security about just who is 'expert' can be revelatory. The disagreement about how biometrics should be used in Senegal, which I discuss in Chapter 6, reveals a distinction between the modernizing vision of local police and the scepticism of European interveners about how technologies fit into broader systems of governance.

Security knowledge goes beyond the specific histories or strategies of individuals. This is why ideas such as 'doxa' cannot account for 'security knowledge' in a satisfactory way for this book's analysis. Zaiotti's (2011) concept of 'cultures of border control' helps us move towards how knowledge is shared and bundled, paying attention to both micropractices as well as how these are reflected in broader policy changes. He defines such a 'culture' as 'a relatively stable constellation of background assumptions *and corresponding practices* shared by a border control policy community in a given period and geographical location' (23, emphasis in original). Thus, there are two important elements in the border control community: its normative or dominant 'common sense' and the constellation of actors that operate within these. The main elements of a 'culture' of border control include (25–27): the 'characteristics that a border should possess', the 'proper approach to manage them', and the 'identity of the relevant border control community' which are all reflected in relevant or symptomatic texts (25). Practices, in turn, are shaped by institutional setting, number of actors involved, the relations between these actors, and how institutionalized the policy process is (26–27). What Zaiotti does is emphasize the agent as well as the community (of which parts can be bundled into 'assemblage', in my understanding), and the ways that their practices are co-produced with knowledges such as official policy pronouncements and texts.

If we understand the practice of borderwork as involving assemblages of security, then it is imperative that we account for the knowledges behind it as being not only social but also *technical*. Building from the approaches above, security knowledge is incarnated in particular standards, best practices, and texts. It should be added that although these ideational capacities are produced by the interactions of human actors, they also depend on – and are reflected by – particular instruments and tools. This is not to attribute a uniquely human intentionality to objects, but rather to broaden the scope of where we can 'see' security knowledge. Non-human elements act in three ways with regards to security knowledge. First, objects play a mediating role in security relationships. Actors can struggle to claim credit for or ownership over a particular technology, for instance, or struggle over the meaning of a particular tool. Second, non-human factors represent and incarnate particular ways of doing border security. A border post incarnates the norm of Westphalian territorial sovereignty, and an EU-funded training manual may draw on expertise from a particular member state's experience. Third, non-humans actively shape practices by producing certain path dependencies: think of the corporate lock-in demanded by the provider of a biometric scanner, or the way that passport scanning equipment lying unused creates an incentive to design new biometric passports. By considering the role of such 'actants' (see Latour 2005 in previous chapter) we can see how non-human factors actively make a difference in modulating who controls the border and how, and what the border is in the first place. This emphasis on the materiality is crucial to the chapters to follow in Part II. It is by foregrounding the material that the importance of patrol vehicles to shifts in regional security cooperation is shown (Chapter 4), that border posts' developmental rationality through utility connections is evidenced (Chapter 5), and that the forms of auditing culture within the Senegalese border police are shown (Chapter 6).

While the specific knowledge or 'cultures' of borderwork are covered in the empirical cases presented throughout Part II of this book, it is worth providing an example here. The need for technological solutions to border control, and the interlinkage of these systems, is a typical demand of international interveners and frequently an aspiration of West African security actors. Actors working from within European border control communities (from which IOM often draws its expert consultants) will likely draw on the Schengen experience of interconnected databases. Given the overlap of social worlds inherent in the transnational assemblages that enact border security intervention projects, these sets of actors will necessarily interact with people from the Mauritanian law enforcement world in which control over border data may factor into perceptions of expertise. In this site of the international, a shared culture around technology might emerge, with each actor applying and drawing different resources from the same security practice. Of course, this question of how knowledge actually functions in different spaces of the international is not always so simple, and some of the mechanics of its take-up (contestation, resistance, hybridization) may tell us about the political relationships at play in border control cooperation. In the section that follows, I leverage the analytical tools of IPS to show that border security knowledge is *mobile* and *mutable*.

Mobility of Security Knowledge

Many of my formal conversations with West African 'security professionals' took place in their offices, in which it is impossible to miss the small markers of how globalized their work is becoming: seemingly banal items such as sticky notes from a migration management workshop, or drug testing equipment from an international partner, are evidence of the assembly of African state officials and institutions with Western aid and 'expertise'. Contemporary border security policies in West Africa are inseparable from the production and transmission of knowledge about security. Security knowledge, produced through the practices that emerge in response to problems such as migration and terrorism, also *moves* between global spaces. This is something that has featured in some existing literature on border control. For instance, in an article on the IOM, Andrijasevic and Walters (2010: 984) argue that the technicalization of migration control is a form of 'normalization' operating through the process of alignment of migration policies with Western technical norms. They speak of the desire to 'generalise a particular model of statehood' (983) but are not specific as to how this model is transmitted. What this literature does not do is provide an account of how these models (knowledges) of border control actually travel (or fail to travel). This is a key question that is under-researched in more theoretical accounts of borders in CSS. Given the contemporary dynamics of north–south cooperation and the cognitive encounters it brings about, knowing what these bundles of knowledge are and how they move is instructive about the types of global relationships being fostered.

The methodological tools of IPS are particularly useful in attempting to overcome this lacuna of thinking about the transmission of security knowledge in/to/from the global south. Although the approaches to CSS mentioned above largely fall within this research sensibility, they too often focus on European and North American examples. An IPS approach, founded on an active re-evaluation of what the 'international' is, and attentiveness to quotidian practice, can be productively applied to think about global knowledge mobilities. The IPS approach provides the theoretical attitude needed to understand the spatial spread of the assemblages in which knowledge production and transmission happen. This builds on the work on security above, leveraging the IPS emphasis on investigating sites where diverse scales of governance meet. Transfers of knowledge between these sites are subject to a constant interplay between mutability and immutability, in that knowledge is transmitted, emulated, adapted, resisted, misunderstood, or used strategically. In short, knowledge is mobile and malleable. The concept of the '(im)mutable mobile' from actor-network theory is particularly useful to understand not only the formation of this borderwork knowledge, but also its transmission and reception across space. A lens attuned to the interplay of global and local, and mutable and immutable, is best positioned to show the mobility of knowledge that sustains borderwork in West Africa. Contemporary security knowledges in border control in West Africa are transmitted through exemplars, emulation, and pedagogy.

IPS has, in critical security studies, generally been 'done' to examine practices and policies in North America and Europe. This is not a cynical or lazy oversight, but rather a lacuna linked to the genesis and sociology of the research approach itself. The 'Paris school', the foremost IPS approach in security studies, has dealt with aspects of European integration such as the divergences between the sociology of EU security agencies and the borders of the union's member states. The origins of IPS are therefore entrenched in the European experience: the binaries IPS-driven approach have tried to contest have been of integration/disintegration, national/European, police/military, and so on. Scholars working in this vein have mapped the social space of EU security (Bigo et al. 2007) as well as examined the mobilization of discourses of insecurity (Bigo and Tsoukala 2008). Other IPS-inspired approaches to borders have produced ethnographies of citizen border patrols in the United States (Doty 2009) and of the Finnish border guards (Prokkola 2013). However, very few IPS works on borders (with exceptions, such as Voelkner 2011; Schomerus and De Vries 2014; Sandor 2016) have used the tools of IPS to look at border security practices in the global south, or the north–south diffusion of security policies and related forms of discipline.

One way that an IPS approach can help us grapple with the politics of security provision in the global south – where knowledge transmission is key – is by refusing to assume a traditional geopolitical view of space. Looking to the French term for IPS pays dividends for more than just pedantic purposes: the term *sociologie politique de l'international* calls for a 'political sociology of the international', which is not the scaled-up form of political sociology as the English translation might suggest. Doing a political sociology of the international is useful to examine knowledge transfer between north and south precisely because the global-local complexity of these transfers defies traditional geography. An IPS sensibility pushes us to critique such conceptions of the international and think of it through its various *sites*. Recalling Salter's (2007: 49) definition of IPS, he adds that the approach 'tak[es] as its subject matter not the grand structure of a universal politics, but more modest examinations of specific sites and institutions where politics are enacted'. This compels us to keep in mind that global and local are not effects of distance alone. For instance, knowledge can be transmitted from 'global' to 'local' within the spatial area of a very small zone in an African country. The international, in this example, is actually not a space of anarchy between two states, but is the site of interaction between intervener and intervened.

Finally, applying IPS thinking to the global south opens up new analytical spaces of critique. The IPS approach to security in Europe is rooted in responses to EU integration, and particularly the changes (and continuities) in approaches to security and immigration that accompany this process. The critique of some of the EU-specific binaries mentioned should, in the global south, take on a rather different tack. In this case, an IPS-led suspicion of binary distinctions should push us to rethink dyads such as expert/non-expert, modern/outdated, and effective/ineffective that are much more specific to security practices in the global south. In fact, given the north–south interactions at play, the very definition of the border security 'community' (to reprise Zaiotti's term) should come under scrutiny, as security *relations* sit at the intersection of different communities of practitioners even though actors may operate in a common site.

Border security knowledge should be thought of as *mobile* and *mutable*. It is mobile because it can move between different sites of the international, and mutable because this process is not always smooth, one-sided, one-way, or successful. The concept of the '(im)mutable mobile' is useful as a heuristic device to understand this rocky and uneven take-up of border security knowledge. Immutable mobiles are sets of bundled practices that move over space and time and retain their shape. Gavin Kendall defines them as 'convenient packages that hold together and maintain their coherence even when they are moved, enabling them to be effective in a variety of settings. So, for example, a map is a conveniently packaged-up "knowledge" which can be transported easily, and which can be used regardless of the war office desk or the battleship where it is spread out' (Kendall 2004: 65). Immutable mobiles can be objects but also practices, discourses, and imaginaries. They are bundles of the kinds of knowledge mentioned earlier: norms, standards, best practices, rules, tacit knowledges, rhythms, procedures, and more. Tony Porter stresses this importance of the micro and of the material, suggesting that global governance is too often

seen as consisting of large forces without sufficient consideration of the specific humans, objects and networks that are needed if these forces are to be transmitted. Alone, humans have great difficulty in transmitting actions across the distances that global governance involves, and they therefore rely heavily on objects such as written texts, electronic networks, weapons systems, transportation systems, and meeting rooms and offices. (Porter 2012: 553)

The classic example of an immutable mobile in ANT is John Law's (1986) study of Portuguese ships in the development of that country's empire. In this work, Law points to the mobility and durability of these ships and how they acted to enact control at a distance. He also points to the network of relations that made this control possible: the role of texts, ports, navigation tools, and more. Law draws our attention to the object under consideration but also the bundle that helps it to be immutable and durable. In the context of borderwork in West Africa, we can think of a patrol plane donated by Spain to Senegal as such an immutable mobile. The principles of flight that allow it to patrol the border remain immutable, but there's more to the bundle that keeps it airborne: the fuel provided by Spain to power it, the bilateral agreement through which Senegal promises to fly daily, and the training programme that builds local patrol expertise. Immutable mobiles help us to think of the human and non-human assemblages that transmit approaches to controlling borders.

Not all knowledges are immutable, of course, and part of the import of border security knowledge is precisely its ability to be mutable which is in turn instructive about the *political* relationships around it. As John Law (1999) argues, to speak of immutable mobiles is also to assume the presence of *mutable* ones. The take-up and reception of objects and knowledges in different contexts can be rocky and uneven. After all, networks are composed of materials (say, a European border training manual) and humans (a Senegalese border guard) that may form precarious or unexpected networks of their own. This can be seen in the interaction between knowledge and infrastructure: a European border management approach reliant on always-on computerized databases, may lack the mutability to exist in a border area with no internet connection (say, in the Mauritanian desert) or with an unreliable electricity grid. In other respects, culture clashes can be important, and '[local] micro-struggles can challenge and shape externally defined programmes' (Bachmann and Hönke 2009: 99). This suggests a degree of agency in the local, disturbing ideas that intervention is about the smooth imposition of outside ideas. For instance, the adaptation of the IOM's entire border registration system (MIDAS; see Chapter 5) to fit onto a low-memory USB stick is specifically intended to make the system as mutable as possible – but this does not anticipate the local uses to which these forms of registration may be put (see Chapter 6).

The first major way that bundles of security knowledge move is through exemplars. Exemplars are very often 'best practices', but can also be behaviours and ideals that are tacitly worthy of emulation. The IOM's border control programmes are heavily reliant on the use of exemplars, as the organization relies on the global diffusion of its relatively standard policy prescriptions. For instance, it is the most active organization globally in terms of spreading the concept of national migration strategies (and their associated dialogue processes) as well as the use of risk-analysis methods at borders. The IOM has even institutionalized structures such as the African Capacity Building Centre (ACBC) in Moshi, Tanzania, which can be understood as a site for the accumulation and dissemination of such migration management exemplars. According to the ACBC's own literature, one of its purposes is to 'develop, institutionalize and deliver on-site and off-site migration management training programmes' (IOM 2010). The construction of border posts in Mauritania and in South Sudan reflects how exemplars about how borders should be managed draw on global ideals as much as project-specific methods. In each case, the IOM construction of border posts follows a global exemplar about sovereignty – the creation of a bounded and defensible space with a state presence – but also a more specific exemplar of how border management capacity-building can work within a defined budget and timeframe.

Exemplars bring us to the idea of knowledge generation, and to the question: where do border control knowledges come from? Here we must recognize the important role that organizations like the IOM play as autonomous yet interlinked *generators* of exemplars. As a case in point, most of the IOM's border management standards draw inspiration from documents such as the EU's Schengen Borders Code. This Code defines border control as

not only checks on persons at border crossing points and surveillance between these border crossing points, but also an analysis of the risks for internal security and analysis of the threats that may affect the security of external borders. (European Union 2006: 1)

This suggests an extension of the border through space (into the EU space and well outside it) but also through time (future threats). This is particularly important as IOM activities in Africa – such as its capacity-building project in Mauritania – explicitly aim to coordinate law enforcement at the border and inland. This reflects how what are considered 'international norms' or 'best practices' of border control actually come from a particular and historically situated moment. In this case, the IOM's growth has coincided with the particular moment in the West – and the EU specifically – in which borders have become more multi-layered and harder to cross.

Exemplars also operate through what Hosein (2004: 189) calls 'policy laundering': the way that 'some countries [...] push for certain regulatory standards in international bodies and then bring those regulations home under the requirement of harmonization and the guise of multilateralism'. Hosein identifies the removal of certain issues from deliberation through such 'high' politics as a crucial part of policy laundering. This reinforces the technocratic aspects of border management, illustrating how – as discussed in the first section of this chapter – security emerges from the interactions of professionals rather than an obvious public-facing securitizing discourse. This is a particularly important factor in semi-authoritarian states (such as Mauritania) in which security policy is more likely to be a 'backstage' matter than a question of vibrant public debate.

Knowledges about border control also flow through emulation: countries, institutions, and individuals take on particular characteristics deemed desirable or advanced. The role of voluntary emulation is reflected in the agency of individual states and contests the idea that borderwork knowledges are always imposed from outside. For instance, the IOM's Development Fund is deployed largely as the request of beneficiary states. Similarly, EU assistance for the formation of national border management strategies like Senegal's is always provided at the formal request of the recipient. Emulation emanates from the sheer power of the signifier of 'modernity' as a source of symbolic capital. The supposed simplicity of the technological 'fix' from countries of the global north provides a powerful source of inspiration for African countries. This is very much the case for biometric technologies, which are seen as remedies for the ages-old problem of unreliable, untraceable paper documents. The technical merits of such systems, even if assessed, take a back seat to their interoperability with and conformity to global standards. Their symbolic importance as markers of technology trumps any objective utility they may have. The importance of biometric documents to the image of a state as trustworthy and 'serious' about security is an almost unanimous viewpoint. This is notable because many security actors in charge of these technologies must 'save face' in the various international police conferences and exhibitions in which they take part. Their emulation of a global standard (which often places them ahead of many Western countries) is a mode of asserting expertise.

The strategic adoption of global standards also provides symbolic capital in a more local context. As Dezalay and Garth (2002) show, such capital obtained internationally is very useful when converted into the local context. They argue that groups of professionals 'can use international credentials, expertise, and connections to build capital that they can reinvest in domestic public arenas' (34). This is certainly the case when it comes to the emulation of global standards, as knowledges of these can help to solidify credibility and expert knowledge domestically. Take, for instance, how Senegalese police commanders make their office decoration illustrate their globally oriented knowledge relationships, displaying badges and certificates from foreign-run training courses.

Emulation is also possible within individual institutions as a means of attempting to replicate practices in different spaces. Some Guardia Civil officers who work in migrant-sending countries in West Africa, as security liaisons in Spanish embassies, have prior experience working in that country's African enclaves of Ceuta and Melilla. This direct experience with what is Spain's 'toughest' border to police provides valued (in a symbolic sense) expertise that coincides with a hope that it can be applied in other migration hot spots such as Senegal or Mauritania. This shows how learning and diffusion do not only go north–south. They can even go in the reverse direction: from intervened to intervener. When a Senegalese navy operational group commander presents his patrol techniques at the Euro-African police conference, it is impossible to imagine the Spanish hosts failing to adopt a single lesson from this. These expert meetings, such as the Africa-Frontex Intelligence Community (AFIC), play a key role in the transmission of approaches to border security. The AFIC brings together Frontex member states and many West and Central African countries into a network of information-sharing structures. It has been in operation since 2010 and regularly holds regional meetings with African and European security officials, replicating in part the 'best practices' of the model of Risk Analysis Networks used by Frontex at Europe's eastern borders (in the 'Western Balkans' and 'Eastern European' border zones respectively) (Frontex 2015). In 2016 alone, this community met in Ghana and Mauritania and the agenda for these meetings has – given the blurry concept of border security – extended to a range of issues beyond migration such as organized crime, trafficking, and terrorism. This type of collaboration is enabled by the everyday practices enabled by a technological backbone, with the AFIC relying on the EU's Communication and Information Resource Centre for Administrations, Businesses and Citizens electronic document-sharing platform.

Finally, the most direct and perhaps most prominent form of transmission of borderwork knowledge is the pedagogical style most associated with statebuilding and capacity-building interventions. To begin with, pedagogy is crucial to contestations over expertise. Although it is seemingly altruistic or at least mildly disinterested, such forms of teaching and instruction are forms of accruing reputational gains through the reinforcement of a (self-)perception as advanced or modern. This educational practice is therefore dependent on the prior existence of an unequal distribution of capital between teacher and learner, which the pedagogical act maintains or even exacerbates. At its root, the politics of border control pedagogy is paternalistic. External interveners claiming to know better, even when attentive to the limits of their local knowledge, continue to bring their material and symbolic resources to bear in African borderlands by the millions of dollars and euros. This is not to erase local agency – and as Chapter 7 argues, arguments about neo-colonialism are wide of the mark – but it is certainly a structure of opportunity in which African actors must operate. For instance, while many of my Western interlocutors voiced strong opinions about the attraction of per diem allowances for training courses, this can be seen as foot-dragging against external attempts to certify and re-certify expertise.

Pedagogy takes place through direct training but also through agenda-setting. For instance, IOM training on border control methods, as Andrijasevic and Walters (2010) highlight, makes trainees interrogate their own learning. This is visible in the IOM's *Essentials of Migration Management*, one of that organization's training manuals for border staff. In each section dealing with themes such as border security, travel documents, or refugee law, the reader is asked to apply her knowledge and test her competencies. Pedagogy also works through face-to-face meetings such as regional law enforcement meetings and migration policy workshops. Bringing together diverse actors around particular policy problems is also effective, as has been the case in Mauritania where organizations such as the IOM and UNHCR 'perform a key role in the [north–south] transfer of cognitive categories and frameworks' about migration in Mauritania (Poutignat and Streiff-Fénart 2010: 203) through, for example, the use of institutionalized migration management study groups. Pedagogy operates to responsibilize on an institutional level. Take the aforementioned case of EU assistance for border management strategies. This assistance is initially made available by the EU through its own funding programmes, but it is up to potential beneficiary countries to apply for this funding with fully formed proposals. This means that such a project is as much an exercise in strategy-building as it is in building up the good governance that generates such successful proposals in the first place. That local EU

Figure 3.1 Mauritanian security officials receiving IOM training on border and migration management, funded in part by the European Union. © IOM 2015. Image used with permission.

delegations will assist with the formulation of such proposals confirms this pedagogical angle (see Figure 3.1).

Pedagogy of border security approaches relies on the adaptability of knowledge. The International Civil Aviation Organization (ICAO) sets standards for aviation and airport security through standards (which are mandatory) and other recommended practices. For the French-run Appui à la sûreté de l'aviation civile en Afrique (ASACA) airport security programme, which delivers ICAO-compliant training to airport staff in twenty African countries, training is based on standardized ICAO Standardized Training Packages (STPs; the French name, *mallettes pédagogiques normalisées*, is more telling as to its pedagogical and normalizing effects). These STPs are taught by ICAO accredited experts in each country, who modify the language and idioms used in each local context. This makes the actual pedagogical moment more effective as the local experts hired are culturally closer to the recipients of the training. The justification for this localism is that 'the French language is not the same everywhere', and so knowledges, even when standardized, must be mutable to fulfil their pedagogical effect.

Exemplars, emulation and pedagogy serve to transmit ways of doing border control, and in doing so also transmit understandings of what the security problem is in the first place. They also reflect the broader worldview that underpins different approaches to security provision in West Africa, and the global south more generally: that security is reliant on state capacity defined through the prism of modernization. This is the rationality of intervention to which I turn next.

Border Security and State Capacity

What dynamics do border security knowledge and its transmission tell us about the politics of security in the global south? What impacts do these practices concretely have in the places in which they are applied? In the West African context, the structures and relationships which enable border security knowledge to move, and the ways this movement is justified, are underpinned by a developmental mindset, shared by global and local actors, that border security is a question of state capacity. The linkage of security and development issues is well developed in the literature on statebuilding, peacebuilding, post-conflict reconstruction, and intervention (e.g. Fitz-Gerald 2004; Buur, Jensen, and Stepputat 2007; Zoellick 2008; *Security Dialogue* 2010; Krogstad 2012). Indeed, it is an appealing way to understand border-work interventions, especially as intervening states and organizations have sought *holistic* ways to address instability, insecurity, and poverty in the global south. Development and institutional 'capacity-building', including security sector reform, are seen as necessary conditions for peace and security (see Paris 2004; Uvin 2002), and a state's 'capacity' to secure itself is essential to the well-being of its population (Zartman 1995). As Zartman (1995) note, 'security' and 'development' have had remarkably similar conceptual evolutions over the last fifty years and share considerable ontological terrain. If we understand borders as functions determining inclusion and exclusion (as in Chapter 2), and security as knowledge about threats and responses to them, then the presence or absence of *capacity* becomes a crucial point of intervention that straddles security and development. One finds this focus on capacity arise consistently when examining border security programmes and speaking to global and local professionals in this community. The common refrain is that only by enhancing capacity can illicit flows be effectively managed and mitigated.

It is impossible to think about the implantation of border security practices in places like Senegal and Mauritania without also considering the modernizing politics that underlie them, and the notion of capacity that this modernizing zeal relies on. That security as an 'ordering' device, particularly at borders, is nothing new (see Van Houtum 2010). But *how* to ensure that order, and the state's *ability* to maintain that order – at the border – is not commonly discussed in border studies or critical security studies. This is where the literature on statebuilding is particularly helpful, in that it reaffirms the continued analytical relevance of a Weberian view of sovereignty for security actors. Jackson and Rosberg (1982) speak of 'empirical' or de facto sovereignty, which requires territory, a relatively stable population and an effective mode of governance. In Jackson's later work (Jackson 1993) he describes as 'quasi-states' those states that, although benefiting from juridical sovereignty and recognition, do not successfully lay claim to the more empirical (proto-Weberian) formulation of sovereignty as successful control and administration. So how does 'capacity' operate?

First, security capacity is conceived of as the ability to sense. It is necessarily about surveillance, which in turn ties capacity to visibility and a broader form of knowability. The idea of legibility, like surveillance, is intimately bound to long-standing techniques inherent to modernity such as surveillance, development, and bureaucracy. The desire for legibility, Scott argues, stems from a 'high-modernist' worldview that predominates in states' grand projects: it thrives in the joining together of Enlightenment will to order and a weak civil society. High-modernism is a response to the 'illegibility' that the state sees in the contingent forms of life represented by the local, the natural, and anything else that escapes the administrative gaze. This gaze is similar to what John Torpey (2000) calls the state's 'embrace' of its population, which stresses the work of identifying and 'filing' that goes into maintaining a body of citizens. The central problem of (il)legibility is therefore fundamental to practices of surveillance and social control. In this sense, I am using the term legibility to describe the state's myriad practices for controlling borders, reading bodies, and managing populations and their movements. This pursuit of legibility, which is associated with grand projects of state reform in developing countries, emanates from a desire for modernization.

Capacity also implies managerial competence and willpower. For instance, 'migration management' implies some kind of bureaucratic capacity to – before control comes into the equation – adequately quantify and respond, at a governmental level, to flows of people. This is why the EU is so insistent on the use of statistics-driven migration profiles as part of its help for migration strategies. Capacity as a managerial category also means managing risks. Capacity as a managerial phenomenon makes itself a type of pre-requisite: before implementing a given security policy, a state must have the capacity to comprehend the policy itself. States in the south are candidates for intervention because, in the words of an ICAO official, they 'often struggle to implement complex specifications because they lack technical expertise and/or funds' (Tiedge 2012). Beyond such issues of ability, motivation is a key part of what counts as a state's capacity. There is a key difference between the 'will' and 'ability' of a state to enact sovereign power (Bain 2011), but the politics of capacity-building seeks to intervene on *both* of those factors. Motivational capacity includes professionalism and expertise, and capacity-building practices often rely on the formation of a cognitive consensus (through workshops or training) as a means of ensuring that all concur on the solution at hand.

Capacity is technological – it is the tangible means through which state power is enacted. Technology is also laden with views of progress and ideas about capacity have a built-in teleological ideal of modernization. One needs to look no further than the way biometric technologies are understood by Senegalese police officials ('finally, we've caught up!') to understand the temporal element that technology embodies. Capacity as technology is also about using technology *well*. Interveners are often keen to stress that 'low tech' solutions work best, and that the interplay of professional culture and technology is more important than sheer advancement. However, this underlines the point that capacity is technological, since technology is by definition a socially embedded factor.

The buttressing or improvement of these aforementioned capacities can be called a form of modernization. In this case, it entails a movement towards Westphalian statehood. The normative assumption in capacity-building practices is that African states, hampered by colonial era borders and weak administrative efficiency, must first attain successful statehood through better territorial control (at borders) and better visibility of population (through identification). Modernization is therefore a form of statebuilding, which Hameiri (2010: 2) defines as 'the broad range of programs and projects designed to build or strengthen the capacity of institutions, organizations and agencies'. Statebuilding does not always concern military or traditional concerns of 'hard' security. Rather, it is a routine and unspectacular practice aiming at buttressing the state. Hameiri notes that this type of statebuilding outside of post-conflict settings has 'taken on a more pre-emptive, risk management form than earlier post–Cold War interventions' (2). This emphasis on risk management explains how statebuilding can be thought of as a form of power on its own. For example, the Frontex missions off West Africa's Atlantic coast have been very successful in reducing the number of migrant departures by sea, but they continue under the guise of managing the risk of new attempts.

Modernization also relies on spillover effects. An example: the Datacard Group, which was charged with overhauling Guinea-Bissau's biometric national ID, speak of this system in terms of 're-establishing' the nation's administrative credibility. According to them, the system will 'go a long way towards helping the country prevent election fraud, fictitious employment, salary remuneration fraud, illegal immigration and related identity issues' (Datacard Group 2012). This brings us back to Huysmans's notion of 'domains' of security, which in the case are not criminological (the way insecurity is linked to street crime in Europe) but rather developmental. The range of meanings to which security is associated is instead one associated with state capacity. But how much does intervening on border security capacity actually transform states and the ways they operate? How effective are interventions?

Assessing State Transformation

The section above demonstrated the degree to which border security in West Africa is underpinned by a logic of intervention that relies on a view of security including elements of control and care. The ways this intervention operates, through knowledge transmission and methods drawn from the development industry, seek to reform the very ways that borders – and the states they bound – are governed: this reforming element at the heart of security practice seeks to 'develop' states through the moulding of security practice, the targeted buttressing of specific elements of statehood, and the re-scaling of certain elements of governance. This is driven as much by international intervention as by local initiative. More specifically, interventions around border control in West Africa operate through the buttressing and transformation of *segments* of the state. The relevance of 'transformation' of the state has found its most direct application to security issues in the work of Hameiri and Jones (2015). Their work on non-traditional security threats identifies security governance as marked by contestation over the very scale at which security should be governed, which in turn emerges from the set of social forces in which this governance is situated. They argue that 'whether and how security is rescaled, and how governance regimes operate in practice, reflect the contingent outcomes of dynamic contestations between socio-political coalitions, whose relative strength is shaped by the broader political economy context and wider social relations' (52). This 'politics' is grounded in a Marxist view of the state as a set of social and political forces, which is the product of contestation and produces particular forms of governing. The transformation of states, in this view, is visible in the changing locus of power across scales and sectors and new types of associations between actors (e.g. public and private). To what extent can we really claim that states such as Senegal and Mauritania are *transformed* by the meeting of border control interventions and local security practices?

The effects of border security interventions in West Africa fall into three categories: transformative, catalytic, and performative. Each of these are consequential, but not all produce the same shifts in the locus and nature of authority. Transformative interventions achieve significant changes in local security routines and forms of knowledge, or transform the self-perceptions of actors to a significant degree as to be politically significant. The bilateral Spanish interventions with Senegal and Mauritania have been successful at changing ways of working on either side, and enabled a stronger Frontex role in the social world of security in the region. As Chapter 4 shows, these interventions have profoundly influenced the everyday routines of the Senegalese navy's patrols. On the Spanish side, these interventions have had a more symbolic impact on the Spanish partners, reassuring an identity amongst them that they have been agents for change and actively changed the mentalities of their African partners. The Seahorse project put in place by the Spanish, with funding from the European Commission, is another equally transformative project, in the sense that it has created a thick social network of communications between West African states and a European partner that previously did not exist in such an institutionalized form. In this case, the transformative effect of intervention is one of creating new social relations that actively change behaviour. Here border control interventions in West Africa come closest to the disciplinary vision of global governance described in contemporary studies of governmentality.

Another important differentiation is to show interventions as *catalysts* for change. In this respect, small-scale interventions are not valued for their own sake, or for their immediate effects, but rather for what types of future changes or policy pathways they enable. The West African Police Information System (WAPIS), funded by the EU and Interpol, is noteworthy in producing the kinds of new linkages that produce new sources and spaces of authority. The system formalizes exchanges of information that have long taken place informally and sporadically between African states' police and intelligence officials. In this sense, it is a catalyst for the routinization of regional security cooperation, but also for an expanding role for Interpol as a technological mediator in the region. Here, 'assembling' of actors is highly local, with the orchestration and motivation role coming from an IGO. The new border posts in Mauritania, as Chapter 5 shows, play a similar catalytic role: while they reinforce physical structures at formal border crossings (in a region where many use these informally or avoid them entirely) the purpose of the project is to reshape the very trajectory of future developments in border security. Similarly, the embedding of specialized 'cells' in key ministries such as interior and justice is intended to stimulate changes in practice and facilitate international cooperation: the EUCAP Sahel mission in Niger, for instance, maintains such a *cellule* in that country's ministry of interior. These efforts aim, as the chapter lays out in more detail, to Westernize over time the informal (and often culturally specific) practices of local security officials – but in the medium-term these arrangements are governed from some distance by their funders, if at all.

Finally, many security interventions and projects are primarily *performative* and produce very few practical shifts in the locus and nature of authority. That is, they operate almost entirely within the symbolic realm. This is not to say that elements of this do not exist in other types of intervention (e.g. the IOM's posters and 'family photos' outside new border posts) but simply that many forms of intervention are not primarily oriented to achieve actual changes in the nature of border control practices, or they quite readily accept their own potential failure. Outside the realm of 'Western' intervention, the adoption of biometric technologies in Senegal and Mauritania epitomizes this. The performative elements of Senegal's biometrics policies in particular exist to adopt a modern self-image – at whatever cost – even when it prioritizes border management in spaces (such as Dakar airport) where irregular migration presents the lowest risk. In the realm of external intervention, the symbolism of EU support to Mauritania (especially in the late 2010s when irregular migration numbers through the country are very low) is particularly striking considering foot-dragging by local security forces who accept help with little enthusiasm.

Given these different effects and ambitions of border security interventions, how can we understand the specific ways states are transformed? We should be cognizant of the limitations of Hameiri and Jones's (2015) arguments, especially in relation to the re-articulation of social forces they emphasize. In the West African context, we can observe a modest re-scaling of governance upwards and outwards towards transnational forms of cooperation (and away from democratic control) yet this is not the result of a profound realignment of the balance of social forces within the state. Rather, intervention targets *pockets* of the state for (dis)assembly, even in their transformative iteration, especially as budgets are often limited. Projects rather tend to be technocratic and reliant on existing modes of international negotiation: memoranda of understanding, bilateral aid, and diplomatic habits. One helpful way of thinking of this circumscribed nature of intervention is in terms of 'pockets of effectiveness'. Roll (2014: 367–369) describes these as organizations providing public services effectively within a broader context of 'weak' overall governance. This argument builds on an ongoing concern in literature on public administration and state formation about how and why 'effective' institutions emerge and persist in supposedly weak states (see Leonard 2010). Given the relatively limited resources of many border control projects in West Africa – IOM Development Fund contributions are below $300,000 – their ambitions tend to be the reform of security practice at a localized level. An example of the circulation of one of these seemingly effective borderwork tactics is the GAR-SI ('rapid action groups for surveillance and intervention') Sahel project funded by the European Union, seeking joint law enforcement teams across the G5 Sahel. Based on a pilot-like operation in Senegal from 2012, this approach is now regionalized, circulated, with new actors (such as EUCAP Sahel in Mali and Niger) assembled into the project as it expands into radically new contexts. In the context of Spanish migration management intervention in Senegal (see Chapter 4), the formation of a joint command centre in Dakar bringing together police, armed forces, and gendarmerie was a highly localized but significant change in the ways these agencies worked together. These types of clustering of agencies create new bundles of authority, and expertise, yet often depend simply on the role of a 'decisive political actor' (Roll 2014: 374) in the emergence of pockets of effectiveness. It is noteworthy that this is the case in many border control projects in West Africa: Senegal's biometric apparatus was kicked in gear in large part due to the recruitment of one technically gifted police commissioner.

My emphasis on 'pockets of effectiveness', and tempering of expectations of state transformation, suggests that the deep roots of the much debated 'African state' may actually be left unperturbed by borderwork practices studies in this book. That being said, we do witness changes in the locus and sources of authority in assemblages of security, and a 'disassembly of the state' and its functions consistent with the current period of globalization (see Sassen 2006). Border security governance in West Africa is effectively re-scaled in many instances, in ways that the survey of actors and their arrangements in Chapter 2 might have suggested: international organizations take on key normative roles, decisions about inclusion/exclusion are made based on databases hosted continents away, and security methods such as forms of profiling are imported from the experience of Western states. Just at a regional level, there are now myriad regional strategies that address security in the 'Sahel', geographically defined in almost as many ways, most calling for better border management. Does this re-scaling of governance, and the meeting of diverse security actors in different international sites – like command centres in Chapter 4, or an airport arrivals hall in Chapter 6 – actually contest anything we know about 'the African state'? It certainly extends the lines of thinking developed in ideas about African statehood such as Bayart's (1989) vision of the 'rhizomatic' state. This idea of the state as a panoply of personal networks, intended to visualize neo-patrimonial relationships, can also capture the ways security apparatuses like Senegal's are 'trans-nationalized' through security cooperation. For example, the pursuit of a more effective border and identification regime in Senegal has meant that the country's national police alone is dependent on UK-based ID card manufacturers, Interpol databases, Spanish border patrolling equipment, and French anti-drug-smuggling training.

The idea of a 'rhizomatic' state here does not only refer to the state's metaphorical roots but also to the ways it might branch upwards reflected by the international sites of security practice it increasingly hosts or participates in. Even when the 'African state' as such as not fundamentally in question, the reasons why are instructive as to the politics of the relationships underpinning border security. Border security interventions are occasionally very light touch, in part due to the fact that the community of interveners itself is often very small and self-contained (see Smirl 2013; Autesserre 2014). In much of my fieldwork, I interviewed ostensibly global actors who sometimes almost single-handedly represented their organization in-country, and who most often knew their regional counterparts personally. This social world of intervention has a relatively small, limited footprint, with often quite limited ability to travel outside of approved safe zones. For instance, the EUCAP Sahel mission in Niger has strict instructions about travel outside Niamey, for reasons of security as well as diplomatic sensitivity. As a result, the ability of international intervention to fundamentally transform the vast 'ungoverned spaces' of Sahel states, let along their ways of governing, is curtailed by their own centralization in the highly governed spaces of national capitals. This concentration of expertise is itself revealing, in that interventions are often weighted towards the urban, elite-driven priorities of the host state.

Conclusion

Security practices are enacted not only by discourse but also in the sociological interactions of security actors. These practices are driven by and generate socially and historically situated forms of knowledge that can be transmitted across international 'sites' with varying degrees of success. This happens through a number of factors such as best practices, interventions, or mimicry, with the north–south flow of knowledge working towards modernizing African states. However, the ways that African states are reshaped by such intervention are inconsistent and showcase the disassembly of the state itself. In the next three chapters of Part II, this book develops empirical arguments that illustrate the theoretical arguments about borderwork and security knowledge made so far. In Chapter 4, I examine Spanish projects to control irregular migration from Senegal and Mauritania as a more routinized form of statebuilding. In Chapter 5, I discuss an EU-funded IOM project to build border posts in Mauritania. Chapter 6 turns to the question of biometric technologies, stressing the differential (and difficult) implementation of global standards in Mauritania and Senegal.

PART II

4 | *From Migration Crisis to* Cooperación

In February 2014, Spain's secretary of state for security Francisco Martínez Vásquez visited Senegal and Mauritania. During his whirlwind tour, Martínez met with the Senegalese minister of interior but also with Spanish police officers stationed in Mauritania. It is hard to imagine such a visit taking place fifteen years earlier, when Spain's political and security footprint in Africa was considerably smaller. Yet Martínez's visit was routine: high level security contacts and visits have become commonplace between Spain and Senegalese and Mauritanian authorities. Senegal and Mauritania are the two West African countries whose police cooperation relationships with Spain have intensified the most since the mid 2000s. These two states are Spain's closest security partners in the region, largely due to their interlinked roles as origin, transit, and destination countries for irregular migration. In this chapter, I examine the work, by security professionals and others at varying scales, which has gone into making a visit like Martínez's seem so routine.

Since the early 2000s, Spain's involvement in the security politics of Senegal and Mauritania has grown dramatically, with relations focused on irregular migration and newer anxieties about drug trafficking and terrorism in the Sahel. Spain has become a central actor in border management in the region, particularly in coastal states prone to irregular migration by boat, and has been a catalyst for a greater EU focus on overseas actions to control its external borders. The most spectacular cause of Spain's involvement in West Africa was the 'crisis' of migration to the Canary Islands, which reached its peak in 2006 when more than thirty-one thousand migrants arrived on the islands, mainly in small boats. This movement, which peaked between 2004 and 2007, was spurred in part by strengthened controls in Morocco and around Spain's tiny African enclaves of Ceuta and Melilla and also by the proximity of the Canary Islands to the coast of Western Sahara. In response to this movement of migrants, Spain initiated unprecedented security

cooperation with Senegal and Mauritania to jointly patrol and observe
the coasts of these countries. It also signed readmission agreements
with both countries, under which Senegal and Mauritania accepted
their own nationals and agreed to repatriate other nationals from the
sub-region that had transited through their state. Spain successfully
Europeanized the migration control issue and put cooperation with
'third countries' firmly on the EU's migration control agenda. Since
2006, Spain's Guardia Civil (gendarmerie) has jointly patrolled the
waters of Senegal and Mauritania with local police and military corps
and reinforced them with training and equipment. Frontex, the EU's
external borders agency created in 2004, continues its 'Hera' coordination operations launched in 2006 and led by Spain, which bring patrol
equipment and expertise from other EU members states to supplement
the Spanish bilateral effort. Spain's role has expanded beyond maritime
patrols towards a more comprehensive involvement, and the Guardia
Civil now work closely with a range of West African states to build
border control capacity on land and against a wider variety of threats.
Spanish intervention – in the form of bilateral police cooperation and
capacity-building – shapes the everyday practices and knowledges of
Senegalese and Mauritanian security actors despite its relatively small
financial and human resource footprint.[1]

This chapter builds on the literature on EU border control, making two main contributions. First, the chapter focuses on the daily
practices of cooperation beyond North Africa, which has to date been
the main focus of literature on the 'externalization' of the EU's borders in the global south. Second, by highlighting the quotidian elements of cooperation between Spain and Senegal and Mauritania, the
chapter brings to light various sites (spatial, conceptual, human, and
non-human) through which approaches to border control are transmitted, translated, resisted, or encounter friction. Since Spain's border is also the external border of the European Union's Schengen
zone of free movement, the relocation of control towards the frontiers of 'third countries' can be seen as an outward shift of the EU's
border function. There is a vast literature on the EU border control
policy (e.g. Zielonka 2001; Carrera 2007; Neal 2009; Léonard 2010;

[1] For instance, the two West Sahel projects have, since 2011, cost the European
Union and Guardia Civil less than €4 million in total and involved only a few
dozen Guardia Civil officers. Similarly, arrangements for joint patrols in both
countries are put in place by fewer than a combined sixty officers.

Carling and Hernández-Carretero 2011; Reid-Henry 2012), much of which focuses on the complex institutional and spatial geography of the Union's border(s). This is visible in work on the dislocation of the EU border through databases such as the Schengen Information System (Apap and Carrera 2004) or the Visa Information System for asylum claimants (Broeders 2007; Balzacq 2008). These render Europe's borders spatially and temporally dislocated. There is now also a considerable literature specifically on the externalization of the EU's borders (e.g. Boswell 2003; Richey 2013) and on new security relationships with third countries (Cassarino 2005; Bialasiewicz 2012; Hernández i Sagrera 2013), but this literature largely focuses on the EU's cooperation with North African partners (e.g. Collyer 2008; Ferrer-Gallardo 2008; Johnson 2013). While the number of migrant interceptions in the 'Atlantic' region dropped over 99 per cent between 2006 and 2012,[2] Spanish cooperation with Senegal and Mauritania has become routinized and institutionalized, with real effects on the local security politics and practices of these countries. Despite this ongoing and intensifying security relationship between Spain, the EU, and West African states in the area of migration control, there is very little work focusing on the ongoing security relationships engendered by this period or on how this new constellation of security actors is actually organized and functions. There are exceptions, of course, such as policy work on migration control arrangements in the Canaries (Arteaga 2007), on the impact of EU migration policies in Mali (Trauner and Deimel 2013), ethnographic work on the Guardia Civil in Senegal and Mauritania (Andersson 2014a, 2014b), and work focusing on deterrence in Spanish migration policy (Godenau and López-Sala 2016). Yet more work is needed on how, as Andersson (2014b: 202) puts it, '[f]or all its apparent might, Europe's emerging border regime takes on a more profane guise on African soil' despite some notable recent exceptions (see Vives 2017). This chapter focuses on these more local and distant impacts of Europe's 'externalized' border, with a particular attention to assembly of professionals that produces local practices which, in turn, undermine the idea of a neat imposition of European border policies. The chapter's approach combines policy analysis with

---

[2] In 2006, the Guardia Civil's coordination centre in the Canary Islands reported 30,246 arrivals in the islands. By the next year, arrivals were down 59 per cent to 12,470 and these numbers continued to drop to a low of forty-five migrants in 2012, a 99.85 per cent drop from the peak six years earlier.

attention to the quotidian in so-called third countries and how this intervention – be it transformational or simply performative – shapes local security politics. The chapter's broader point is that while critiques of the 'externalization' of European borders are laudable, we must highlight local agency in this process and acknowledge the complex social and technical (border)work that makes this possible.

By paying attention to the level of practice, the chapter's second main contribution – on the transmission of border control knowledge – becomes apparent. Spanish intervention in Senegal and Mauritania has been an important catalyst for the formation and transmission of security knowledge. With capacity-building and training playing such a central role, agencies such as the Guardia Civil have created a space for the institution of new ways of *doing* border control. Materials play a key role in this normative aspect of border control: vehicles donated under capacity-building projects or the sensory infrastructures used to detect migrant movements are all the material of which border control knowledges are composed and through which they are transmitted. Spanish involvement in Senegal and Mauritania has moved the EU's external border function to the shores of West Africa, and the quotidian interactions in this Euro-African borderland create and transmit knowledges about how border control is to be done. It has also been an exercise in reinforcing local capacity to fight migration and, as security in the Sahel has become more prominent, reinforcing security capacity beyond migration issues. The Spanish role in patrolling the coasts of Senegal and Mauritania has provided normative and technical transfers to each state. Paying attention to the 'things' that make up border control – vehicles, concepts, tropes, command centres, medals – highlights how small non-military interventions (like Project West Sahel, which cost under €4 million) reflect and impact ways of doing security.

In terms of historical coverage, my focus here is on tracing the emergence of 'crisis' in the Canary Islands from 2006 onwards, the new socio-technical space of security that emerged from it, and the turn towards migration control as risk management. The 2006 'crisis' represented by a spike in migrants from sub-Saharan Africa stimulated the formation of a new security assemblage. This arrangement should be thought of not as a tight, coherent 'field' of security actors but a broad socio-technical space in which a range of security officials, boats, police officers, smugglers, migrants, satellites, planes, and cameras act to make the border what it is. Despite the end of the crisis, Spanish cooperation with Senegal and Mauritania has actually strengthened due to a risk management approach to potential migration. This is reflected in capacity-building projects such as the Guardia Civil's West Sahel project, launched in 2011 and funded by the EU, which seeks to improve overall border policing capabilities in countries beyond coastal states (such as Niger) and respond to a broad range of threats. The chapter goes on to argue that interior security attachés or 'security liaisons' (law enforcement personnel largely based in embassies) have been key players in the Spanish-African space of border control. Spanish security liaisons and their Senegalese and Mauritanian partners occupy different professional spaces and cultures – each primarily originates from and operates in different social worlds – but they work together in a common socio-technical space on a common mission. Rather than being competitive or only rhetorical, the ideal of cooperation so cherished by the security actors interviewed for this chapter reflects their desire to integrate and smoothen security relations and build an autonomous local policing capacity. While there is prestige inherent in the provision of expertise, there is not a dynamic of competition between Spanish and African actors. Turning to technologies of border control, the third section of the chapter argues that vehicles – planes, boats, and 4×4s – are key material elements that shape (and reflect) the everyday practices of border control in Senegal and Mauritania. These are important sites for the transmission of knowledge, reflect the complexity of the sovereignty they uphold, and illustrate the rise of new anxieties (e.g. about land borders) and are the sites of struggle over the fine details of border control capacity-building. These technologies, such as infrared binoculars or the Seahorse communications system, also operate to observe and to sense, thereby fostering the ideal of the border as a technological and integrated space. The fifth section of the chapter discusses the large power of small, mundane symbols and rhetorical devices. These include the medals, pins, and other tokens of cooperation that circulate in this borderwork assemblage, as well as linguistic shorthand such as 'Le Frontex' that refer to maritime patrols but also crystallize opposition to technical, bureaucratized border management practices. The chapter concludes with a discussion of the growing use of joint land patrols and police stations by

Spanish security cooperation in West Africa, activities launched since 2013 suggest a turn towards a more holistic security capacity-building agenda.

Crisis, Risk Management, and the Socio-Technical Space of the Border

With large-scale migration to Spain only growing since the 1970s, the country has transitioned from a migrant-sending country to one that has increasingly attracted labour migrants from South America and North Africa. While earlier forms of irregular migration were primarily due to visa overstays and gaps in the consular system, more spectacular forms of irregularity have become prominent since the 1990s. Most of these more visibly irregular forms of migration – the type more likely to provoke media spectacle and security framings – have come from North African countries whose proximity makes clandestine journeys to Spain appealing. Throughout the 2000s, there was a constant interplay between inducement through regularizations and ease of access on one side, and control achieved through policing and surveillance on the other. In this section, I give a quick overview of irregular migration to Spain since 1990, with the bulk of attention devoted to the turn towards migration in the Canary Islands. I go on to argue that although the number of migrants landing on the shores of the Canaries from 2005 was significant, it is rather the sense of emergency it created, and the enduring understanding of migration as a risk, that has dictated the Spanish (and EU) response to migration since then.

The story of border control between Spain and North and West Africa is one of an interplay between crisis and control. With the imposition of tougher visa requirements on the Maghreb and sub-Saharan Africa in the early 1990s, irregular migration grew. In response to an emerging crisis of irregular migration, primarily along the Straits of Gibraltar and the enclaves of Ceuta and Melilla, Spain introduced better policing cooperation internally and with 'origin' countries. For instance, Spain signed a readmission agreement with Morocco in 1992 and installed fences around its African enclaves of Ceuta and Melilla in 1993. In response to an increase in irregular migration from North Africa, which featured growing numbers of migrants from sub-Saharan Africa, Spain also boosted its maritime surveillance operations through the Sistema Integrado de Vigilancia Exterior (SIVE) maritime radar project announced in 1999. In all of these cases, the vision of security laid out in Chapter 3 as a practical, routinized form of governance – through key technologies – is evident. Beyond control, Spain also regularized migrants in 2000, 2001, and 2004. These amnesties, however partial, arguably acted as an incentive for labour migration (De Haas 2008) and increased migratory pressure at Spain's southern borders. The hardening of control at Spain's borders with Morocco (at its enclaves of Ceuta and Melilla) and within Morocco itself meant that West African migrants started finding new routes into Europe. The otherwise perilous trip to the Canary Islands – the part of the EU's Schengen zone closest to Mauritania and Senegal only one hundred kilometres off the coast of Western Sahara – suddenly became more appealing.

From 2000 to 2008, Spain experienced consistently high volumes of irregular migration via the straights of Gibraltar (and the country's African enclaves of Ceuta and Melilla) and later to the Canary Islands. While sub-Saharan Africans have consistently represented a large part of those seeking to enter Spain through the enclaves of Ceuta and Melilla, it was the shift of point of entry farther south to the Canary Islands, peaking in 2005 and 2006, that added an element of urgency to the 'crisis'. According to the Spanish coast guard, emergencies involving *patera* type boats for the Las Palmas rescue command centre had started rising in 2000, suggesting that migrants had begun leaving from farther south before SIVE and the reinforcement of control in Ceuta and Melilla. Indeed, the Canary Islands route was a longstanding route for irregular entry into Spain, but had never been used by so many in so short a time (Willems 2007). The 'crisis' of 2006 was therefore a *productive* moment: of migrant irregularity but also of the Canary Islands themselves as a space of security intervention. It also obscured other crises that were productive of migrants' choices to move: structural adjustment policies and declining fish stocks in Senegal, to name but two. The sense of 'crisis' in the Canary Islands was fed not only by numbers, but also by the humanitarian situation. From my interviews with Spanish police personnel involved at the time, it was a genuinely jarring situation marked by overcrowding and by a desperate health situation. In 2006 alone, 30,246 migrants landed in the Canary Islands (Guardia Civil 2013), having taken small fishing boats from Senegal for a long journey along the coast of West Africa, or taken the shorter journey from Nouadhibou in Mauritania. Indeed, the sharp reduction in migrant numbers between 2006 and 2012 mentioned earlier has retroactively continued to produce the traumatic power of the crisis.

The Canaries crisis acted as a watershed moment for policy and policing. While Spain had negotiated readmission agreements and police cooperation with its North African neighbours, the country had never had close security ties with sub-Saharan African states. From crisis came unprecedented security cooperation with Senegal and Mauritania, primarily through an immediate increase in policing. Spanish police had already used a model of joint border patrols with Morocco, starting in 2005, and replicated the model in Spain's new agreements with Senegal and Mauritania. On 24 August 2006, Senegal and Spain signed a memorandum of understanding allowing joint patrols between local gendarmeries and navies and the Guardia Civil. The patrols, Operation Gorée in Senegal and Operations Cabo Blanco and Atlantis in Mauritania, began in May 2006, the same month that logistical assistance from Frontex became available for identification and repatriation of migrants in the Canaries. The process of identification itself became a site for the application of 'local' knowledge, with Senegalese police using intuitions based on migrants' knowledge of their purported countries of origin (naming heads of state) or cities of residence (asking them about their neighbourhoods).[3] The agency's Joint Operation 'Hera', formally hosted and coordinated by Spain, also brought together aircraft and naval resources from other EU member states such as ships from Iceland and aircraft from Luxembourg.[4] There have been three such operations: Hera I (July–October 2006), II (August–December 2006), and III (February–April 2007). The initial response to migration pressure was swift, but cooperation has intensified since 2006 and created a growing 'assemblage' of transnational actors, practices, and knowledges.

In response to the 'crisis' of the Canaries and the need to prevent the risk of renewed irregular flows, new transnational clusters of security professionals and practices have emerged in Spain, at the EU level, and in 'third countries' such as Senegal and Mauritania. It is too simple and analytically unhelpful to speak of a unified 'field' of

---

[3] Interview, Police Nationale du Sénégal, Dakar, 18 January 2013.
[4] Interview, Marine Nationale du Sénégal, Dakar, 13 March 2013.

security between Europe and Africa, or of a unified apparatus of control. Migration governance consists of 'disparate strands of practices, provisions and principles' (Kunz, Lavenex, and Panizzon 2011: 3–4) and existing approaches to EU border control policies in third countries have referred to an 'archipelago' of border control (Bialasiewicz 2012) or a 'Euro-African borderland' (Andersson 2014a), hinting at the complex geography of the geographical and policy of migration control. Here, I consider this Euro-African space to be a *socio-technical one* in which the governance of migration occurs by actors from the worlds of policing and the military, migrants, smugglers, bureaucrats, as well as the tangible objects that make the border what it is. Since the border is not simply a line in the sand, nor simply a social institution, it is a socio-technical space (as argued in Chapter 2). By paying attention to the technical, we can account for the borderwork done not only by humans but also the role of boats, satellites, concepts, tokens, idioms, and more in everyday border control practices such as knowledge transmission.

Who participates in this transnational space? Who is assembled into it and who orchestrates the relations that hold this socio-technical space together? Most prominent are Spain's Guardia Civil officers who are the country's paramilitary police force equivalent to the 'gendarmerie' found in many francophone countries. The tendency for gendarmerie organizations' mandates to be in the administration of 'territory' outside of cities and more militarized policing operations is reflected in the Guardia Civil's affiliation to the Spanish ministry of defence for operational activities. This mandate has put it in an ideal position for peacekeeping missions abroad but also joint operations aligned with its mandate of land and sea border surveillance, anti-trafficking, and responsibility for international cooperation. Since 2001, the Guardia Civil has had a specialized borders command (the Jefatura Fiscal y de Fronteras) and the agency has since built up a degree of institutional credibility for border control missions. The Spanish national police, the Cuerpo Nacional de Policía (CNP), also work alongside the Guardia Civil in third countries where they have their own cooperation activities. In Mauritania, the Guardia Civil works mainly alongside the local navy (Marine Nationale) as well as with the gendarmerie's maritime patrol units (the Brigades Maritimes et Fluviales). In Senegal, the navy's operations group

(GNO – Groupement Naval Opérationnel) and the border police (DPAF – Direction de la Police de l'Air et des Frontières) coordinate the operational and logistical cooperation, but the Senegalese gendarmerie and air force also participate in patrols. Farther afield, Warsaw-based Frontex provides technical assistance under Article 8 of its regulations, and the Brussels-based International Centre for Migration Policy Development (ICMPD) contributes to the Rabat Process launched by the July 2006 Euro-African Conference on Migration and Development. The European External Action Service (EEAS), which is essentially the EU's foreign service, acts as a local project management organization and through its network of 'delegations' and its staff is the first point of contact for local projects. For instance, the West Sahel project, although implemented by the Guardia Civil, is administered through the delegation in Nouakchott, and Guardia Civil staff periodically report on their activities to the delegation. Migrants and those who smuggle them also play a key part in this socio-technical space as their agency is the original act that brings about the security response. Smugglers also use many of the same tools (e.g. boats) and logics (capacity-building) as their security counterparts. In short, the social space of border control cuts across different social spaces of practice. Despite a decline in the number of migrants, it continues to grow in size and complexity.

The approach towards migration in the border space between Spain and West Africa has turned away from interrupting flows and moved towards pre-empting movements and managing the risk of resumption. This risk-based understanding of migration is one common element of the border security knowledge that circulates within the assemblage produced by the so-called crisis. Spanish and Senegalese/Mauritanian actors are aware of the net regression of the number of migrants, and the narrative that patrols and policing have been wildly successful was a point of universal agreement amongst the totality of my interviewees, with surprisingly few wanting to claim sole credit for this work. According to the Guardia Civil's figures, migrant arrivals in the Canary Islands are down over 99 per cent from 2006. Despite this drop in numbers, the sheer risk of a resumption of irregular migration has set the agenda. Frontex (2011: 133), in its 2011 Programme of Work, mentioned that '[t]here is a risk that if the control is gone, the arrivals at the Canary Islands will start again'. The same document for 2013 explicitly links low figures to the possibility of recurrence:

According to reported detections, the situation on the western African route has been mostly under control since 2008 but remains critically dependant of [*sic*] the implementation of effective return agreements between Spain and western African countries. Should these agreements be jeopardised, irregular migration, pushed by high unemployment and poverty, is likely to resume quickly despite increased surveillance. (Frontex 2013: 20)

Similarly, most of my interlocutors were adamant that their presence was the only thing staving off a renewed crisis. In Mauritania, the Guardia Civil largely see themselves as the guarantors of this lower figure, due to a belief that local security forces are unconcerned with migrant departures.[5] The lower numbers are therefore charged with meaning: high numbers demanded intervention, but low numbers still require increased vigilance. As a high-ranking officer in the Senegalese navy told me, policing the sea is like policing in town: 'just because there's no crime, that doesn't mean you get rid of the police'.[6]

These numbers produce a risk-based approach to security, which responds to the low and diminishing irregular migration figures. Numbers, regardless of their content, are ripe fodder for an increase in control. It is important not to overstate the *turn* to risk, however, as the very positioning of Spanish ships in the territorial waters of Senegal and Mauritania in the first place was always a means to spatially and temporally pre-empt migrant departures. The number of migrants using the sea route from West Africa has dropped dramatically since 2006, but the consensus amongst the security personnel I spoke to – Spanish, Senegalese, and Mauritanian – is that sea and land migration routes in the area could reopen at any time, once others through Mali, Niger, and Libya are inevitably closed off. Multiple interviewees used some version of the metaphor of *vases communicants* (communicating vessels or pressure valves) to describe migration patterns in North and West Africa. This analogy suggests that migration pressures are mechanical and reactive to control – which effectively foregrounds the agency of the security actor, rather than that of the migrant. One Mauritanian army official suggested to me that migrants might even be guided by the Islamic concept of *qadar* (predestination) as a means of making

---

[5] Interview with Spanish interior security attaché, Nouakchott, 20 February 2013.
[6] Interview with head of Frontex cooperation, Marine Nationale du Sénégal, Dakar, 30 June 2013.

sense of their otherwise risky movements.[7] In addition to this, the idea of migration pressures as shifting (say, from Ceuta to the Canaries to Lampedusa and back again) reinforces the idea that migration is a phenomenon that can be managed by professionals. With this consensus perspective, it is not surprising that the policy and technical apparatus of joint Spanish-African border surveillance remains in place, and is indeed being strengthened, with this eventuality firmly in mind.

The EU-funded West Sahel project launched in 2011 typifies this risk management thinking, through its mix of capacity-building assistance and training. The project is run under the EU's Thematic Programme for Migration and Asylum and aims to boost the migration management capacities of security agencies in Mauritania, Senegal, Niger, and Mali. Most of its €2.44 million funding (80 per cent) comes from the European Union and the remaining 20 per cent from the Guardia Civil (European Delegation Nouakchott 2011). The project is three-pronged, and provides material and training in border surveillance, training on assistance to migrants, and the coordination of regional law enforcement meetings between the beneficiary states (which are all origin and transit countries for irregular migration). West Sahel contributes to the expansion of cooperation between Spain, the EU and 'third countries', and more importantly showcases the importance of capacity-building and training as modes of managing the risk of migration 'at the source', through transfers of equipment and expertise. In the next section, I use key human and non-human elements as narrative devices with which to showcase such everyday practices of knowledge transmission and cooperation in the expanding socio-technical space of border control straddling Europe and Africa.

Interior Attachés as Security Professionals

When one speaks to Guardia Civil officers in Mauritania, one of the words that figures most prominently is *cooperación*, and the same applies to gendarmes and police officers in Senegal, who stress the honest, close, and sincere nature of their *coopération* with the Spanish police. The emphasis on this close symbiotic relationship is telling as to the types of security relationships that occur across international

---

[7] Interview, official from Direction de la Sûreté de l'État (DSE), Nouakchott, 25 February 2013.

divisions between security agencies. Since the emphasis has been on building a collaborative response, dynamics of competition have taken a back seat. In this section, I argue that interior security attachés participate in an emerging assemblage which flattens out the distinctions of global and local, actively working across different law enforcement cultures by virtue of their cooperation and knowledge diffusion activities. Against the idea that police liaison work is competitive (Bigo 1996) or that cooperation in this field is disingenuous (Gerspacher and Dupont 2007), I argue that liaison work in the Spanish-African borderland does show some elements of competition over expertise but only between national actors – leaving relations between intervener and intervened cooperative and sincere. The broader significance of this point about the role of *agregados* is that while their pedagogical efforts may reflect the paternalistic politics of capacity-building, they are also operating in a security assemblage in which their partners agree with the catalytic element of their presence.

Security liaisons have been essential in smoothing the interaction between the different security services involved in policing migration in the Euro-African borderland. In Spanish embassies, they are known as *agregados de interior* (interior attachés), and they act as liaisons for the activities of the Spanish ministry of interior in the country in which they are posted, without formally being its representatives. The Spanish embassies in Nouakchott and Dakar each have two such attachés, with one each from the Guardia Civil and from the Cuerpo Nacional de Policía. French embassies have a similar arrangement, with *attachés de sécurité intérieure* (interior security liaisons) who are usually high-ranking officers in the French national police. Although Spanish embassies have defence attachés (*agregados de defensa*), migration management is still considered as a police responsibility. This is partly because their focus is on fighting trafficking (a criminal procedure) and much of the work relating to migration involves border procedures (a police responsibility) and interviewing of migrants (investigatory work). More generally, the treatment of migration management *cooperation* as a police issue reflects the fusion of internal and external security responsibilities highlighted by Bigo (2001). This is particularly striking given that gendarmeries (such as the Guardia Civil) are paramilitary corps, that local partners are often military (navies), and that the solutions adopted (border surveillance and maritime patrols) are militarized in their symbolism. The assembling of expertise, in this case, brings together actors who seem in many ways incompatible or difficult to arrange around a common mission. Spain's first security liaisons in West Africa were posted in Dakar in 2002,[8] and their role has been increasingly defined by coordination on migration issues. This network is growing and Spain now has liaison officers in Portugal, Morocco, Algeria, Tunisia, Mauritania, Senegal, Gambia, Cape Verde, Guinea-Bissau, Mali, and Niger.

These security attachés have relations of their own, to their civilian bosses in Madrid and to commanders in centres such as Las Palmas, but also do the work of assembling new sets of actors from social worlds that go beyond this. A Guardia Civil *agregado* based in a West African country is very much a part of the world of Spanish law enforcement, in which claims to expertise might be buttressed by a stint in 'tough' Ceuta or from training African police forces. Similarly, the police patrolling the beaches in Dakar under the terms of the Senegal-Spain MOU are actors in Senegal's law enforcement culture, reaping prestige and bonuses from their work. This does not, however, mean that these are incompatible or competitive relations. The bundling of actors across national law enforcement worlds through practices of police cooperation reinforces forms of authority that rest on institutional similarity and interoperability. For instance, in all West Sahel project countries with the exception of Niger, the Guardia Civil works with local gendarmeries. This cooperation is spurred on by an institutional similarity, since the Guardia Civil and francophone gendarmeries have very similar mandates and histories. They also have a great level of trust between them, as their African colleagues greet the Guardia Civil as 'brothers in arms' with a similar *esprit de corps*.[9] On the technical level, the similarity of mandates means that gendarmeries share similar modes and scopes of operation, and are more receptive to transfers of equipment and expertise. The very structure of gendarmeries, which straddle internal and external security (Lutterbeck 2004), has been a catalyst for the Guardia Civil's role in transnational security cooperation.

Cooperation is the watchword from abstract policy pronouncements all the way down to quotidian practice. In July 2006, the first Euro-African Conference on Migration and Development was held in the

---

[8] Interview, Spanish internal security attaché, Dakar, 19 March 2013.
[9] Interview, security attaché at EU delegation, Nouakchott, 19 February 2013.

midst of the Canaries crisis. At this conference, which launched the ongoing Rabat Process on migration, the need for better cooperation on preventing irregular migration was high on the agenda. The Africa-EU declaration that came out of this conference noted that '[l]arge spontaneous and illegal or irregular migratory flows can have a significant impact on national and international stability and security' and suggested '[c]ooperating to develop border control measures [. . .] and addressing the need for swift contacts between the EU and Africa in exceptional situations' (Africa-EU Ministers 2006). Such measures amount to what De Haas (2008) calls 'declarations of good intent', but do not have more than a minute power in terms of shaping actual everyday practice. However, 'discourses of cooperation' are central claims to position in what could be termed the 'security field' (Bigo, Guild, and Walker 2010: 14) and in the case of Spanish police cooperation in West Africa, it acts to obfuscate unequal power relationships and create a sense of unity behind solutions to the migration 'crisis'.

The bulk of migration cooperation happens at the level of everyday practice, and security liaisons have proven to be policy innovators – deploying their 'practical knowledge' – building up novel governance arrangements on which Spanish-African cooperation rests. The most prominent of these is the memorandum of understanding (MOU) between Spain and Senegal, which was one of the first of its kind in the region. A commissioner in the Senegalese national police drafted the MOU, and the document was put through an iterative drafting process and was approved by all of the police, gendarmerie, air force, and navy.[10] Such governance by MOU emphasizes speed, flexibility, and technical governance. It was practitioners rather than politicians who drafted the MOU in the midst of the 2006 crisis, and it was thus able to short-circuit true political discussion about how to respond to migration movements. While this is evidence of how security practice operates outside deliberative politics (see the discussion early in Chapter 3 on this), it also reflects how ad hoc bundles of actors can produce new institutions and forms of authority. This particular MOU has taken on a life of its own as an explanatory tool, with Frontex in 2016 put low migration numbers along the Atlantic route down to the Memorandum of Understanding between Spain, Senegal and Mauritania, that includes joint surveillance activities and effective return of those

---

[10] Interview at Police Nationale du Sénégal, Dakar, 18 January 2013.

detected crossing the border illegally (Frontex 2016: 21). The question of returns, which is politically tricky in EU-Africa relations, is effectively sidestepped by the re-scaling of governance down to such 'backstage' technical instruments. This approach is reflected in the more recent approach towards informal migration 'compacts' between the EU and select African states is, according to the European Commission, 'avoids the risk that concrete delivery is held up by technical negotiations for a fully-fledged formal agreement' (European Commission 2016b: 3) The use of MOU as a governance tool is also a practice which reflects the *background assumption* (recalling 'cultures of border control' from Chapter 3) that rapid, technicalized cooperation represents the most effective means of dealing with migration.

Vehicles as Security Technologies

Standing at the gate to the port of Dakar – in my case waiting to be admitted for an interview in the midday sun – it is impossible to miss the white 4×4s that speed Guardia Civil officers to and from from their living quarters in the city centre. Vehicles figure in all sorts of ways in this world of border security into which I am allowed to intrude: next up is the unmissable Guardia Civil boat docked in the port, but also the pirogue the is the backdrop to any conversation with a smuggler. Although human actors such as security liaisons play a crucial role in the quotidian practices of border control, we must not lose sight of what Bruno Latour (1992) calls the 'missing masses': the non-human actors that, without usurping human agency, extend it and shape it in important ways. As argued in Chapter 2, it is impossible to speak about the emergence of social relations of security without including the tangible surveillance technologies and vehicles that help them function. In particular, I am interested to show the 'international political sociology' of these absent technologies and objects and the roles they play as some of the 'sites' (see Chapter 3) for the consolidation of security relationships and the transmission of particular understandings of border control. Below, I examine the role played by vehicles in border security in Senegal and Mauritania, where they serve as sites for knowledge transmission but also as reflections of the knowledges that accompany new security relationships.

Boats are essential to the routines of patrolling that make up the daily reality of Spanish-African cooperation on maritime border control. When visiting the Senegalese naval base in Dakar, which sits alongside the commercial port, one is first struck by the multitude large commercial vessels in the distance. Just next to the headquarters of the Senegalese Groupement Naval Opérationnel – the navy's operations group – sits a small Guardia Civil patrol boat. In Nouadhibou, I knew I had found my interview location when I spotted the same type of 4×4 – this time with Spanish number plates – I had seen in Dakar. The Guardia Civil has three boats operating from the port of Dakar, the largest of which is an ocean-going vessel based in Las Palmas, whose crew members serve in fifteen-day shifts. Under the terms of the Senegal-Spain MOU signed in 2006, patrols must take to the seas daily. These routines blending international and local actors seem to both confuse and augment sovereignty at the same time: they are 'mixed' and incarnate an awkward blend of authorities but also act to improve the surveillance capacities of all partners. When Spanish patrol boats roam the coastal waters of Senegal, they must have a Senegalese officer on board. This is an obligatory concession to the juridical sovereignty of Senegal, whose officers retain the exclusive right to make arrests. It was made clear to me by the Senegalese navy that Spain is not allowed to 'be the policeman' and their presence is intended only to improve 'capacity to see'.[11] This catalytic form of intervention (augmenting a local partner's 'capacity') also aligns with its performative and symbolic element visible on the Guardia Civil boats' masts, on which both the Spanish flag and that of the host country fly. This complexity of de jure sovereignty should not detract from the fact that patrol boats seek to enhance the de facto sovereign power of each country. For Spain, the routines of their Senegalese and Mauritanian partners improve their power to intercept and pre-empt migration. For Senegal and Mauritania, the additional maritime power of the Guardia Civil provides additional sets of eyes and ears for their daily surveillance activities.

Boats are brought into this emerging assemblage of actors by featuring as essential pedagogical sites for the inculcation of security knowledge. While the types of training sessions that officers have tended to receive from Spain (such as theoretical training on clandestine migration in Las Palmas) reinforce *techne* – rational knowledge – it is

---

[11] Interview with head of Frontex cooperation, Marine Nationale du Sénégal, Dakar, 30 June 2013.

repeated and routinized local interactions that solidify the unconscious rhythms, intuitions, and reflexes required for quotidian border control. These are what James C. Scott calls *metis*. This type of knowledge involves 'knowing how and when to apply the rules of thumb *in a concrete situation*' (Scott 1998: 316, emphasis in original) and relies on the type of spontaneous knowledge described in Chapter 3. Joint patrols, which are the essence of bilateral cooperation between Spain and its African partners on migration control, effectively provide the physical site for this global-local transfer of *metis*. Most of the Senegalese security officials I spoke to mentioned that they did not have much to learn in terms of basic technique, but instead benefited from more advanced surveillance skills and techniques facilitated by the opportunity to use more advanced equipment.[12] In short, the gap in capacity is not inherently one of human resources, but rather of the material equipment required to improve *metis*. Nevertheless, pedagogy is still dependent on an unequal distribution of power – in this case a very tangible form of 'capital' – between teacher and learner (see Chapter 3).

While the figure of 'assemblage' is helpful to think through new relations between largely fraternal security cultures, the agency of the subjects and objects being controlled shapes how far this authority goes. Boats, in this case, are not only control technologies: they also represent its subversion by the migrants and smugglers who also 'do the borderwork' (see Chapter 2). Smugglers' boats, mainly small wooden fishing boats (pirogues) benefit from being easy to dissimulate. For the purpose of facilitating control, and with this camouflage in their sights, Mauritanian authorities in Nouadhibou have insisted on the registration of fishing boats to facilitate control and more easily identify their owners in the event of attempts at outward migration. This further reflects the risk management imperative behind the policing of boat migration. Rather than glorify or romanticize smugglers' attempts to subvert control, their practices should point us to their own *metis* – which mirrors the transmission of knowledge that happens between security actors. In the case of the smuggler, the 'knack' manifests itself in profiling the passengers that the boat is to carry. From the smuggler's standpoint, the transport of migrants to Europe is not an archetype of market exchange. Rather, there is a keen interest taken in precisely *who* is being transported. Women, for example, are not considered

---

[12] Interview, Armée de l'Air du Sénégal, Dakar, 27 February 2013.

ideal candidates and 'any old person can't just get on this boat'.[13] The gendered division of migration rather considers women to be beneficiaries of primarily male attempts to gain economic advancement through movement. Similarly, a migrant smuggler will draw on existing navigation experience built up over years of fishing to make the longer trip to the Canaries. While the police tend to portray smugglers as GPS-toting opportunists,[14] smugglers themselves see their work as an opportunity to refine their *metis*. This smuggler capacity-building extends to material improvements, too: a fisherman taking migrants to the Canary Islands could net up to 15 million CFA francs (€22,800) for one trip – money that is reinvested. According to smugglers, this money helps to add improvements to boats such as better engines or repairs to the hull.

The forms of authority that are produced through Spanish-African police cooperation are reflected in the aerial dimension to efforts to stop boat migration, provided by aeroplanes and helicopters. Unlike its maritime counterpart, the aerial dimension of patrol is entirely a surveillant presence, assuring reconnaissance and extending the vertical reach of border control. When I spoke to officers from the Guardia Civil detachment in Nouadhibou, they were very clear that their aerial support was a supplement to the work of the Mauritanian gendarmerie's maritime patrol units, and solely intended to speed up interceptions.[15] The Senegalese air force, similarly, does not directly carry out any interceptions. Rather, it acts as a reconnaissance service, using BN-2T and CASA 212 patrol planes and a UH-1 helicopter donated by the Guardia Civil. Senegalese air force officers have participated in missions facilitated by aircraft provided under Frontex cooperation, where they work alongside officers from the EU member states involved. In my interviews with the Senegalese air force, they insisted that the material capacity provided is welcome but primarily provides a site for learning 'new search techniques'.[16] The material therefore facilitates the transmission of knowledge, and the extent of material capacity-building is summed up by the fact that, under the terms of the Senegal-Spain MOU, Spain even provides the jet fuel for Senegalese air patrols.

[13] Interview with migrant smuggler, Dakar, 17 January 2013.
[14] Interview at Police Nationale du Sénégal, Dakar, 18 January 2013.
[15] Interview with Guardia Civil patrol team, Nouadhibou, 18 June 2013.
[16] Interview, Armée de l'Air du Sénégal, Dakar, 27 February 2013.

Four-wheel drive vehicles – 4×4s and quad bikes – are reflective of the forms of authority such as the turn to pre-emptive policing as well as the emergence of new security anxieties about migration over land. As Andersson (2014a: 128) shows, the use of quad bikes to patrol the beaches of Dakar involves a radically different type of work than patrolling the high seas: 'The patrols were instead an exercise in what police chiefs called "visibility" – to show "candidates" that the police were ready to cut short any attempted boat journey to Europe'. This work is a further reflection of the risk management ideal, whereby the need to pre-empt and profile migration is as important as the more complex humanitarian task of stopping migrants at sea. By seeking out 'candidates' for irregular migration, pre-emptive patrol and policing practices are central to the *production* of irregularity, in that they undertake border control well inland while relying on a profile on the behaviour and possessions of an irregular migrant. According to migrants' rights defenders, accusing people of planning to emigrate provides states such as Mauritania justification to quickly deport other African nationals.[17]

The use of such vehicles reflects European funders' change in anxieties: policing the territorial border has taken on a greater importance. Under the West Sahel project, the Mauritanian gendarmerie received Nissan 4×4 vehicles and quad-wheel 4×4 bikes from the Guardia Civil. The West Sahel project's official description from the EU includes only Senegal, Mali, Mauritania, and Senegal, but activities have also taken place in Cape Verde, Guinea-Bissau (a major drug smuggling hub) as well as Burkina Faso and Chad (both landlocked countries).[18] This expansion in the project's scope highlights the turn to a focus on land borders but also to threats beyond irregular migration.

Four-wheel drive vehicles, though they dictate approaches to controlling the border, often do so tenuously. Some forms of equipment have proven more mutable (see Chapter 3) than others. For instance, the original batch of Nissan 4×4s given by the Guardia Civil to the Mauritanian gendarmerie was a formidable set of brand new vehicles, yet spare parts for these were not readily available in-country. These parts could not, in the words of an EU official, be purchased by a

---

[17] Interview, Association Mauritanienne des Droits de l'Homme (AMDH), Nouakchott, 23 June 2013.

[18] Interview with security attaché, EU delegation, Nouakchott, 19 February 2013.

gendarme 'along with his sugar and his flour' in a local market.[19] In the end, these vehicles were replaced by Toyota 4×4s, for which parts are more ubiquitous in Mauritania. This suggests that the design of the West Sahel project was not responsive to local conditions and perhaps based on procurement processes far removed from the African context. Indeed, in many of my interviews with European funders, it was suggested that 4×4s may not always be devoted to patrol duties, with some officers requesting superfluous premium features in the vehicles, or using the vehicles to drive their wives around town. While these may be rumours or unfair characterizations of local partners, such visions show how attempts to produce 'catalytic' forms of intervention can fail when the technical and social are misaligned. The effectiveness of 4×4 vehicles aside, they are reflective of funder priorities but also of local forms of appropriation.

Surveillance Technologies and Security Cultures

The border function is dependent on technologies and other non-human actors that work to sense, detect, communicate, and visualize. These technologies include cameras, canine units, and communications infrastructures which help to proliferate of the border function and create new routines of border control oriented towards an ideal of an integrated, rapid border function. As part of the West Sahel project, the Guardia Civil gave thermal imaging binoculars to the Mauritanian gendarmerie to facilitate border controls at night, and on land, suggesting that controls should take place away from official border crossings (which are run by the police) and in desert areas – away from the sea migration route. The Mauritanian gendarmerie have also been given thermal imaging cameras and while these were initially considered ideal for patrolling vast expanses of desert, particularly from a good vantage point, the dust from this same desert has interfered with their functioning and made gendarmes go back to their original methods of border control.[20] These 'local' methods are more rooted in the traditional approach to policing outside of urban areas, focused on mobile patrols and tapping into local populations' observations. It is also worth noting that the 'local' does not represent a symmetrical

---

[19] Interview, security attaché at EU delegation, Nouakchott, 19 February 2013.
[20] Interview, Spanish internal security attaché, Nouakchott, 20 February 2013.

opposition to the 'global' (European) approach to border control, as many methods pre-dating Spain's intervention are rooted in longer colonial histories. For instance, the very division of policing between police and gendarmerie in Senegal and Mauritania is the result of the colonial encounter with France. That being said, the abandonment of external advice or technologies in the present shows the persistence of local routines coupled with the opportunistic acceptance of help from outside. In contrast to technologies' propensity to fail to adapt to new contexts, as the desert dust proved, other 'non-human' elements in border control such as canine units have proven to be quite malleable. As one Spanish attaché joked to me, dogs are the same everywhere,[21] noting that the upkeep needs for canine units mean that do not succumb to the Mauritanians' supposed lack of interest in maintaining donated equipment. In this way, the low upkeep required by canine units overcomes the differential in commitment to migration control between different partners. These canine units have also been an important element of 'function creep' – a surveillance tool's functioning driving it beyond its intended scope of application – and have been deployed for policing beyond migration alone, and even beyond the border. For instance, canine units have facilitated searches for narcotics at the Nouakchott airport. Further evidence of the spillover effect of border control capacity-building is reflected in the use of these canine units for night-time patrols in peripheral areas of Nouakchott.

The Euro-African security assemblage formed by international police cooperation around the Canaries crisis draws from and links into a broader world of European border security practice. In 1999, in response to increasing levels of irregular migration across the Strait of Gibraltar, Spain announced the Sistema Integrado de Vigilancia Exterior (SIVE). First deployed in 2002 in Algeciras at the southern tip of the Spanish coast, the system uses radar sensors, video cameras, and infrared cameras to track boat movements and alert Guardia Civil units. As a policy innovator, Spain has been able to push for a Europeanization of this exemplar of automated border surveillance through EU-funded research projects such as Seabilla which tries to 'define the architecture for cost-effective European Sea Border Surveillance systems' (Seabilla 2013). This north to north policy diffusion, built on Spanish border knowledge, yielded EUROSUR, a common European

---

[21] Interview, Spanish internal security attaché, Nouakchott, 20 February 2013.

border surveillance system, which was launched in December 2013. The Europeanization of border control, even more deeply institution-alized by Frontex's creation in 2004, would also be the backdrop for similar but less prominent efforts farther afield. One of the uses of 'assemblage' as a theoretical tool is that it helps to understand how such initiatives and practices connect. In this case, we can see a clear linkage between Spain's initial technological approach to border control and the ways these have been folded exported through the forms of border security cooperation with third countries such as Sene-gal and Mauritania. The Seahorse information-sharing programme, announced in 2004, has provided an infrastructure for daily interac-tions between local forces from Senegal, Mauritania, Cape Verde, and more to the Guardia Civil's coordination centre in Las Palmas.

The Seahorse project reflects the ways that bundles of technology can actively facilitate the assembly of new transnational configurations of actors and the re-scaling of some elements of the state's surveillance functions. This international information-sharing system was funded under the EU's AENEAS migration cooperation programme from 2006 and 2008 and since 2009 has relied on national contact points (NCPs) in Senegal (Dakar), Mauritania (Nouakchott and Nouadhibou), Por-tugal (Lisbon) and Cape Verde (Praia) and Spain (Gran Canaria). The Seahorse system is not primarily concerned with visual surveillance, but rather with speeding up the communication of surveillance infor-mation through information transmitted by secure satellite communi-cations and made available to all participants. The system allows file sharing, sharing of geographic information system information, chat, and email and Senegalese navy officials consider this system to be a very useful means of aggregating surveillance reports. Officials were thrilled by the sheer simplicity of the system and its powers of aggregation and coordination, recalling with enthusiasm the daily routine of logging in to the system and finding new reports from the different NCPs.[22] The Senegalese navy's implication in the growing Seahorse system also adds another layer to the its claims to operational competence for migra-tion control, since the service is in contention with the police for who claims true 'leadership' of border control operations against irregular migration. These claims are salient since Senegal's operations against irregular migration by sea are split between operational control by the

---

[22] Interview at Marine Nationale du Sénégal, Dakar, 13 March 2013.

navy and logistical command from the ministry of interior. Although the initial spur for the Seahorse project was human migration, the tightening of information-sharing has been enabled by the Spanish provision of capacity in the form of secure communications infrastructure. Following from the typology of state transformation developed in Chapter 3, this intervention has been transformational in terms of the formation of new linkages across national security sectors, and stimulated a re-scaling of the intelligence elements of maritime border security.

Symbols and Rhetorical Devices

As I walked into the office of the police commissioner in charge of security at Dakar's international airport, I noticed a West Sahel award lying prominently on the desk next to a stack of business cards. Small Guardia Civil pennants also hang in the offices of police officers from the DPAF who coordinated the response to the 2006 migration crisis. What this type of interaction shows is that the politics of border security is not only a technological and bureaucratic space but also functions through symbols, tropes, rhetorical devices, and widespread perceptions. Items such as pins, certificates, and other types of souvenirs would often betray the 'security cultures' of my interlocutors as much as any discussion or policy document. Such badges, certificates, awards, banners, maps, and even stationery also testify to the importance and prestige accorded to interactions between local security professionals and their foreign partners. These symbols wield a double-edged role: they are representations of success and tokens of prestige, but also manifestations of the tokenism of capacity-building interventions. They reflect the *performative* (see Chapter 3) nature of many of the capacity-building interventions that shape borderwork in West Africa: frequent but ultimately low-impact training courses and equipment donations. Regardless of interventions' actual impacts, Guardia Civil emblems and West Sahel tokens are play an important symbolic role as artefacts of expertise, which are the physical manifestation of a successful career. For some, they are also a source of pride. For others, such as a lower-level gendarme I spoke to in Mauritania, saw these tokens of cooperation as confirmations of their undesirable status within their profession. This particular gendarme, having undergone Spanish-funded training, had been given a small Guardia

Civil Tráfico (traffic police) pin at the end of his training session, and a training certificate. This certificate was not even his to keep, but was kept in his personnel files, as if to show how little the training achieved for anyone involved beyond the senior officers, who did not transmit their own acquired knowledge down the chain of command.[23] Even amongst those who work closely with the Spanish day-to-day, there is a perception that the capacity-building assistance they receive is minimal compared to the help their European partners devote to themselves.[24]

Looking beyond the tangible tokens of security cooperation, rumours and popular nomenclature shape the ways that border security 'assemblages' are understood in the public imagination, and by extension how they are resisted. For example, the EU's border agency Frontex is well known beyond Europe's shores, even if only by name. In everyday terms, people on the streets of Dakar are well aware of Frontex, which emerges as a shorthand term standing in for the wide-ranging and heavy-handed European response to migration. In popular parlance, the 'MOU' or the Spanish police presence effectively melts into a larger category of European migration control encapsulated by Frontex, notably in the press. This particular public understanding of migration control echoes with Andersson's (2014b) anecdote, relayed in Chapter 2, about how migrants frequently identified Spanish Red Cross workers as involved in border policing. Even at the highest levels of the security establishment, talk of the *dispositif Frontex* circulates as a shorthand for a security practice that is primarily a bilateral affair with Spain. Given that Spain is actively pushing for a 'European' approach to controlling the border, and Guardia Civil officers self-consciously understand themselves as guardians of the continent's borders in Africa, perhaps this shorthand is quite apt. The term 'Frontex', whether or not it actually refers to the organization itself or its coordination role, has also given focus to opposition to Spanish border control efforts in Senegal and Mauritania. For instance, Migreurop has worked in concert with local agencies such as the Mauritanian human rights association (AMDH) on a campaign called 'Frontexit', launched simultaneously in Brussels and Nouakchott. While on the side of security, 'le Frontex' provides focus on the mission, for human

---

[23] Interview with gendarme, Nouakchott, 14 June 2013.
[24] Interview with head of Frontex cooperation, Senegalese navy, Dakar, 30 June 2013.

rights campaigners it provides means of making visible a security cooperation that remains technical, opaque, and bureaucratized. These discursive tropes are crucial parts of the identification and delimiting of the Spanish-African police cooperation assemblage.

Finally, the relations within this security assemblage are smoothed over by the rhetorical power of the concept of 'capacity'. It plays a large role in Spanish-African cooperation on migration because the question of capacity to control borders, or of policing capacity in general, rests on temporal assumptions and rhetorical devices. The interaction between Spanish police and their Senegalese and Mauritanian partners rests on an ongoing assumption that the initial intervention of the late 2000s was needed because African states were uninterested in or unable to control irregular emigration. Their intervention is therefore necessarily remedial, to improve capacity. Capacity, in turn, is an idea intimately linked to an idea of temporal progress. The interveners (the Guardia Civil) place themselves temporally ahead of the intervened, with their expertise and equipment advantage standing in for claims to a greater temporal advancement and justifying their authority to guide their African partners. For instance, Spanish security attachés I spoke to wielded the Spanish experience as a way of attributing some kind of institutional capital to the Guardia Civil, noting that Senegal faces 'the same problems [they] had in the early 1980s'.[25] This experience gap is not straightforwardly paternalistic – it is actually quite sympathetic and draws on Spain's own post-Franco statebuilding – but it nonetheless betrays how self-evident the Guardia Civil considers its claims to expertise to be. The rhetorical importance of 'capacity' does not always follow a north–south direction of travel. Senegalese authorities are keen to highlight their existing naval expertise and their preexisting initiative to prevent irregular migration. Officers I spoke to at the Senegalese navy were quick to recall that interceptions of irregular migrants were occurring well before the Guardia Civil or Frontex intervened, pointing to past efforts such as a 1998 interception of a Sri Lankan ship heading to Canada.[26] This is also an important reminder that it is not only the European border being policed, but also the Senegalese border. Indeed, officers are quick to place caveats on the Spanish role, which is described as providing greater 'assurance' and

---

[25] Interview, Spanish internal security attaché, Dakar, 30 January 2013.
[26] Interview, Marine Nationale du Sénégal, Dakar, 13 March 2013.

'coordination', rather than ascribe a foundational role to their foreign partners.[27] Even though Spanish-African security relations are founded on the idea of a capacity differential, the pedagogical nature of border control is not to be oversimplified as a form of one-way tutelage dominated by constantly unequal power relations. Recalling that assemblage is open to dispersed causality and agency (see Chapter 2) helps us to grasp this multi-purpose way that border security cooperation works in practice.

The rhetoric of capacity is also used by local actors to contest the elements of the European border security culture that tie technology to capacity. It is difficult to quantify capacity, particularly when African police forces are compared to well-equipped European forces, with the latter operating as the benchmark. My police interlocutors in Senegal were proud of what they achieved against the irregular migration 'problem' given their resources, and suggested they may even be more *efficient* despite lower capacity. 'If we had what they had', one Senegalese police commander told me, 'we would be far better than them'.[28] Senegalese security officials are also more *familiar* with their territory. One commander in the national police spent so much time in the Canaries in 2006 that police came to consider the islands 'like [their] village'[29] or backyard, considering Madrid to be more distant than Dakar (in every sense of the term) from the tangible effects of clandestine migration. Capacity is also relative because capacity-building also flows from south to north, with opportunities for African security forces to 'speak back'. Migration has provided an ongoing issue area for police cooperation well after the 'crisis': the Euro-African police conferences on irregular migration (hosted by Spain) have continued to be held in the Canary Islands despite the reduction in numbers. At the conference's seventh iteration in 2012, the head of the Senegalese navy's Groupement Naval Opérationnel provided a masterclass on his unique experience in handling irregular migration. The eighth conference was held in April 2015 in the Canary Islands, under the auspices of the West Sahel project, with officers again invited to present on their areas of expertise. This ongoing security relationship, initiated by the crisis of migration and the need to manage risks around it, has provided

---

[27] Interview, Marine Nationale du Sénégal, Dakar, 13 March 2013.
[28] Interview, Police Nationale du Sénégal, Dakar, 18 January 2013.
[29] Interview, Police Nationale du Sénégal, Dakar, 18 January 2013.

opportunities for the rhetoric of capacity, efficiency, and experience to be wielded in both directions. In this assemblage of security, we do not see one dominant logic but rather elements of contestation and flows of knowledge in all directions.

A Territorial Turn: On the Expansionist Nature of Security Practice

As argued in Chapter 2, the border is 'more than a line in the sand'. That being said, policing lines drawn in the sand has become an increasingly important part of Spanish police cooperation with Senegal and Mauritania. This is not to say that the socio-technical border control arrangement between Spain and African states has not had territorial outposts: these have taken the form of command centres in Las Palmas, Nouakchott, and Dakar but also beach patrols and intelligence gathering in areas housing potential migrants. Territory is simply increasingly appearing as a prime site of intervention in this space, reflecting the desire for greater security integration as well as new anxieties about drugs and terrorism. With the dramatic reduction in irregular migration to the Canaries removing the veneer of 'crisis' from security cooperation, Spain has increasingly directed its police cooperation activities inland, planning joint police stations and reinforcement of regional cooperation.

The years since 2006 have seen the emergence of a more comprehensive security approach, which deliberately amalgamates cross-border flows and subsumes the response to them under a general banner of better policing capacity. The second phase of the West Sahel project, West Sahel II, was launched in March 2014 and encapsulates this comprehensive approach to security cooperation. As an extension to the first phase launched in 2011, the new phase moves the focus away from 'migration and asylum' towards regional security integration and closer cooperation with landlocked states of the Sahel such as Mali and Niger. One of the keystones of this approach is the creation of joint police cooperation centres in new and existing police stations. For instance, the PK 55 border post on the border between Mauritania and Western Sahara is a *commissariat conjoint* (joint police station) bringing together officers from Spain's CNP as well as Mauritanian police and gendarmes. This joint post has been in place since the spring of 2013. As part of the West Sahel project's extension, there are plans for a Centro de Cooperación Policial International (international police cooperation centre) in the Mauritanian town of Sélibaby (Guardia Civil 2014). The location of this city – in the southeastern corner of Mauritania, at the borders with Mali and Senegal – reflects the triple concern with land migration, drugs, and terrorism that has been the impulse behind the West Sahel project from its inception. Border officials (police, gendarmerie and customs) from Mali, Senegal, and Mauritania will be housed in the new centre and patrol this tri-border area together. Sélibaby sits both geographically and mentally at the nexus of traditional migration routes as well as more recent drug trafficking routes, and the new joint police centre fits into the drive to cooperate at the level of daily practice. This cooperation centre mirrors existing Spanish arrangements such as the joint police station at the Tanger Med port where Guardia Civil agents work alongside Moroccan gendarmes. Under West Sahel II additional Guardia Civil officers will be sent to Nouadhibou and Mauritanian liaison staff will go to the Guardia Civil's command centre in the Canary Islands, and for the first time Spanish and Mauritanian gendarmerie will undertake *land*-based patrols together. As Chapter 2 noted, determining the extent of 'assemblages' can be difficult – in this case, the actors and forms of cooperation are at some temporal and physical distance from the initial MOU signed at the height of the Canaries crisis. That being said, current Spanish practices combating overland flows are the direct inheritance of the initial ad hoc assembly of police actors in 2006.

The growing Spanish reputation for migration management expertise has been leveraged in Niger, with which Spain signed a cooperation agreement on transnational organized crime in early 2015. While there are traditionally very few political or economic links between the two countries, there is a Spanish *agregado de interior* in the capital Niamey, who oversees the implementation of the agreement and liaises with the local IOM and EUCAP Sahel missions on border security issues. The agreement signed between Spain and Niger is not only reflective of the technical governance discussed above in the context of MOUs, but also of the growing consideration of 'cross-border threats' as a singular category into which diverse issues such as migration and drug trafficking fit. This approach relies on a facile association between migrant smuggling and other forms of trafficking or criminal flows, with the idea that trafficking networks are amorphous and 'always there'. According to one Spanish officer, the degree of threat to the border is simply a question of whether these networks are 'activated' or not.[30] Under the agreement with Niger, Spanish officers mentor and train Nigérien law enforcement agencies and share intelligence, transmitting European 'security culture' around personnel management and how to lead judicial investigations. These new forms of cooperation beyond sea patrols are perceived as security 'innovations'[31] amongst the different actors I spoke to and they illustrate the role of the global south as an incubator of new security practices and as a space of experimentation. Although posts such as PK 55 or Sélibaby are conceivably global spaces, the differential in knowledge between 'north' and 'south' continues to act as the overarching framework of justification for continuing security cooperation, with each donation or new construction reaffirming this gap even through its attempts to close it.

Conclusion

There is a large socio-technical space created by the meeting, overlap, and interaction between different clusters of Spanish and African security professionals. This space must be investigated because it provides a view into the externalization of the EU border in practice, in an area that has largely been overlooked by academic literature on this phenomenon. The various objects, concepts and actors who compose this borderscape make excellent narrative devices through which to explore the relationships fostered by this cooperation. Looking forward, the consolidation of security relations between Spain and West African countries has correlated with a dramatic fall in the numbers of migrant departures and interceptions. As the number of migrants using the sea route to the Canary Islands has dropped, interveners' focus has shifted towards a more generalized view of security and of the response needed. This has coincided with a growing concern with terrorism in the Sahel region triggered by the intensification of jihadist violence, particularly in areas bordering northern Mali. As such, border control has become more than just a migration issue, and security actors in the region have pointed to trafficking in drugs and small arms, as well as terrorist infiltration. The threat is no longer 'migration' but

---

[30] Interview with policy officer, EU delegation, Nouakchott, 28 February 2013.
[31] Interview with Mauritanian gendarmerie commander, Nouadhibou, 18 June 2013.

rather 'porous borders' more broadly. Spain has become an important player in security in the Sahel, and the Guardia Civil participates in naval exercises such as Saharan Express 2013 and the US-led Flint-lock military exercises. This has served to push for a broadening of the assemblage to include a raft of other organizations and relations. Agencies such as the International Organization for Migration have provided border management assistance, and bilateral technical assistance now serves to improve general security capacity beyond migration alone. The European Union has also come to play a central security role in West Africa, first through migration concerns but increasingly in other questions surrounding drug trafficking and military training. One programme that reflects this trend is the EU-funded construction of border posts in Mauritania. This programme ostensibly began as a response to the same irregular migrant movements discussed here, but has morphed into a catch-all security solution for Mauritania. It is to this programme, and the broader assemblage of security in Mauritania, to which I turn in the next chapter.

5 | Border Infrastructures and Statebuilding in Mauritania

On the night of 8 August 2009, a suicide bomber blew himself up outside the French embassy in Nouakchott, the capital of the Islamic Republic of Mauritania. No one other than the bomber was killed, but the embassy attack confirmed Mauritania's status, at least to outsiders, as a locus of diverse cross-border threats. Mauritania's border control arrangements were already a source of concern, with the country deemed a 'transit' space following the 'crisis' of migration to Spain from West Africa (see Chapter 4). With a spate of attacks on security personnel, aid workers, and foreign tourists occurring in the country between 2005 and 2009, largely blamed on Islamist militants straddling the Sahel-Sahara space, terrorism joined irregular migration as a new threat angle in the minds of local and global policymakers and security professionals. In the face of a multi-faceted security threat, the pursuit of better *border management* – not just migration control – has become paramount in the eyes of local and foreign security officials and bureaucrats. Transit migration, infiltration by terrorist groups, and a growing West African drug smuggling route linking South America to Europe all created a situation through which securing Mauritania's borders became paramount.

The focus of this chapter is Mauritania's decision to rebuild its border control infrastructure through the renovation and construction of its border posts. In 2010, the Mauritanian government decreed that the country would have forty-five exclusive legal points of entry along its more than four thousand kilometres of borders with western Sahara, Algeria, Mali, and Senegal, as well as three international airports. The national migration strategy, in force since 2011 and developed with help from the European Union (EU), called for this project under its section dealing with 'control over migration flows'. Since then, largely with €8 million of funding from the EU's European Development Fund (EDF) and Instrument for Stability, the EU and International Organization for Migration (IOM) have led a project to build and renovate

Mauritania's border posts, helping to train staff and install new techno-logical infrastructures. This border post programme in Mauritania has catalysed the formation of a community of security professionals com-posed of representatives of international organizations, embassy secu-rity liaisons, and even development agencies. This chapter provides an entry point into the diverse and growing assemblage of border man-agement actors, practices and technologies which has cropped up in Mauritania, one that has – largely for reasons of access – been neither mapped nor explored in much detail so far.

Existing work on borders and mobility in Mauritania and the Sahel/Sahara region (e.g. Robin 2009; Choplin and Lombard 2010; Poutignat and Streiff-Fénart 2010; Brachet et al. 2011) provides novel insights into migratory patterns and policies, often through ethno-graphic methods, but does not give detailed accounts of the social and technical world of security professionals and technologies, and their role in the production of knowledge about border control. The every-day roles of security professionals and other bureaucrats, especially of organizations such as the IOM, are not researched in much detail in the region. This is despite the fact that organizations like the IOM have pushed strongest for the language of 'border management' as a means to greater security. In response to this lacuna, this chapter asks two major questions: first, 'Who are the actors that make up the border security 'assemblage' in Mauritania, and what are their roles, routines, and struggles?' and second, 'What rationalities of border control are transmitted, adapted, or resisted in border governance in Mauritania?' To answer these questions, the chapter draws on the theoretical frame-work established in Chapters 2 and 3.

The first section of this chapter builds on the theoretical framework of the previous chapters, highlighting the socio-technical nature of the Mauritanian border by using an understanding of 'assemblage' devel-oped in Chapter 2 which focuses our attention to the socio-technical elements of the border. The remainder of the chapter pulls the empiri-cal analysis deeper, focusing on four key actants of border control: the border posts, the landscape, the biometric entry–exit system and train-ing practices. In each of these empirical vignettes, the (partial) mapping of the assemblage of border control in Mauritania undertaken in this chapter re-emphasizes the central concerns of this book: showing the socio-technical forms of borderwork that build and sustain the bor-der, whether these are done by humans or not, and asking what type of understanding these practices reflect about who should control borders and how. Each one also provides a broad entry point into the practices, knowledges, routines, technologies, and struggles of border security in Mauritania. The conclusion sums up the main points and segues to the next chapter on biometrics.

Mauritania's Socio-technical Border

The framework established in Part I of this book sets out a vision of borderwork as a heterogeneous and disaggregated practice. Assemblage, in turn, illustrated the often sporadic social and technical relations that emerge in attempts to shore up West African borders such as Mauritania's. This lens is attuned to the nature of projects like the border posts in Mauritania, with EuropeAid, the EU organization that administers the European Development Fund (EDF) through which the project is funded, evaluating the programme in 2013 and noting that

design and implementation of the EC support was rather guided by the type of events that prompted this support (drastic increase in irregular migration flows) and the experience of implementing organisations (esp. Guardia Civil, IOM) rather than by overall EU policies or programming documents.
(EuropeAid 2013: 152)

This testifies to the disaggregation of Mauritanian border security as well as to the complex social space in which the various actors who work in and around the border operate. In this respect, the project confirms a key insight in critical border studies, namely that the border is diffused, abstracted from the territorial line, and part of a broader process of governance (Paasi 1998; Walters 2002; Rumford 2008). For the border posts project alone, multiple agencies and actors are involved. The EU's local presence is assured through the European External Action Service's (EEAS) delegation, which oversees the implementation of EU-funded projects in the country. Projects are funded through lines such as the European Development Fund and the security-focused Instrument for Stability. The EU's main implementing partner, the IOM, is an entrepreneurial and project-based international organization whose activities are largely shaped by its donors' specifications. In addition, European states have independently contributed to the project: France has built some posts through its security cooperation, as has Germany through its development agency (GIZ), which also provides police training in the country. Spain's Guardia Civil have also provided border patrol training and equipment to the Mauritanian gendarmerie through another EU-funded project, West Sahel. The International Centre for Migration Policy Development (ICMPD), a Brussels-based international organization that coordinates migration management projects around the world, has used its own direct EU funding to help Mauritania manage biometric data for its border management system.

Recalling the analytical lenses on borderwork discussed in Chapter 2, the complex blend of actors involved in and around the Mauritanian border posts project could be considered part of a 'field' in the Bourdieusian sense. They do appear to fit his vision of it as a 'network, or a configuration, of objective relations between positions' held by actors (Bourdieu and Wacquant 1992: 97). The concerns of this chapter also overlap with the vision of habitus and capital that Bourdieu puts forward. However, there is more to the sociology of the border posts project, and to border governance more generally, than such concepts allow us to see on their own. The project, along with the social relations around it, is shaped by the agency of material factors such as the posts themselves, the biometric entry–exit databases they host, and the training programmes created and modified for the police and gendarmes who staff them. This is where concepts from an actor-network theory vision of assemblage help us to see the border as socio-technical. Actor-network theory, with origins in science and technology studies, is not a holistic theoretical approach, but rather what Law (2007: 2) calls a 'diaspora that overlaps with other intellectual traditions'. Actor-network theorists' emphasis on the world as nothing more than contingent sets of associations between humans and non-humans alike puts the approach in stark contradiction to what Latour (2005) calls the 'sociology of the social' – which includes Bourdieu's oeuvre. The radically flat ontology characteristic of actor-network theory (generalized as an 'assemblage' approach in Chapter 2) approaches sees little difference between the human and the non-human in their capacity for agency. In the light of these radically different foundations, Bourdieu's sociology and actor-network theory are seemingly not commensurable. ANT concepts help us to paint a fuller picture of border control in practice, and help us to grasp many of the same social dynamics (competition, struggle, and actors' histories) but add in some more helpful corollary concepts to complete the picture: the concept of 'actant', through which we can theorize the border as socio-technical, and that of the '(im)mutable mobile', which can describe border control knowledges and their transmission. The former appears briefly in Chapter 2, while the latter has been discussed at length in Chapter 3.

The concept of 'actant' (Latour 2005) is particularly crucial to our understanding of project's like the Mauritanian border posts because it removes the analytical difference between humans and non-humans in terms of their possibility for agency. The concept of stops short of attributing intentionality to the non-human by defining agency simply as the ability to make a difference. This does not remove the importance of human agency, but simply highlights the ability of non-humans to be of consequence. Much of this was visible in the preceding chapter, in which the narrative was organized around actants such as vehicles and surveillance technologies. An attention to non-human agency is compatible with sociological approaches to the relational construction of security, as recent work on 'policy tools' (Balzacq 2008) and 'technologies' (Guittet and Jeandesboz 2010) has shown. By considering the agency of the non-human, we are better able to account for ways in which technologies exert agency in Mauritanian border governance. Agents struggle over different objects: the EU delegation and IOM representative may seek to enhance their respective status over the same object or project output. The biometric entry–exit tracking system is a bearer of a norm of how border control should be done: its technical linkage to national ID systems demands that the border be stretched inwards from the territorial line. Technologies also shape the trajectory of the border. For instance, a border post is a security tool that weds its users to specific security solutions (biometrics, e-passports, etc.). By examining these non-human actors we do not give them human intentionality, but rather highlight their ability to incarnate cognitive relationships and shape human action. They are also lenses through which we can observe the social and technical items being assembled: by studying border posts in Mauritania, we necessarily bring in the passports they read, the internet infrastructures that connect this passport information to centralized databases, and the risk-analysis techniques used in mining these databases. Security is therefore not *only* the result of an institutional or professional interplay; it is also an outcome of material processes, the deployment of security tools and the agency of objects.

In sum, with the Mauritanian border being a transnational space governed as much from Brussels as from Nouakchott, we must use theoretical tools that are attuned to the diverse personal dispositions and social interactions that shape how the border is governed. The selective and careful use of concepts from actor-network theory usefully draws our attention to socio-technical factors, notably the importance of non-humans in shaping border governance. Concretely, speaking of actants helps account for the agency of materials and objects, and the concept of the (im)mutable mobile (cf. Chapter 3) highlights the motion of knowledges about border control.

Border Posts as Infrastructural Security Technologies

The border posts in Mauritania are significant because they are *infrastructures* of border control. Every actor is also a network, and the border posts in Mauritania are no different: they assemble disparate knowledges, technologies, and funding arrangements to extend the reach of state surveillance – a form of surveillance mediated by external actors. These border posts also provide reputational capital for border control actors, and solidify particular policy paths through the introduction of new ways of controlling the border. First, we should think of the posts as infrastructures of legibility (Scott 1998) of the border area itself, as well as of the populations that cross it. This capture by the administrative gaze is similar to what John Torpey (2000) calls the state's 'embrace' of its population, which stresses the work of identifying and 'filing' of citizens. In places, Mauritania's border posts are quasi-developmental tools that boost the capacities of local communities, providing the only source of electricity or market space in some villages. These border posts are the state's broader footprints in a locality, providing a new interface for populations previously out of reach of central government. As such they are not a circumscribed migration policy tool, but a much more wide-ranging infrastructure of state visibility. This visibility extends both ways, however, and the primary purpose of the posts remains one of identification – making visible and legible those who cross the border.[1] This dual purpose of the border post as an infrastructural tool is significant in terms of the broader

[1] Interview with journalist from Agence Nouakchott d'Informations, Nouakchott, 16 June 2013.

assemblage of border control in Mauritania because different actors provide largely different justifications and emphases. The local Direction de la Surveillance du Territoire (DST), on one side, emphasizes the utility of statistics and of document fraud reduction.[2] The local EEAS delegation, however, emphasizes the developmental aspect of the project. Despite these conflicting justifications, different goals coexist in the same project.

There is little prestige available to foreign security actors in Mauritania, but the infrastructural nature of the border posts project means that the buildings are sources of reputational advancement. Although Mauritania's somewhat undeserved reputation as a large desert haven of terrorism has attracted funding and programmes, it has made it an unattractive work destination for border management experts. For instance, the Brussels-based ICMPD found it very difficult to find personnel to go to Mauritania precisely because so few wanted to relocate, especially without their families.[3] The generalized view of Mauritania is that it is far from a dream work destination, and the makeup of international actors in the security assemblage around it is overwhelmingly male. Yet the border posts project has provided donors with opportunities for the accumulation of prestige and pride, to varying extents. Various funders bring different strategies and levels of resources to the project, and gain differing levels of prestige as a consequence. The IOM Development Fund, drawing from IOM member state contributions, offers only moderate levels of funding, typically below $500,000 and mainly for training. Although the IOM uses UN pay scales and adopts a blue-and-white corporate identity, it is not formally a UN agency (despite a formal affiliation to the UN in 2016) and therefore does not have the same degree of continuity or funding. By contrast, the EU's millions in migration management aid to Mauritania enable the local EEAS delegation to reap the benefits of a very visible intervention. The funding for the posts comes from €8million in European Development Fund (EDF) funding Mauritania receives for the implementation of its integrated migration strategy. The EEAS's desire to implement visible projects, near which a placard bearing an EU flag can be placed, is much more pressing than the IOM's. Each new post opening is marked by a press release from the local EEAS delegation,

[2] Interview with DST director, Nouakchott, 27 February 2013.
[3] Interview with ICMPD staff, via phone, 18 March 2013.

and is attended by an official from the delegation, the IOM head of mission, and local security actors. Pictures are taken, and this photographic aspect of the project is central to the day-to-day routines of EU staff: before-and-after images of the border posts line the walls of the local EEAS delegation, alongside posters for other border control projects. The IOM's global capacity-building website also features these side-by-side comparison photos, which show border posts going from dilapidated shacks held up by four sticks to brand new concrete buildings. This is testament to a self-perception of transformational presence and to Mauritania's role as an exemplar.

Mauritanian security officials are also in hot pursuit of the reputational gains that participation in global security assemblages confers. The Mauritanian exemplar confers greater credibility with their neighbours and from the transnational border control community. The IOM considers Mauritania by far the most 'advanced' country in terms of border control in West Africa[4] and border posts also provide a physical manifestation of progress, which can be shown off to neighbours. However, an evaluation mission by EuropeAid (which administers the EDF) suggested that the Mauritanians 'appeared more concerned by short term benefits (access to funding to modernize relevant institutional bodies) than by a long term strategy for improving border management' (EuropeAid 2013: 152). This suggests something that international security professionals informally highlight in most interviews: that local security forces tend to be myopic (in the interveners' terms) or at least have radically different beneficiaries in mind in their pursuit of foreign assistance. This is not to say that private gain trumps the public good, but rather that a Mauritanian security professional's incentives may lie with the prestige of a particular unit or corps rather than of the DST or of the state as a whole. Regardless of any manipulation or resistance in the project, these actors still accrue a Bourdieusian 'symbolic capital' through the promotion of the Mauritanian exemplar overseas, and the EU and IOM have organized meetings between Senegalese and Mauritanian officials to facilitate transfer of best practices, which is quite a feat in light of the two countries' often tenuous diplomatic relations. The EEAS delegations and IOM missions in Dakar and Nouakchott are in competition to earn credit for this facilitation of knowledge transmission. This highlights how infrastructural

---

[4] Interview with IOM staff, Dakar, 25 January 2013.

advancement is as much reputational as it is tangible, and also shows the degree to which the 'international community' in globalized security assemblages is itself asymmetrical and disaggregated. As Martin Geiger has argued in the context of IOM intervention in Albania, the organization is 'not just the henchman of the EU' (2010: 154) and its pursuit of an independent role as an effective and prestigious actor in Mauritanian border control is essential to accrue the credibility it requires to access more donor funding.

Mauritania's border posts are also a material infrastructure of pedagogy, enabling the transmission of intangible 'best practices' of border control. The newly built border post at Rosso, Mauritania's busiest post along the southern river border with Senegal,[5] shows precisely how material infrastructures act to instil new routines through the global border management norms they convey. At Rosso, the separation of incoming and outgoing flows of people from Mauritania, essential to avoiding the goods or travel documents passing between people in each line, was not respected. As with many West African border posts, the reality of mostly pedestrian crossings and the informal practices (such as leaving an ID card at the border while crossing for the day) at Rosso exists in stark contract the international standards developed in the Schengen zone and beyond. By building a new border post, the new standard is effectively 'built in' to the material infrastructure of the border. Although IOM's border management project cycle normally determines 'big' normative questions such as legal frameworks before turning to 'smaller' concrete infrastructure-building and equipment provision,[6] it is clear that even when concrete actions such as border post construction come first, they always embody knowledge about how borders should function. This reflects how rationalities of border control are present at *all* stages of the process.

Mauritania's border posts shape the range of possible trajectories in border control by favouring a technologized, speed-focused answer to the question of porous borders. By substituting paper registries (which are consulted 'in case' of a problem) for real-time interconnection with a point-to-point internet connection (satellite internet technology was considered too expensive at €360,000 per year) these posts privilege

---

[5] Senegal renewed its own post at Rosso in September 2013, complete with issuance kiosks for its biometric visa launched in July 2013.
[6] Email correspondence with IOM head of mission, Mauritania, 3 March 2013.

a turn towards data analysis – widely used for border control in the West – as a response to border security problems. This is something that the IOM's entry–exit system, to which I turn later, facilitates. The importance of having a real-time account of the border is quintessential to the leadership in the Mauritanian national security directorate (DGSN), who privilege the speed and better situational awareness provided by this system.

Part of the role of border posts as infrastructure networks is their *modular* approach to security – a view which understands them as small steps towards a more whole and totalizing approach. The posts are therefore considered something of a start – since progress 'has to come from somewhere'[7] – rather than as an end product, and provide plenty of room for upgrades. For instance, the Personal Identification and Registration System (PIRS) system used for entry–exit recording is a piecemeal software package that allows the post-purchase inclusion of different features, allowing border guards to attach new hardware (webcams, fingerprint scanners) and new software features (saving of scanned passport images) down the line. In this way, the software *acts* to dictate and constrain future policy paths, by prefiguring the progression of border control modernization. Similarly, the adoption of a modular technology also acts as a signal of commitment, whereby the country adopting the system demonstrates its willingness to buy in to the particular path dependency offered by the system. This importance of signalling showcases the role of border posts as symbolic infrastructure, in that they highlight the centrality of state presence to the assurance of sovereignty. As the EuropeAid evaluation mentions, border post design 'does not stem clearly from a detailed analysis of flows and prevailing threats at the border' (EuropeAid 2013: 157). They are, in this sense, a product of aligning incentives amongst the assembled actors in this socio-technical project: all seek the successful completion of the project in line with a vision of appropriateness of border security rather than objective threat analysis. These actors all appear to converge on the idea that the border posts are an incarnation of the state's commitment to security, both to outsiders and to its own citizens, regardless of the borderwork they are designed to do in terms of inclusion/exclusion.

---

[7] Interview with IOM regional border management expert, via phone, 10 February 2013.

The Role of Terrain and Landscape

The infrastructures of border control in Mauritania are shaped by the terrain they occupy, and recent work in critical security studies has acknowledged the role of such material settings. Aradau (2010) and Nyers (2012) both draw on the nascent literature on the 'new materialisms' (e.g. Bennett 2010; Coole and Frost 2010), itself related to ANT, to point to the agential role of infrastructures and border landscapes respectively. Aradau looks beyond discourse alone to see the way that 'things' like critical infrastructure actively shape security problems, while Nyers points to the mobility of the physical terrain. Mauritania's terrain, from the green Senegal River basin in the south to the windswept Saharan dunes of north, has been essential in framing what security problems are responded to and how. As a result, new security relationships emerge around the desert as a problematic and its conditions 'make a difference' (recalling the agency of actants) in terms of the approaches applied to controlling different parts of the border.

The Senegal River, along which most of Mauritania's border posts are situated, provides the natural border with Senegal to the south, and the Senegalese border post at Rosso is reachable from the Mauritanian side by ferry or by pirogue and there are plans for a road bridge to be built. Prior to the border posts project, the Mauritanian border security services (police, gendarmerie and customs) were housed in a building owned by the ferry operating company. The EEAS delegation, insisting on a neater separation of public and private sectors at the border,[8] preferred a purpose-built structure, which now stands a hundred metres upstream from the previous location. This reflects the delegation's position that *acceptable* border management standards include a clear demarcation of sectors, a situation brought about by the particular landscape in question. This is reflective of the broader EU agenda in Mauritania which, unlike the IOM's, is more holistic and centred more clearly on ensuring good governance. This is also part of a tendency to build a standalone police capacity, to ensure that the state is eventually able to independently police its border.

Beyond the Senegal River, the Sahara plays an agential role in shaping the kinds of technologies deployed at the border posts. While wired electricity connections are available in bustling border towns

---

[8] Interview with security attaché at EU delegation, Nouakchott, 19 February 2013.

like Rosso, almost every other post in Mauritania is necessarily remote or, in the case of those in the north, in desertic conditions. The landscape therefore shapes the types of expertise and learning required to make the border posts project 'work' in Mauritania. France, having built border posts in Mali under its JUSSEC (Justice et Sécurité en région sahélo-saharienne) programme, shared its experience with the EU and IOM, suggesting that posts use solar panels[9] and be built near sources of water in order to gather useful intelligence from nomads or other passers-by.[10] The bundling of multiple international actors in this borderwork assemblage enables a south-south transmission of security expertise which is itself required by the landscape itself. The landscape also dictates the types of material infrastructure that must be put in place, as equipment in the border posts must be amenable to the production capacities of solar equipment and the speed limitations of the internet connection. The IOM's entry–exit tracking system, to which I turn later, is one such adaptable technology.

The Sahara also represents a vast space of what lies 'in-between', and as such is a blank canvas onto which anxieties about migration and terrorism are projected. The desert, which spans most of the country, has long been a space of vibrant exchange and circulation (Scheele 2012). However, a discourse of threat has tended to prevail with regards to the flows that criss-cross it. Since 2000, Mauritanian discourse has increasingly aligned with Western perspectives on its role as a sufficiently democratized Islamic bastion against terrorism (Jourde 2007), and the country has extensively played up its experience of irregular migration since 2006.[11] Between late 2007 and mid 2009, a string of attacks against Mauritanian army personnel and European tourists, culminating with Mauritania's first suicide bombing outside the French embassy

---

[9] I later learned that this was because unlike solar power, fuel can easily be siphoned off by staff, who tend to be (or feel) underpaid.

[10] Interview with interior security attaché, French embassy, Nouakchott, 4 March 2013.

[11] In the second half of 2006 almost thirty thousand people from across West Africa left the coasts of Senegal and Mauritania, mainly in fishing boats, attempting to reach Spain's Canary Islands, which are only one hundred kilometres off the coast of Morocco. This spurred an increase in EU – particularly Spanish – involvement in migration management in the region that continues to this day with maritime patrols (via EU external borders agency Frontex), migration and development programmes, and technical assistance of the sort seen in Mauritania.

in Nouakchott, created the impression of an onslaught of terror. As a result, the state has taken a sharp turn towards a security orientation, and portrayed its territory as vulnerable and vast, requiring external assistance to secure. Mauritania has allied itself to European rationalities on migration management, and Spain's interest in reducing transit migration through Mauritania has helped its president Mohamed Ould Abdel Aziz avoid the full brunt of European censure for the 2008 coup that brought him to power (Foster 2010). Part of this security problem came from the desert's lack of natural obstacles, which made policing the border much tougher.[12] Members of the Mauritanian security forces describe the eastern desert border with Mali as easily penetrable, due to the sheer radius each patrol has to cover.[13] In turn, the desert reflects strategic battles about what is to be secured against, with the Mauritanian government more concerned about terrorist infiltration from Mali,[14] while EEAS and IOM staff play up the migration, asylum, and human rights justifications for the project, largely due to EDF funding objectives. What is notable is that although the landscape provides different incentives and security rationales, the assembled actors in the world of border control have converged on a comprehensive solution in the form of the border post project.

Finally, the physical landscape shapes the institutional division of border control, which in turn shapes the institutional cultures and methods that are applied to each border post. Mauritania, like most former French colonies, assigns policing duties through a roughly spatial division of labour, with the Police Nationale tasked with urban policing and the gendarmerie that of rural areas and the desert. The same applies to the border posts, with the police tending to take charge of airports and urban posts. This literal landscape of policing is a window into the routines, strategies, and forms of competition between Mauritanian security actors. The police run most border posts along the Senegal River, as these are near cities and experience large population flows, but maritime patrols on the river itself are carried out by the gendarmerie. Police, competitive with their colleagues in the gendarmerie (whom they perceive as better equipped), have had requests

---

[12] Interview with French interior security attaché, French embassy, Dakar, 22 July 2013.
[13] Interview with gendarme, Nouakchott, 5 March 2013.
[14] Interview with DST director, Nouakchott, 27 February 2013.

to the EU for boats of their own rebuffed,[15] with a reminder that this is beyond their mandate. However, gendarmes often work in areas of the landscape where there are no border posts, particularly along the riskier eastern border with Mali. Here, some gendarmes are sent for six-month shifts, sleeping in their vehicles in the desert, often to make room in the more desirable gendarmerie posts for officers who are friends or relatives of the regional commander.[16] Although the gendarmerie (as a military corps) is best equipped for the dangerous task of policing the desert, it is this perceived advantage of equipment and professionalism that paradoxically puts it lower down the list for new border posts. The landscape is therefore intimately tied to questions of prestige (a key symbolic pursuit for security actors), modes of institutional competition, but also the tension between state directives and local practices.

The IOM's PIRS System: A Technology of Border Proliferation

West Africa is not immune to the global trend towards the inclusion of digital technologies in borderwork – and in many cases it at its forefront. In the case of Mauritania's border posts, information technology is a site for struggles between security professionals and also helps proliferate the border function both inward and outward. Mauritania's border posts bring together, and play host to, two important technological trends: the use of biometric identifiers and the creation and integration of databases. The first extracts and isolates human attributes to facilitate control, and the second makes possible a range of bordering practices such as internal controls and deportation, effectively centralizing many ways that border crossing is governed. The Personal Identification and Registration System (PIRS),[17] an entry–exit tracking system designed in-house by the IOM, is an entry-level border management technology designed to be a key first step for nations in the developing world towards computerized immigration processing. The

---

[15] Interview with security attaché, EU delegation, Nouakchott, 19 February 2013.
[16] Interview with gendarme, Nouakchott, 5 March 2013.
[17] The system has since been renamed MIDAS, for the Migration Information and Data Analysis System. I have forgone the use of this name as it was not in use during my fieldwork period. However, it is noteworthy that the system's new name is reflective of the desire to move beyond 'registration' towards better 'analysis' of data gathered at border posts.

system 'offers high-quality performances at an affordable price […] is suitable for installation in remote areas' (IOM 2011), and has mainly been installed in countries from the global south, from South Sudan to Zimbabwe to Belize. PIRS is the type of technology that, following Mutlu's (2013) vision of the role of materiality, should be understood as both a form of *emergence* of a new security actant but also as a *by-product* of existing social relations in the assemblage at hand.

The PIRS system's implementation in Mauritania remains an ongoing process, with the IOM continuing to train and equip border officials as of 2017, but it already highlights the coexistence of digital and analogue approaches to border control. The system is in place at the two busiest posts, Nouakchott international airport (where it was piloted) and the town of Rosso on the border with Senegal. On one hand, PIRS represents the IOM's push to technologize and integrate border security in developing countries. It connects to Interpol databases of stolen vehicles and wanted persons, and affords travellers quicker border clearance times than the paper registers used beforehand. On the other hand, PIRS has not entirely displaced analogue practices: Watching the system in action,[18] one sees that Mauritania's border posts are not yet equipped with webcams and biometric scanners, so police must still rely on face-to-face verification of passport photos and the confirmation of entry stamps for citizens of Senegal and Mali (who have visa-free travel to Mauritania). The daily routine of border control in Mauritania, even in the presence of technological mediation, is still very much a hybrid of digital and analogue cultures. That being said, the system is progressively eliminating the need for Mauritanian officers stationed on the borders to phone neighbouring countries' border posts to get data about its own entries and exits.[19] Of course, all border regimes are hybrid in this way: passing through a US airport can involve a mix of in-person profiling and biometric registration – but in Mauritania this mix is due to the meeting of two different rationalities of border control: one based on local identification practice and another on global technological standards.

Systems like PIRS providing a means of accruing a form of 'symbolic capital' within the security assemblage. It provides IOM staff a

---

[18] Participant observation with police at Nouakchott international airport, 28 June 2013.

[19] Interview with IOM head of mission, Nouakchott, 20 June 2013.

certain amount of credibility as development-oriented security actors in Africa. The very basic nature of the system means IOM can claim that it is building up the 'basics' of border management on which further progress can be made.[20] A key task of IOM staff is therefore to actively try and 'sell' the PIRS technology to partner countries, but not by competing with the private sector. Rather, IOM must be altruistic and remind countries of the cost-effectiveness of PIRS. IOM Mauritania had to gently remind the authorities of PIRS's cost-effectiveness when French ID company Morpho proposed its own immigration processing solution as part of a 'bundle' with the biometric civil registration system the company was already implementing in the country.[21] The IOM logo is displayed prominently on the PIRS software, in much the same way as the EU flag is on the outside of the border posts: it represents a claim to symbolic capital akin to that of a development donor.

PIRS also highlights relationships of mistrust between different actors who do border control. A common 'esprit de corps'[22] helps a former European gendarme working for the EU delegation in Nouakchott when dealing with colleagues at the Mauritanian gendarmerie, but technology proves to be a source of controversy. Some Mauritanian actors do not trust the system itself – one official called for all computers to be removed from border posts[23] – and the country's security officials are keen to control the source code to prevent 'backdoor' access to their data. That the Mauritanians have been worried about clandestine access shows that relationships based on obtaining rents (in the form of border infrastructure) may not correlate with *trust* between security professionals. The reluctance to discuss data protection provisions with the ICMPD,[24] which uses EU funding to improve Mauritania's national biometric database, shows how the technology's linkages have not led to the wholesale adoption of a corresponding culture around the treatment of data.

[20] Interview with IOM regional border management expert, via phone, 10 February 2013.
[21] Interview with IOM head of mission, Nouakchott, 19 February 2013.
[22] Interview with security attaché at EU delegation, Nouakchott, 19 February 2013.
[23] Interview with security attaché at EU delegation, Nouakchott, 28 February 2013.
[24] Interview with ICMPD staff, via phone, 18 March 2013.

The PIRS technology makes it possible for borders to be controlled well inland, through its deployment of identification technologies linked to emerging biometric systems in Mauritania. The country has since 2011 proceeded with a vast 'renewal' of all documents, including passports, national ID cards, and foreign resident cards, assured in part by making all persons resident on the territory re-register with the state's civil documents agency (this is a central focus in Chapter 6 which follows). The new Registre de Populations, replacing the last national registration exercise from 1998, will be linked with police records of criminal activity as well as to the existing border control databases maintained by the police and gendarmerie and aggregated by the DST. In theory, data from Mauritania's ubiquitous internal controls, from its borders, and from its ID databases will eventually be interlinked. In 2013, risk-analysis techniques provided by the United Kingdom[25] were deployed at the DST in order for officers to be aware of the unique threats each faces. This is to enable better profiling techniques, representing a further transmission of well-documented European norms of risk management (Aradau and Van Munster 2007; Amoore and De Goede 2008) into the global south. As one IOM regional border management expert told me, part of the work of intervention is about moving from 'capture' to 'treatment' of data.[26] In other words, it is not only about the ability to see, but rather the ability to make mobility legible in a way that is effective. The proliferation of borders in Mauritania therefore dovetails neatly with the tendency towards government through identification and data capture seen in countries of the global 'north'.

If borderwork is a socio-technical practice, as this book has consistently maintained, we must examine the social context of security into which technologies such as PIRS are inserted. The inward movement of the border that such technologies facilitate has raised the social stakes of border control in a state where relations between 'Arabo-Berber' and black African populations have always been uneasy. The question of how the social stakes interact with 'imported' cultures of security in Mauritania is impossible to unlink from the 'local' context in which race and racialization play a key role in structuring the security sector. Most significantly, the upper echelons of the country's

[25] Interview with IOM head of mission, Nouakchott, 20 June 2013.
[26] Interview with IOM border management expert, by phone, 10 February 2013.

security services tend to be dominated by the country's Arabo-Berber population, which has traditionally been closest to political power since independence. This does not permit us to draw a neat line of causality from an institutionalized racism which may not exist towards a border security system that is heterogeneous and disaggregated, but should push us to think about what dynamics this reflects. Amongst these are the personal closeness between commanders of certain security agencies (such as the Groupement Général de la Sécurité des Routes or GGSR) and the presidency, or the ways promotions may be informally tied to social relations such as such as clan and family. While there is no blanket racial exclusion in the security sector – with black Mauritanian officials at all levels, including the minister of interior during my fieldwork period – it is readily apparent from who gets promoted or passed over that racialized bias exists in the Mauritanian security sector. This shapes *which* borders become relevant as security concerns, and what measures are applied to them. In Mauritania, a simple glance at the map of where the border posts have been refurbished or newly built shows a cluster along the southern river border with Senegal, in which one finds twelve new posts. This builds in part on Mauritania's withdrawal from regional bloc ECOWAS in 2000 – and therefore from free movement commitments that go with it – which has freed it to have a more restrictive border control policy in relation to its neighbours. Mauritania formally provides visa-free access to Malian and Senegalese citizens, but these rights are undermined by the vast network of internal checkpoints at which racialized citizenship verifications are carried out. From my own experience travelling overland and northbound in Mauritania, these forms of checking tend to target darker-skinned people who might be ineligible to travel through Mauritania. This racialized nature of the border also shapes *how* the border function is applied in an age in which data and identity become crucial ways of doing the borderwork, that is, determining who to include or exclude. In response to the renewal of Mauritania's ID infrastructure, which is to be interlinked with the border management system, a movement of black Mauritanian activists called Touche Pas à Ma Nationalité ('don't touch my nationality') has contested what it calls a 'racist' biometric system.[27] This *social* context of a racialized reality is crucial to understanding how the

---

[27] Interview with TPMN coordinator, Nouakchott, 13 June 2013.

technical elements of border control actually affect security governance in Mauritania.

Training, Routines, and Rationalization

Borderwork practices in West Africa rely heavily on workshops, seminars, presentations, and other pedagogical styles of practice. This is such a standard practice, and not only on irregular migration, that most security actors I have encountered across the region are blasé about whether these achieve anything. For many Mauritanians I met at a two-week training workshop in 2013, it was far from their first such experience. Yet practices such as these produce and reveal *effects* even if they lack effectiveness. Organizations such as the IOM 'perform a key role in the [north–south] transfer of cognitive categories and frameworks' about migration in Mauritania (Poutignat and Streiff-Fénart 2010: 203) through such methods. The border posts project reflects the importance of routinization to this cognitive transfer. Most training practices aimed at border police are short (usually fourteen days) and even the Essentials of Migration Practice (EMP), IOM's flagship training programme for border control personnel, only takes a maximum of six weeks. In many ways, this reflects the 'performative' type of intervention discussed in Chapter 3. The IOM favours 'on the job' learning and training for PIRS was done at the Nouakchott airport, in a setting familiar to trainees. The EMP also proves to be a 'mutable mobile' and has been modified through academic input – 'Mauritanized'[28] by a local sociologist – to better reflect local legal and social realities. Through 'training of trainers' workshops, norms are diffused through the ranks of the security forces at low cost. This approach seeks to reduce dependence on external donors[29] by ensuring the autonomy of the intervened country. This autonomy is limited by the fact that there are only four dedicated trainers in the national police and most of them are not dedicated to this task full-time (see Figure 5.1).[30]

Part of the everyday routine of border governance in Mauritania also involves planning and attending workshops that bring together

---

[28] Interview with Université de Nouakchott sociologist, Nouakchott, 6 March 2013.

[29] Interview with IOM head of mission, Nouakchott, 19 February 2013.

[30] Interview with IOM head of mission, Nouakchott, 19 February 2013.

Figure 5.1 A meeting in Nouakchott marking the donation of border and migration management equipment to the Mauritanian government by the EU. © IOM 2016. Image used with permission.

the small border management community in Nouakchott. This is to the point that there is a sense of 'workshop fatigue' setting in.[31] One use of workshops has been ensuring consensus. The IOM's primary emphasis is moving Mauritania towards integrated border management (IBM). In September 2012, a workshop was held in Nouakchott to evaluate threats and risks at which participants, according to the IOM press release, agreed on 'the importance of an integrated and coordinated border especially in the current security environment' (IOM 2012). These threats and risks are typically not divulged to the public (or researchers!) but a consensus around IBM in principle – even through the simple performance of bringing actors together – already sets the cognitive path. Local civil society are occasionally involved but human rights organizations such as the Association Mauritanienne des Droits de l'Homme, which has consistently protested the treatment of migrants at Mauritania's borders, have considered their role to be nothing more than rubber-stamping conceptions of the border devised elsewhere.[32] The 'assemblage' of borderwork, which *includes* civil society as much as security professionals, remains weighted towards control by *excluding* and failing to give weight to their framings of the common problem.

---

[31] Interview with IOM head of mission, Nouakchott, 19 February 2013.
[32] Interview with representative of AMDH, Nouakchott, 23 June 2013.

The border post project inculcates a common culture of profession-alism, officialdom, and bureaucratic rationalization. Professionalism is a key tenet of the project as described in the national migration strategy, which counts amongst its assessment metrics the 'quality' of a Mauri-tanian delegation to be sent to Spain, results on standardized tests, and the number of agents trained (Islamic Republic of Mauritania 2011: 75–76). The professionalization of Mauritanian security forces is done independently of any national approach to border management, but still pushes for a respect for existing global norms.[33] Similarly, offi-cialdom is imposed through pressures to abandon previous informal and unrecorded practices. For instance, the local EU delegation keeps a database of trainees to avoid double dipping by trainees,[34] as train-ings and workshops tend to provide modest daily allowances to offset costs, and therefore a financial incentive to participate. Such incentives are often controversial as Western actors rail against the self-interested ways these are taken up, but Mauritanian security actors understand them through an economy of fairness and compensation for time spent. While these differences of opinion are intractable, the EU has also urged Mauritania to keep border guards at a specific post for a certain amount of time to build up a stock of local experience, but staffing practices at the micro level – in each regional security zone in Mau-ritania – mean that 'best practices' are balanced against family com-mitments, clan preferences, and personal entrepreneurial ventures. One Mauritanian gendarme I spoke to expressed indifference at his border control training and instead detailed his own smuggling activities at the border with Western Sahara.[35] Best practices have been forced to be mutable. Finally, bureaucratic rationalization is a common goal of the culture of border control being imposed. Multiple interveners from IOs based locally point to the fact that the DGSN does not have a clear strategy for training, and even when a common proposal is submitted by the DGSN, requests are still received from departments lower down the hierarchy.[36] This is something that the EuropeAid evaluation also found, noting that 'various actors tend to follow their own logic and no clear common vision on short and long term priorities has been

---

[33] Interview with GIZ project manager, Nouakchott, 10 June 2013.
[34] Interview with security attaché at EU delegation, Nouakchott, 28 February 2013.
[35] Interview with gendarme, Nouakchott, 14 June 2013.
[36] Interview with GIZ project manager, Nouakchott, 10 June 2013.

developed yet' (EuropeAid 2013: 153). In the view of foreign interveners, this is largely the case across the security sector in Mauritania, not just for the EU/IOM project, but this criticism also applies to the disaggregation between different global approaches. Workshops, training, and rationalization may not always be effective, but they assemble key parts of the police in states like Mauritania into new entanglements of authority.

This 'basics first' approach to border management training in Mauritania attributes a self-evidence to the task of reinforcing border control in Mauritania, and solidifies cooperation within the assemblage of security. Capacity is so low – many border agents had to be trained how to type before being trained on PIRS[37] – that the mission hardly seems to need rhetorical justification, as practices justify their own performance. The border posts project was put in place with minimal threat assessment, and was chosen because it represented, in the IOM head of mission's words, 'low-hanging fruit': it is a project that is easy to put in place and, and as the before-and-after photos referenced earlier show, it was *obvious* that the border posts needed to be brought up to scratch. This has the effect of minimizing many of the dynamics of 'competition' that we might attribute to the social relations in this assemblage, as there is a perception of a common mission. Competition is also mitigated by the diversity of different actors' own trajectories and histories: personnel working in the EEAS delegation in Nouakchott and local IOM office do not have an exclusive 'security' orientation. The IOM head of mission has had to learn a lot about border management on the job[38] while staff members at the EEAS are just as likely to be professional project managers as detached officers from EU member state police forces. By contrast, on the Mauritanian side, most are career police officers, with some parlaying their experience into doctoral studies related to security and sovereignty.[39] A cooperative element is visible in the gestures of respect for local ownership that are visible in the very architecture of the border posts, which showcase Mauritanian architecture.[40] There is an understanding that reinforcing the very basic capacities of Mauritanian forces is a self-evident task which mitigates dynamics of competition. The devil is always in the

---

[37] Interview with IOM head of mission, Nouakchott, 19 February 2013.
[38] Interview with IOM head of mission, Nouakchott, 20 June 2013.
[39] Interview with head of training, DGSN, Nouakchott, 5 March 2013.
[40] Interview with IOM head of mission, Nouakchott, 19 February 2013.

details, but the perception is that local capacity is not sufficiently high for an engagement with the fine details of border management.

Conclusion

The Mauritanian case shows us that borders are socio-technical spaces in which we can observe the interplay of mobile and mutable security cultures by examining infrastructures (the border posts), terrains (the landscape), technologies (the PIRS), and training practices. This socio-technical aspect of border security is particularly clear in the focus by the Mauritanian state and its external partners on border posts as key forms of developing border control *capacity*. This infrastructural focus not only seeks to enhance the physical presence of the state, but also to enable it to multiply its ability to monitor and record data from mobile populations in new places. This importance of the technical reaffirms the catalytic element of efforts at transformation of the Mauritanian state, and the developmental mindset that underpins it. All four empirical sections of the chapter showed some implicit linkage between border control and statebuilding efforts whether in the non-security actors involved in the project, the importance of infrastructures, or the purpose of training practices. The Mauritanian case is particularly consequential as it has provided an exemplar of best practice which circulates in IOM projects elsewhere in Africa as well as in the popular consciousness of security interveners who laud the country's 'advanced' efforts in the area of border security. Mauritania's is indeed an early example of the contemporary rollout of complex border security intervention in the African context, from the involvement of public and private actors in border crossers' data collection and processing, to the multiplicity of external donors spending and branding together. It neatly illustrates the interplay of global and local practice that is inherent in statebuilding efforts. Border control intervention in Mauritania is just one instance of the increasingly multi-faceted border security interventions across the global south: the EU funds border management training in central Asia, the IOM's construction of border posts in South Sudan is instrumental in buttressing that new state's emerging sovereignty, while internationally funded biometric identification programmes play a dual role across Africa as development (elections, population registration) and security (border control, denationalization, deportation) tools. The next chapter brings together a number of the strands in this present one, particularly in relation to the interplay of technology, security cultures, race, legibility, and identification. Building on the theoretical approach used here – attentive to borderwork knowledges – it turns to the emergence of biometrics as key technologies for the determination of inclusion and exclusion in West Africa

6 | *Biometric Borderwork*

When arriving in Senegal through Dakar's Léopold Sédar Senghor (LSS) international airport, a traveller's first encounter is with a Police Nationale border service agent, who scans their travel document, photographs them, and takes digital prints of both their index fingers. The biographic and biometric information collected at LSS airport is stored as part of a computerized register of entries and exits and verified against local and international databases and watch lists. This system is but one of a rapidly growing number of digital biometrics systems across the African continent, many of which are used for border control. Spurred on by international standards, African countries are adopting biometric passports, ID cards, and visas, but also less obvious borderwork tools such as national biometric enrolment. This chapter focuses on the use of biometrics in West Africa, and in Senegal and Mauritania in particular, with attention paid to the role of knowledge diffusion and to the socio-technical nature of their everyday deployment in these two countries. Biometrics are the technology of choice for solving governance problems across Africa: in Ghana and Kenya, voter registration has been tied to citizens' biological features, while Nigeria has seen efforts to enrol public sector workers to monitor pay and attendance. Observing this rapid proliferation of digital forms of biometrics – the use of physiological elements such as bodily characteristics and behaviours for identification and surveillance – this chapter asks a number of questions concerning the spread of digital biometrics as a tool of border management in West Africa. First, in relation to knowledge diffusion practices behind the adoption of biometrics in West Africa, it asks, 'What drives states in the global south, such as Senegal and Mauritania, to adopt biometrics for border management?' Second, this chapter seeks to understand the social and technical elements of biometrics, asking, 'What are the practices that emerge around biometrics deployments in these countries, and what forms of resistance do they engender?'

142

In asking these questions, this chapter applies the political sociology developed in Part I to trace the multiple and overlapping security assemblages that shape the implementation of biometric technologies in Senegal and Mauritania. Biometrics are fundamentally concerned with many of the practices of identification, profiling, and international interoperability that the projects in Chapters 4 and 5 covered. As a result, the bundles of authority and expertise described here contain many of the exact same law enforcement, policy, and international intervention actors as the 'assemblages' described in the preceding chapters. It is not the case, therefore, that the security assemblages described here are somehow completely distinct, hermetic bundles of social and technical elements. That being said, many of the sets of relations in the world of biometrics bring in new actors: many of the usual suspects appear, such as in European security attachés and local border police officials, but new ones emerge such as private algorithm developers, local notables charged with corroborating identification, and citizens excluded from state registration practices. This chapter speaks of particular local bundles of security authority and expertise, but these assemblages are also global by virtue of how they connect into broader global circuits of knowledge and practice.

This chapter builds on but also challenges existing work on biometrics in critical security studies and surveillance studies, making two main contributions by examining the knowledge politics and everyday practice of biometrics deployments in Senegal and Mauritania. The first main contribution is to describe the kinds of knowledge about biometrics that are produced and how they move between different scales of the international. This chapter focuses on a level of practice composed of formal standards and intangible ideals created and implanted through professional practices. The basis of this argument comes from a dissatisfaction with existing literature on biometrics, which has been directed either towards large-scale modalities of power on one side or towards embodied subjects and corporeality on the other. This is particularly the case in work that relies on Foucauldian theoretical foundations. In *History of Sexuality Vol. 1*, Michel Foucault identifies biopolitics – the form of power that takes human life as its main point of regulation – as being organized around just this macro-micro bifurcation: discipline relates to the '*anatomo-politics of the human body*', while regulation is to do with the '*biopolitics of the population*' (Foucault 1990: 139). This approach holds some explanatory power, to be sure, but work in this vein has overlooked the 'meso' level of practice. Contributions have either stressed the corporeal nature of biometrics as 'shift of focus away from nation states to embodied individuals' (Pugliese 2010: 99) or focused on what this technology tells us about larger modalities of governance in the Western world, focusing on risk (Amoore 2006; Muller 2010), traceability (Bonditti 2004), or the government of marginal populations (Magnet 2011). Answering the question 'how do security knowledges travel?' the chapter finds that there is an emerging global ideal around the effectiveness of, and necessity for, biometric technologies which is reflected in standards, policy documents, the literature of key corporate actors, as well as in the discourses and everyday assumptions of security professionals. These forms of knowledge are of varying formality and are geographically disaggregated, but together compose an ideal of biometric security in which biometrics are a solution to porous borders, a mode of reinforcing the state's grasp of mobile populations, and a token of integration into global border control arrangements. Examining biometrics knowledge helps to explain why biometric technologies are appealing to states in the global south, and helps to elucidate the sources of epistemic authority in borderwork assemblages more generally.

The second main contribution of this chapter focuses on the failures of biometrics in Senegal and Mauritania – failures which are still instructive about the socio-technical systems they emerge from. There is a growing body of empirical work biometrics in Africa or elsewhere in the global south: Keith Breckenridge (2014) has written about ID and biometrics in South Africa, and others have written on the effects of the massive enrolment under the Unique Identification (UID) project in India (Jacobsen 2012; Thomas 2014). However, there remains little literature on biometrics in sub-Saharan Africa more specifically, and none from an IPS perspective focused on security professionals. Biometrics deployments are not monolithic and, since their use is subject to the people and materials in assemblages of practice, these modular systems often fail to come together in ways that show the persistence of analogue practices, reveal divisions between security actors, and exemplify different rationales and actor strategies. The idea from one of my interlocutors that 'technologies do not make systems'[1] directs us to think that these systems fail for social and technological reasons: it is

---

[1] Interview with project manager, EU delegation, Dakar, 29 January 2013.

not only the social systems in which biometrics are embedded that are worthy of analysis but also the ways that technical systems act to shape borderwork practices and, in some cases, to frustrate even the best laid plans.

The first section of this chapter returns to the central question of security culture, arguing that there is a 'biometric ideal' emerging from a combination of standards and norms but also through knowledge produced in professional sites such as workshops and specialist magazines read by the global border management elites. This knowledge about biometrics relies on tropes about the smartness of borders or the need to know who is crossing them, and is reflected in and produced by a range of documents and other key texts that reflect the thinking of the globalized community of border managers. The section selects key publications such as the International Civil Aviation Organization (ICAO) *MRTD Report* and reports by the World Bank and Center for Global Development as key texts reflecting the global biometric ideal. With the biometric 'state of mind' developed, the chapter then proceeds to select key practices, institutions, groups and technologies to highlight how, in Senegal and in Mauritania, the adoption of biometric systems is mediated by security actors' struggles and strategies as much as by technical failure and local politics. The second section of the chapter discusses how this biometric ideal moves, with particular emphasis on forms of security intervention as well as dynamics of emulation. The third section on airport security draws on fieldwork at the Dakar and Nouakchott airports to argue that registration and biometric enrolment of travellers, and the deployment of new entry–exit systems, function as mimetic elements of the biometric ideal which show African states' commitments to practically integrate into global security arrangements. The fourth section of the chapter focuses on the passports and visas which are the documentary illustrations of the biometric ideal. It argues that the visa as a token of modernity facilitates claims of credible border control and also reflects the role of technological solutions in displacing some security officials' resistance. The fifth section of the chapter turns to biometric data, the informational basis of legibility, arguing that its collection is central to strategies of good governance and its possession a source of expertise and prestige for security actors. The sixth section of the chapter focuses on national identification structures in Senegal and Mauritania, contesting the idea that biometrics are a technology of legibility. ID structures are undermined by competing private interests, lack of integration of systems, as well as by struggles over the social determinants of identity. This latter point is illustrated by the case of local committees that have presided over Mauritania's mass enrolment process. The final section turns to those who are caught by the historic and bureaucratic prejudices spawned by the paradox of biometric enrolment. Drawing on interviews with citizens protesting the biometric enrolment in Mauritania, it argues that the pursuit of legibility, rather than a fundamental recasting of citizenship, is a central political strategy of groups such as Touche Pas à Ma Nationalité in Mauritania.

The Biometric Ideal

Biometric technologies use physiological elements such as bodily characteristics and behaviours for the purposes of identification and surveillance. Practices such as criminal fingerprinting, airport iris scanning, and facial recognition in passports are premised on attempts to link fluid identity (as an intersubjective relation to the world) or bodies to a fixed identification (an assigned, usually recorded mode of recognition that aspires to be unchanging). Although this mode of verification has long been in use, and in West Africa has strong links to the colonial period, the use of digital biometric technologies is a newer application whose promotion has relied on a new form of security knowledge. Recalling Chapter 2, borderwork is networked and cultural: it stretches the border function inward and outward, by bringing together an assemblage of disparate factors that cannot be limited to that geographical space, and also relies on a *normative* or cultural basis. This refers to the range of ideas, norms, hunches, statements, documents, and ways of doing that make the adoption of biometric systems possible, logical, and seem like common sense. The use of digital biometrics across the African continent is associated with efficient border management through modernization and improvement in the state's ability to make legible. As argued in Chapter 3, security knowledge is produced by, as well as instructive about, the socio-technical formations from which it emerges. These formations that emerge around borderwork are, as argued earlier in this book, heterogeneous assemblages made up as much of human as non-human actors. These 'assemblages' include creators of knowledge, such as border security professionals, but also actants such as texts which are bearers and transporters of knowledge.

In the case of biometric systems, these include formal policies and technical standards, reading material and promotional material from the ICAO and biometrics vendors, and from reports framing biometrics as a development issue.

There is now a vibrant literature on biometric technologies in international politics, which pays particular attention to their role as security devices at borders and beyond. This literature has dissected the forms of governance that biometrics incarnate, such as Ajana's (2013) work on biometrics which sees them not only as a form of governance of bodies but also as a means of regulating a new form of neo-liberal 'biometric citizenship'. In similar vein, Bonditti (2004) sees biometrics through a Foucauldian lens, focusing on a turn to 'traceability' of bodies, while Epstein (2007) considers the type of guilty subjectivities governed by biometric borders. All of these contributions see an in-built promise or purpose to these technologies: building on the idea that the body can 'speak' and be a source of data, biometrics have been analysed through the prism of how they disaggregate the body itself into information (Van der Ploeg 1999) and how they fit into the broader turn towards data and algorithms as border control technologies (Amoore 2006; Muller 2010). All of these contributions have come to the conclusion that biometrics – and the security actors who want them – are dependent on, or bearers of, understandings of what border security should look like. These contributions to work on biometrics have undoubtedly driven the research interest and questions this chapter poses. Yet few segments of this literature have considered two aspects that an analysis of security practices in West Africa yields. First, we do not know much about the contours of the transnational inflections of security practice emerging with around these technologies, nor how knowledge about biometrics circulates to security professionals outside the West. This is despite the fact that such practices assist the transformation of African states' security practices towards valuing 'high-tech' solutions. Some contributions on biometrics have looked beyond the West, focusing on the Unique ID system in India for instance (Jacobsen 2012; Thomas 2014), but most contributions in this field are focused on Western-specific experiences, notably the Europeanization of security fields (Broeders 2011) and biopolitics in 'advanced' liberal societies (Pugliese 2010). Second, we do not know enough, in light of the tremendous uptake of biometrics for border security in Africa, about the particular local inflections of failure these deployments present in contexts such as Senegal and Mauritania.

The appeal of biometric technologies to security professionals in places like Senegal and Mauritania rests on the labour of a transnational community of professionals who shape a 'biometric ideal' specific to states in the global south. The biometric ideal is a set of knowledge claims about the effectiveness and symbolism of biometrics that circulates through the interactions of international (usually European) and West African security professionals. There are two key elements of this 'biometric ideal'. The first is the promise of *legibility* of populations both within the state and of those who cross it. This idea drawing on the work of James Scott (1998) captures the state's desire to not only know but also to better record and analyse information about mobile populations. Activities aiming to buttress the state's 'infrastructural power' (Mann 1984) – the use of bureaucratic and technocratic rather than despotic forms of state power – enhance this ability to make legible. This includes international interventions around border control such as police training and capacity-building, which are increasingly common across the Sahel states of West Africa (see Sandor 2016). Legibility through biometrics at the border furthers the 'polysemic' nature of borders, a term Étienne Balibar (2002: 79) uses to describe how 'borders never exist in the same way for individuals belonging to different social groups'. In this sense, the ideal is of a border whose functioning is selective, but also one whose filtering is increasingly 'smart' and efficient. Biometrics are held up as tools to better identify who is 'out there', and to provide better information for the state to make decisions about admission.

The biometric ideal can be studied by paying attention to the articulations about these technologies – and about mobility more generally – found in the publications through which actors in this area put forward and receive knowledge about biometrics. In the case of biometrics, magazines and reports 'speak' for actors but also for the social relations in which they are embedded. This idea of biometric technology as a border control device is one that has needed to be constructed and performed, and one that has taken hold strongly as various groups of professionals (in the security and transport industries) have pushed to have this technology represent efficiency, security, modernity, and credibility. The literature generated by those who govern global migration in support of this hope reflects this linkage between smartness and efficiency. For instance, the International Civil Aviation Organization (ICAO) – which pushes biometrics due to its role as a global regulator of civil aviation – encourages these technologies through the logic of efficiency, claiming that:

The ability to identify rapidly and precisely 'problem cases' allows governments to spend their always-limited border control and law enforcement resources on those who should be given a more detailed inspection. That efficiency also reduces the need to hire additional government personnel and facility costs. (ICAO 2010)

The ICAO's MRTD Report, a quarterly magazine largely aimed at a tight-knit community of travel security, aviation, and border management professionals, reinforces this trope of 'efficiency' in its reader. In its very first issue (ICAO 2006) an advertisement for ViiSAGE, a US-based firm selling document readers, asks, 'Do you know who's traveling?' in an ad for its passport chip-reading scanner. In similar vein, a full-page ad for Gemalto in volume 2, issue 1 asks, 'Who's behind?' above a picture of a passport behind handed from border guard to traveller, both of whom remain unseen. The MRTD Report's content sells the idea of biometrics as proving the credibility of travellers, but also that of states: the 'you' targeted by the advertising is the globally mobile border security professional who, competing for limited resources within their state security apparatus, can justify their acquisition of technology as a reliable and efficient means of boosting the state's capacity to see and control flows at borders.

The second element of the biometric ideal, the promise of *modernity*, is closely linked to the first and is at once a source of prestige and a technical achievement. Modernity here stands primarily for the sense of symbolism that comes from the adoption of high-technology solutions (such as biometric visas with real-time security screening) but also from the achievement of locally and internationally integrated security systems. For instance, border police officers from both countries are keen to stress examples of data from border posts facilitating criminal investigations, and take considerable pride in the inter-linkage of local data solutions with international databases such as Interpol's. Many pursue the symbolic modernity afforded by digital biometrics, and relish (and are promised) the possibility of integrating their security systems into global (read 'Western') arrangements. There is also a developmental element to this modernity, which aims at the reduction of inefficiencies within the state itself. The World Bank's (2014: 2) Digital Identity Toolkit for Africa claims that developing countries 'lack robust identification systems' which leads to 'inefficiencies in the way the government and firms interact with the population'. These claims are reprised in the work of development think tanks like the Center for Global Development (CGDev), whose *Identification for Development: The Biometrics Revolution* report refers to an 'identity gap' (Gelb and Clark 2013: 8) to describe how the lack of identification hampers government service provision. In countries like Senegal and Mauritania, what Muller (2010) calls the 'biometric state' is therefore not oriented towards risk management but rather towards an initial knowledge of population. The drive towards a biometric state with integrated and efficient systems represents, to those who buy into the biometric ideal, the fulfilment of a promised radical technical break from the inefficient past. This, of course, is just a promise on the part of those whose work it is to create and transmit the biometric ideal. This is the world to which I turn in the next section.

How the Biometric Ideal Moves

On 19 October 2017, a ministerial meeting was held in Paris between the prime ministers of Senegal and France around a number of bilateral agreements, including one on migration (RFI 2017a). While key elements of the migration were quite familiar to the observer of Euro-African borderwork – readmission logistics and a deal for a few more visas – most notable was a clause on the *état civil* in Senegal. As part of the patchwork of procedures against irregular migration, Senegal reasserted its pledge to produce a biometric national identification system. While this is a long-standing goal in Senegal (as the section about ID below shows), the explicit linkage of irregular migration and national ID reveals the ways that the vision of biometrics-as-best travels. The transmission of the biometric ideal is undertaken at the level of cooperation and intervention between politicians but also between experts from global north and global south. In Senegal and Mauritania, French bilateral security cooperation is particularly dominant, but Spain is increasingly active in shaping each country's local security agendas on migration issues. Officials like *attachés de sécurité intérieure* (interior security liaisons) play a key role in implementing programmes that include biometrics, or set the agenda in their interactions with local bureaucrats, police officers, and gendarmes. Under the French ASACA airport security capacity-building programme, immigration and security experts (*conseillers sécurité immigration*) shortlisted by France are implanted in intervened states' ministries of interior as border management consultants.[2] Similarly, the ICAO runs gap assessment missions as part its Traveller Identification Programme. This program, funded by the Canadian government, held assessment missions in Costa Rica and Honduras in 2013 and 2014 respectively (ICAO 2014), and in Niger in January 2015 as part of the 'Sahel and Neighbouring States' facet of the project (ICAO 2015a). These knowledge-generation and -sharing practices put forward both an image of borders (as identity management tools) and how to control them (through technology and integrated systems). These practices also generate demand by raising awareness amongst local security elites and signalling best practices. It is noteworthy that trainees are often brought outside their home country for training, to prevent their everyday routines (work and family life) getting in the way of their acquisition of the requisite airport security skills. Study tours in French airports – which have a similar institutional setup to francophone African countries' – are frequently used as means of experiential learning for police trainees.[3]

Expert meetings and workshops are key spaces in which the transmission of the biometric ideal happens. The ICAO has been instrumental in bringing together security professionals to share a common agenda. The International Organization for Migration (IOM), an intergovernmental organization dedicated to all aspects of migration from border security to resettlement, has also urged states in West Africa to adopt biometric technology as an answer to the question of weak border security. Both organizations have regional offices in Dakar, and carry out training and capacity-building activities across the region. The ICAO Regional Conference on Aviation Security was held in Dakar in October 2011 (ICAO 2011) and Senegalese police officers have participated in ICAO trainings on airport profiling, for instance. The IOM has sought to position its own entry–exit tracking system, which is deployed at Mauritania's main airport in Nouakchott, as a low-cost alternative to expensive privately marketed

[2] Interview, European aviation security expert #1, Dakar, 11 March 2013.
[3] Interview, European aviation security expert #2, Dakar, 11 March 2013.

immigration management systems and provided workshops on fraudulent document detection for West African police forces.[4] Other examples of these social spaces of knowledge transmission include the
ICAO's MRTD Regional Symposia, where key actors coalesce around
common views of how borders (and travel documents) are to function.
This is akin to the 'workshopping' approach common in the development industry which facilitates getting actors in the global south on
board with the importance of traveller identification. It also recalls the
Euro-African police conferences discussed in Chapter 4, which provide
opportunities for lessons learned and for the exchange of ideas from
south to north.

Finally, it is important to acknowledge the importance of African
agency in the transmission of ideals about biometrics. West African
security professionals – like many of their counterparts in the region
– adopt these technologies as a means of ensuring conformity to what
are perceived as 'global' standards. This is not to suggest a 'copycat'
mentality, but rather to point out that claims to modernity function
through emulation (see Chapter 3) and are often made relative to the
states that are considered leaders in the area of border security. This
can in some cases refer to Western states (notably the United States
and France), but many in the border security professionals in Senegal
also consider Mauritania to be a regional border security leader worthy of emulation. Perceptions of what are truly 'global' standards are
also shaped by perceived expertise: while Spanish expertise is highly
regarded in terms of reducing irregular migration, French expertise tri-
umphs in the context of airport security due to a similar institutional
setup (evidenced by the shared Police de l'Air et des Frontières moniker
for their border police forces). The case of the biometric visa is particularly pertinent in this case, as Senegalese police justified it in relation
to the restrictive visa policies of EU states specifically. Local agency is
key not just to the biometric ideal but also to the *malleability* of this
ideal: local law enforcement, airport authorities, technologists within
African ministries of interior, and local political actors all have habits
and registers in which they frame their work, and personal trajectories that eliminate any pretension to smooth transfer of 'international
standards'. In the next section, I suggest that the biometric registration of passengers at Dakar's main airport is one such site in which

[4] Interview with IOM officials, Dakar, 22 January 2013.

we can observe the failures of the biometric ideal to live up to its own terms.

Tracking and Tracing at the Airport

In Peter Adey's (2002: 501) words, we 'learn useful lessons at airports' about security and the ways mobility is sorted and controlled. Indeed, recent work on border security has taken the role of airports seriously as sites for the analysis of security policies. For instance, Salter (2007: 53) describes the airports as places that 'represent the policing power of the sovereign state, that contain the dangerous or risky elements of the unknown, and that render certain mobilities visible and others impossible or invisible'. Brenda Chalfin's work on Kotoka International Airport in Accra seeks to understand 'how the aura of sovereign intimacy is sustained and internalized by those actors considered to be its source and its object' (Chalfin 2010: 193–194). Leese (2016) argues that airports are increasingly subject to the efficiency-driven managerial logics of the private sector. The airport is therefore a microcosm of the heterogeneity of borders and the ideals that go into securing them. Airports are crucial sites at which we see the (dis)assembly of border security in West Africa, precisely due to the overlapping social and technical elements that interventions bring together. In the case of Dakar's airport, the use of biometrics is intended to push towards the efficient movement of travellers, and testifies to the integration of Senegal into global security systems. Despite this, specifics of local practice – its status as a privileged border point and the technical limitations of its systems – undermine the claims of the biometric ideal.

On arrival at Dakar's LSS airport, travellers immediately come face-to-face with biometrics, and registration of travellers begins with the scanning of their travel documents. The Senegalese police have electronic document readers which scan the machine-readable zone of travel documents. After this, a still image of the traveller is taken via the webcam which sits in the border guard's booth, and the traveller is then asked to provide her right and then left index fingerprints on the scanner. Traveller records are integrated, and each entry or exit can be visualized in the police's system as an individual 'transaction', which is held in a police database on-site. When I asked to view my own records, I was able to see my photo, citizenship, fingerprint image, flight numbers, and dates of entry and exit, all from a simple search by surname. Remembering some of the difficulties that many Western states have faced with the implementation of 'smart' borders and the tracking of entry and exit, this struck me as remarkable (even if only applied at some border crossing points). All of these security procedures are seemingly routine interactions at a border post but also reflect the role of transnational technology transfer in this sector. The 'transactions' of biometric registration are part of a broader comprehensive security system in the airport known as the SICM, provided by US-based Securiport LLC.[5] In addition to the biometric registration of travellers, the SICM also manages video surveillance of the airport grounds. This integration of border and airport security is not accidental, and international interveners (notably French bilateral assistance) devote considerable efforts to training about access control. The imperative to capture and record data is one element of the drive towards a border that is not only intelligent in terms of what information it can capture, but also able to filter this information. Much like the application of risk analysis at the Mauritanian border posts (see Chapter 5), the Securiport system at Dakar airport enables the triage of passengers as well as data analysis techniques: when a Senegalese national was able to fly to Washington, DC, without proper documentation, the US authorities were able to ask Securiport to reconstruct the person's itinerary and, using data from the system in Dakar, identify the passenger (Securiport 2014). The biometric ideal of borders as intelligent tools is effectively implanted through this technology and the international collaboration it facilitates, even though the Senegalese authorities were left red-faced by the relative weakness of their *exit* controls.

One of the elements of the biometric ideal, which promises the integration of local practices into global aviation security assemblages, is the promise of interconnection and the implementation of internationally recognized security procedures. The SICM enables Senegal's integration into global security arrangements at a very practical level, by being connected to Interpol's database of Stolen and Lost Travel Documents as well as the I-24/7 database which allows Senegal to receive 'red notices' from Interpol for wanted persons. In this case, it is the security tool (the actant) itself that facilitates the transfer of a 'culture of border control' (see Chapter 3) favouring database-driven

[5] Interview with unit commander at LSS airport, Dakar, 22 July 2013.

verification and authentication. Any flag raised by the system shuts it down and the supervisor – a more senior police commander – manually examines every flag and can override the system in cases of erroneous identification. In addition, the system is integrated with local databases held by the police and gendarmerie stipulating who is prevented from leaving the national territory.[6] This system's global interconnections and attendant practices are a source of considerable pride within the Senegalese police, even though they appear to partly re-scale the site at which borderwork is done in Senegal. When I spoke to the police commander in charge of security procedures, he mentioned the speed with which data retention and information-sharing facilitates cooperation between the police and Gendarmerie Nationale, making it easier to arrest locally wanted suspects whether or not they were in the Interpol database.[7] The technical therefore plays a crucial part of the assembly of local knowledge and distant international databases to produce clear effects on inclusion/exclusion. This also illustrates the inculcation of practices of inter-agency cooperation that feature in training meted out to Senegalese officers by international interveners such as ICAO, IOM, and the UN Office on Drugs and Crime (UNODC).

Senegal's entry–exit system is shaped by growing aviation security intervention in the country in which Western security professionals push for what they deem to be 'smarter' borders and 'smarter' border guards. These interventions are key ways of transmitting ways of approaching biometrics and are most often led by European security professionals under the guise of capacity-building. For instance, a French-funded modernization programme aimed at the Senegalese police (Appui à la modernisation de la Police sénégalaise) has provided €700,000 for an assortment of activities: training of prosecutors, equipment donations to the drug squad, but also the provision of equipment and training at the airport to improve 'prevention'. Prevention of cross-border crime and irregular migration function in part by trying to make the border 'smarter' and more efficient. The presence of immigration liaisons (*conseillers sécurité immigration*) – shortlisted by France but chosen by the host government – is one such way to ensure a friendly voice for the cause of 'smarter' borders within the

---

[6] Participant observation at Dakar airport, Dakar, 22 July 2013.
[7] Interview with unit commander at LSS airport, Dakar, 22 July 2013.

local government as it shapes its border security policies. While the ideal of entry–exit biometrics as a 'modern' solution for prestige is shared by European and Senegalese security professionals, the former tend to be of the opinion that there is little point in gathering data if there is no emphasis on the *analysis* of data on which better filtration rests.[8] The meaning of the much-vaunted smartness of borders is itself subject to divergences between security professionals. There is also a need to make the border guard herself 'smarter', and Western interveners put great effort into ensuring, for instance, that border guards at LSS stay in post long enough to internalize key practices of airport security,[9] but this aim is often frustrated. This also includes trialling new biometric approaches centred on profiling arriving passengers' behaviour and body language, promoted by the ICAO, even though there is a view that African airports may be too 'stressful' as a baseline for such practices to be effective ways of screening risky bodies from safe ones.[10] This practice does have some approval in the local context, with a Senegalese police official telling me that biometrics cannot signal a person's intentions, so there is a need for such profiling.[11] This is underpinned by an understanding of the airport as a 'laboratory' of border control, where new practices can be tested in a relatively controlled environment. This emphasis on speed and efficiency comes from the prioritization of the *flux rapide* (a quick flow),[12] showing how Scheel's (2013) observation that biometrics link together technology, security, and freedom of movement applies in the non-Western world.

Technical failures underline the pitfalls of implementing the biometric ideal in West Africa, and reinforce the idea that assemblages of security often bring together social and technical elements without a singular functional logic. Although the Senegalese border police does collect biometric information from passengers, the optical reading and ultraviolet light equipment at the border does not allow the reading of the more securely stored (encrypted) biometric information found on a passport's microchip. This information should also be compatible with the ICAO's Public Key Directory, which is this organization's means of

[8] Interview with European security attaché, Dakar, 11 March 2013.
[9] Interview with European aviation security expert #2, Dakar, 11 March 2013.
[10] Interview with European aviation security expert #2, Dakar, 11 March 2013.
[11] Interview with head of Senegalese DPAF, Dakar, 11 July 2013.
[12] Interview with ICAO official, Dakar, 21 July 2013.

fostering international collaboration on passport security through the proliferation of a common technical standard for reading encrypted information (ICAO 2015b). These keys for decoding are the backbone of biometric systems, as they are the necessary supplement for one state to read another state's biometric documents, yet Senegal is not yet an implementer of this single standard. This is significant as the inculcation of a *cultural* security standard proceeds apace through forms of training and auditing, yet the adoption of a *technical* security standard undermines the desired outcome. Through the collection of biometric data, Senegal participates in the biometric ideal but, by not verifying this data, fails to be completely integrated into one of the backbones of the global airport screening system. In this case, Senegal's entry–exit system is symbolically integrated to global security systems but is not practically, at a technical level, reaping the enhanced legibility that is integral to the biometric ideal. Such technical failures are also found in Mauritania, whose government declined an American government offer of the PISCES entry–exit system, opting instead for the IOM's PIRS. As the PIRS source code is handed over to client states, Mauritania built its own software solution on top of the IOM's code. Yet this locally adapted system has not been completely linked to the Morpho ID system whose main selling point is integration of all national identification procedures, from population enrolment through to criminal Automated Fingerprint Identification System (AFIS), the electoral register derived from it, and the document issuance system it enables.[13] This reflects another instance of failure of implementation of the biometric ideal: although the technology itself is not contested and flows smoothly from one security context to the other, approaches to its rollout illustrate technical limitations and policy failures within the local security assemblage.

Finally, one of the key elements of biometric screening is its digital nature, yet the entry–exit system at Dakar airport is marked by the persistence of paper solutions, and Senegal's other borders are often run with analogue solutions. While more senior Senegalese police officials dismissed the utility of paper landing cards, street-level officers actually preferred analogue techniques: most I spoke to lamented the decision to do away with these paper visitor landing cards, as these

---

[13] Interview with IOM border management expert, Nouakchott, 19 February 2013.

in the past provided an important backup for officers who forgot to save traveller transactions in the SICM. Indeed, given the strict punishments meted out by the border police for forgetting to register travellers, the paper landing cards functioned as indirect guarantees of job security. Bonelli and Ragazzi (2014) discuss the use of papers, files, and memos in the French intelligence service, pointing out that these represent the persistence of a particular way of doing security work on the part of intelligence professionals. This is one of the elements that also reflects a crucial divergence between security actors in Senegal and can undermine the best laid plans: in this case, the upper levels of the Senegalese police are assembled much more directly into global security ideals about biometrics, while their lower-level colleagues (and those at rural borders) remain in the analogue security culture that the biometric ideal excludes. At the time of my fieldwork, most posts in Senegal still used paper registers for the recording of entries and exits into the national territory. Many police and customs officials based outside of the capital who, as I observed, mostly do not have computer or internet facilities and must rely on paper documents and personal wireless internet sticks.[14] This has changed at some higher-traffic posts, with the police in Rosso apprehending a terrorist suspect in 2017 through fingerprint matching (RFI 2017b).

Passports and Visas

Passports and visas are crucial to the global mobility system, determining rights to access and vouching for citizenship and permissibility. Visas are a 'necessary supplement to the passport system' (Salter 2006) and effectively delocalize the border function inward (to verification systems) as well as outward (to points of issue), and are a central part of the facilitation of global mobility. As Shamir (2005: 212) points out, visas are essential profiling tools that have become increasingly data-driven and increasingly rely on 'technologies of examination that are by far more sophisticated than the impressionist judgments of police officers and security guards'. In this section I argue that beyond inscribing sovereignty on the bodies of citizens, these technologies facilitate security actors' claims to modernity and prestige and inculcate the

---

[14] Participant observation at customs post, Rosso, 12 January 2013.

polysemic nature of borders. However, in the case of the biometric visa specifically, biometrics face contestation due to the slowing effects they have on desirable types of mobility.

In 2008, Senegal launched its biometric passport and in 2013 confirmed it would be using biometrics in a new visa. The need for a retooled visa was brought about by the then 'reciprocity' policy, which meant that any state requiring visas of Senegalese citizens would have its own citizens subject to a visa requirement to enter Senegal. The roll-out of the biometric visa was driven by a desire for pre-emption on the part of political actors and the higher levels of the Police de l'Air et des Frontières. The upper levels of the Senegalese police, more tightly integrated into the security assemblages in which the biometric ideal enjoys the most currency, considered biometric screening to be a means of better profiling travellers as well as overcoming the 'randomness' of existing approaches.[15] The biometric visa also aided the pursuit of a comprehensive view of who was in the country: in order to issue visas within forty-eight hours, the border police's territorial surveillance directorate (DST) in Dakar had access to real-time data from visa applicants in Senegalese embassies across the world. This screening process, however, was significantly undercut by the informal crossing procedures that persist at most land border crossing points, which includes allowing citizens of neighbouring countries to 'deposit' their ID card at the border post when visiting Senegal for daily errands. Nevertheless, the upper echelons of the national police command considered the biometric visa an essential token of 'modernity' whose adoption largely went without saying.[16] This reframed debate about the visa from a political one (about what type of border control was best) towards a technical one (about whether the visa was more efficient or not).

The biometric passport and visa are notable for being local technologies in their conception, even though their rise is facilitated by the circulation of a global ideal through a security assemblage. While the exemplar of conforming to ICAO standards is powerful, the Senegalese biometric passport was *not* spearheaded from outside, but rather by a

---

[15] Interview with head of Senegalese DST, Dakar, 11 July 2013.
[16] Interview with director of the Senegalese border police (DPAF), Dakar, 15 July 2013.

particularly technologically keen commissioner of police in 2007. This particular commissioner was brought into the police for this project from a previous job in the IT world. While the passport is considered a 'sign of modernity',[17] its rollout was unrelated to the pressures for international link-up that have been exerted in the cases of airport biometrics and the national ID card. In the case of the biometric visa, the justification for its use testified to the post-colonial logic inherent in the policy of visa reciprocity: that in a world in which formal political equality is underpinned by state sovereignty, operating on an equal footing with Western states requires the assertion of the rights to sort and filter citizens' rights of passage in both directions.

The infrastructure behind the biometric passport and visa is revelatory of the multi-sectoral nature of security assemblages: it draws equally from the private sector and from overseas expertise, much to the discomfort of local security professionals. The Senegalese police's upper echelons expressed concerns about the visa being subject to commercial considerations.[18] Although these doubts about the attribution of the contract and data management to foreign companies lingered, the supposed technical benefits of the biometric visa were never in doubt. The company charged with administering visa issuance was the Côte d'Ivoire-based SNEDAI (the Société Nationale d'Édition de Documents Administratifs et d'Identification), and the biometric visa made SNEDAI into a major actor at the border posts through its donation of ten patrol vehicles to the Senegalese police (AllAfrica 2013). SNEDAI deployed equipment by Belgian ID card maker Zetes to Senegal's border posts, some of which were newly built. The corporate contribution to this security assemblage reveals the sheer diversity of how the seemingly finished technical object (visa) is actually produced through practices of sub-contracting: Zetes provided the enrolment kits to Senegal under a five-year 'build, operate, and transfer' (BOT) contract for sixty-six enrolment stations, the technology to individualize biometric records, and the installation of a payment system through its subsidiary FasTrace for three hundred thousand visas per year (Zetes 2013). The biometric visa enrolment machines used featured fingerprint sensors

[17] Interview, senior Senegalese police commander, Dakar, 12 February 2013.
[18] Interview with director of the Senegalese border police (DPAF), Dakar, 15 July 2013.

made by US-based Lumidigm. This variety of private sector actors made the project feasible but also created tension within the world of public sector security professionals.

These efforts towards better legibility and efficient filtering at the border are generally lauded by Western security professionals in Senegal. Western officials interpreted the creation of a fraud bureau in the heart of the Senegalese police as a sign that document security had 'entered the habits' of Senegalese security officials.[19] It is a mistake, however, to assume that Senegal's efforts towards achieving a biometric 'ideal', through passports and visas, are always met with cheers from security professionals from the global north. Many of those based in Senegal as liaisons express a *suspicion* of biometrics and consider these technologies to actually entrench a status quo in which there are many fraudulent documents around – including many of the ones on which biometric documents rest. True to the tensions within any security assemblage, there is also an element of disagreement between global and local security professionals with how the technology is meant to be used even when all agree that it fulfils a modernizing role. Western security actors deployed in Senegal tend to resent what they perceive as the deployment of biometrics for their own sake, and many of my interlocutors were keen to point out that this technology was of no use unless local practices could ensure that proper *procedures* and a suitable 'culture of security' were followed.[20] In the words of one European diplomat, the technologies themselves are nothing without the right political and infrastructural *systems* in which to frame them.[21] While the rollout of biometrics is a source of the kind of 'shared knowledge' that I identified in Chapter 3 as crucial to cultures of border control, there is disagreement over what precisely is a successful and appropriate use of the technology.

Within the Senegalese law enforcement world, the biometric visa reflected a pre-eminence of its top strata. This visa was largely a prestige technology, targeted mainly at Western foreigners (citizens of ECOWAS countries do not need visas to enter Senegal) and other travellers who mainly transit via LSS airport in Dakar. The visa was not

---

[19] Interview with aviation security expert #1, Dakar, 11 March 2013.
[20] Interview with aviation security expert #2, Dakar, 11 March 2013
[21] Interview with EU official, Dakar, 29 January 2013.

just a token of modernity but also facilitated the projection of a modern identity. My interlocutors at the top level of the police claimed, for instance, that stamp visas are outmoded and any country that takes its security seriously must have something more modern,[22] without providing technical rationales. Dezalay and Garth (2002) capture this idea of a split within any given 'field' of practice in which one part is internationally oriented and seeking symbolic recognition from abroad, and the other remains rooted in existing local or informal practices and oriented towards local gains. This is very much the case in Senegal, where the highest ranked officers tend to be invited to international border management workshops – internalizing the knowledge and habits of the transnational community – while others lower down the ranks remain confined to routines devoid of technology, away from the capital, and disconnected from the world of policy.

The elimination of the biometric visa requirement in May 2015 testified to the limits of the biometric ideal when faced with divergences in police practice but also to limits exogenous to the world of security. The suppression of the visa, amidst complaints from the country's tourism sector, hard hit by international fears following the Ebola outbreak in the region, highlighted how the implementation of security practices associated with the biometric ideal may not always guarantee frictionless mobility: knowledge in the name of security was pushed aside in favour of a greater facilitation of leisure travel. This undermines the idea of biometrics as a facilitator of mobility – in fact, at the same time as the removal of the visa, Senegal's airport taxes were also reduced (Jeune Afrique 2015) as part of a broader removal of financial obstacles to visiting Senegal. The visa had made the work of the border police at the airport confusing – they frequently faced confused travellers arriving without visas in hand – so the actual *functioning* of the visa, beyond its symbolic and performative (see Chapter 3) importance, was a source of consternation. By 2015, the arrivals area of Dakar's LSS airport was littered with two material reminders of the failures of the biometric ideal: on one side sit the unplugged automated passport scanning gates provided by Iris Corporation as part of the twenty-year biometric passport contract and abandoned when the SICM was installed, and on the other the visa application machines

---

[22] Interview with head of Senegalese DST, Dakar, 15 July 2013.

which had been provided for travellers who had – in defiance of the ideal of legible mobility – arrived in Senegal without one.

In Mauritania, whose biometric 'sticker' visa is part of the overhaul of that country's ID system promised by Morpho, this visa is not ubiquitous. There are no biometrics used at Nouakchott airport and passenger profiling mainly takes place through physical examination of passport documents (such as prior stamps)[23] and the verification of places of residence during stay. Here, biometrics have not yet in practice won out over the old-fashioned 'hunch' and local knowledge of the border guard, even though – like in Senegal – the official discourse favours technological solutions (such as the border posts in Chapter 5). The entire experience of visa issuance is also decidedly informal. When I applied for my visa at the Mauritanian embassy in Dakar, it just took my passport, photos, and the application fee, slipped through the gate to the security guard. No biometrics are taken of applicants, and the visa is a simple ink stamp in the passport rather than the printed 'sticker' commonly associated with biometric visas. Mauritanian police do carry out manual crosschecking of sequential visa numbers (via email) between embassies and the DST in Nouakchott, but plans for real-time verification and sticker-based visas are not fully implemented. The slow rollout of the Mauritanian biometric visa, and the places where it *has* been implemented, reflect how these technological deployments bifurcate the world of Mauritanian security professionals, as noted above in the case of Senegal. This new visa launched first at the Mauritanian embassy in Paris but also at the PK-55 border post in the north of the country which has proven to be a site of experimentation and security innovation on migration issues (see Chapter 4). Biometrics, in this particular case, are at once a representation of modernism in the former metropole (France) but also a technology associated with the forefront of security practice. The cases of Senegal and Mauritania are indeed similar: higher-level security officials participate in many of the same workshops and training that bond together the global border security community (in some cases on issues such as migration rather than biometrics per se) while everyday practice succumbs to the failure of attempts at state transformation to reach all the way down.

---

[23] Interview with police commissioner at Nouakchott airport, Nouakchott, 28 June 2013.

Data: What They Enable and Frustrate

Biometric borderwork is reliant on *data* which are used not only for identification but are also themselves reflective of state priorities and the social relationships within security assemblages. Contributions from surveillance studies and sociology have located biometric technologies within the historical arc of techniques of bodily identification. Joseph Pugliese (2010), adopting a genealogical approach in his study of biometric technologies, calls them the 'culmination of a series of anthropometric technologies' (164), such as physiognomy, phrenology, and anthropometry. In doing so, Pugliese follows influential studies of the importance of identification practices to modernity, such as Simon Cole's (2002) history of criminal identification. Cole and Pugliese both highlight the role of early forms of measurement of the body, such as Alphonse Bertillon's anthropometry and Cesare Lombroso's physiognomy, both of which were instrumental in the development of anthropometry as a form of criminal identification. But data are not just a question of identification through the information extracted from the bodies and biographies of people enrolled into biometric systems. They are also a tangible reflection of development funding priorities as well as a tool through which social relations of security are mediated. In many ways, the idea that more and better data lead to better security, and more development, has come to be conventional wisdom. In Senegal and Mauritania, biometric data collection shows a fusion of development and demographic anxiety, is a point of contention between security actors, and allows the state to surveil itself.

The need for the collection of biometric data arises in part from a fusion of developmental goals with anxiety about demographic change. In Mauritania, the justification of biometric enrolment has also been driven by the perceived security threat presented by the country's increasingly large non-native population. The relative success of the operations to prevent Mauritania becoming a space of 'transit' (see Chapters 4 and 5), halting the mobility of potential migrants from the sub-region, has reframed the focus towards how to deal with 'settlement'. As a result, the security focus is shifted from 'who is crossing the border and how can we stop them?' to 'who is here and how can we track them?' The 2012 anti-terrorism strategy released by the Mauritanian foreign affairs ministry testifies to this change in mentality, calling for measures to (Ministère des Affaires Étrangères et de la Coopération

2012: 18, emphasis added) 'reinforce border control and the *tracking of persons* [. . .] tougher visa issuance procedures and the development of civil registry and document security systems using modern technologies (like biometrics)'. My interviews with security officials in Mauritania, who rely on the biometric system for their work, revealed that the system is used primarily for national security purposes,[24] with these tending to be defined broadly. For instance, the verification of residence permits for foreigners (the *carte de séjour*) is heavily policed (especially at night) under the guise of national security and often facilitates the expulsion of foreigners. In Senegal, similarly, the biometric visa was not only intended as an entry credential also a means of knowing who is in the country at any given time. This biometric borderwork, as Chapter 2 argued, is not only about policing the territorial line but refers to practices of filtering and exclusion across sovereign territory.

This security imperative has fused with externally sanctioned measures intended to boost the state's ability to make legible. Mauritania's ministry of interior, as part of its Poverty Reduction Strategy Paper (PRSP), has included the collection of biometric data as part of its strategic planning process. In a document produced for the PRSP period for 2011–2015, the ministry included the goal of 'renovation and reinforcement of the production of an unfalsifiable national ID card based on biometrics' (Ministère de l'Intérieur 2010: 33) under both 'Security of people and goods' and 'National security' categories. The national security category calls for a 'census of foreigners, issuance of secured forms of residence permits and visa application forms, and the creation of a digital database of foreigners' (41). The PRSP document includes a separate category for the *état civil* which includes harmonization of records, production of new forms, and the creation of a uniform register of family names. The latter is of great importance in a country where Arabic and French coexist in national identity papers, creating inconsistencies in transliteration. This echoes Breckenridge's (2014: 15) linkage of current practice to colonial histories, arguing that 'this project – of fixing the names of illiterate African subjects in particular – remained the driving justification through the whole of the twentieth century and it is still the raison d'être of the current round of large-scale biometric systems, both in the former colonies and at the gates of the imperial capitals' (Breckenridge 2014: 15). In the Mauritanian case,

---

[24] Interview with official from DSE, Nouakchott, 25 February 2013.

this 'fixing' also goes beyond names and towards a genealogical basis, with enrolment dependent on family ties and the prior registration of family elders – the Mauritanian president Mohamed Ould Abdel Aziz has himself emphasized the potential for a digital family tree through this system. In Mauritania, security, statebuilding, and identity rationales combine to animate a pursuit of data.

Biometric data are also an object of struggle and 'disassembly' within security assemblages. First, the collection of biometrics is part of a broader security culture, put forward by security actors in the West, of fusing internal and external security (see Bigo 2001). The Mauritanian anti-terrorism strategy of 2012 calls for biometrics to be used as part of a 'new military and security doctrine in which notions of national defence and defence of the national territory fuse with those of internal security' (Ministère des Affaires Étrangères et de la Coopération 2012: 16). This reflects preoccupation with the global discourses around the Sahel as an 'ungoverned space', with biometrics acting as necessary modern tools for the reinforcement of actions against a threat that is at once exogenous and internal. Second, the collection of biometric data is a key element in struggles for recognition (or 'symbolic capital' in the Bourdieusian sense) and there are institutional scraps about who controls or accesses data. In Mauritania, the police and gendarmerie have competed over how to organize data gathered from the new border posts (see Chapter 5) and there has also been tension between the police and Agence Nationale du Registre des Populations et des Titres Sécurisés (ANRPTS), the civilian agency tasked with biometric enrolment, over ownership of and access to databases. The decision to have a new standalone agency – a new site of authority (and a 'pocket of effectiveness' of sorts) rather than entrust one of the security services has been seen in some quarters as denying the prestige of Mauritania's security agencies. In my interviews at the national security directorate in Nouakchott, police downplayed their role in the enrolment and insisted that the ANRPTS is not a police agency.[25] This is partly due to the fact that the Mauritanian police has since 2008 been relatively side-lined in broader space of security provision due to a perception of corruption and association to previous regimes, losing symbolic ground to new services such as the Groupement Général de la Sécurité des Routes (road traffic control) and the ANRPTS.

---

[25] Interview with head of training, DGSN, Nouakchott, 5 March 2013.

When I walked into the office of the police commissioner in charge of security at Dakar's LSS airport, the most striking aspect of the office was the sheer number of monitoring screens showing video surveillance images. These video feeds not only reinforce the state's ability to see travellers, but also to see *itself* through the monitoring of staff. The state in Senegal and Mauritania relies on biometric data collection – and the surveillance around it – to watch over itself. Returning to computerized immigration processing, data are crucial not only for having a comprehensive picture of mobilities but also for the control of borderwork labour. 'Seeing like a state' is achieved by disciplining police themselves, with data from computerized immigration processing acting as a disciplinary and anti-corruption tool, appending the names of immigration officers to each entry–exit record to facilitate accountability in the case of errors in processing. Beyond this, the state's ability to collect data also implies an ability to *anticipate* through analytics. Securiport, which provides the entry–exit system at LSS airport, has also used its experience in data analytics to track passengers arriving from countries with a high number of Ebola infections (Securiport 2014). Securiport's deepening involvement in the security assemblage around biometrics in Senegal is not only dependent on an identity as credible, but also on showcasing its its ability to handle data, as much as the positioning of police commanders' is reliant in part on their ability to surveil passengers and each other. What this transnational bundling of actors produces, in the Senegalese case, is new forms of both private expertise and public authority. In the next section, I turn to national identity papers and how these succeed and fail to enact biometric border security away from the border.

Borderwork through National Identity Systems

One of the key elements of biometric border security is the adjudication of citizenship and non-citizenship, which is managed through systems such as national identity cards. Ajana (2012: 852) points to the two-way interlinking of biometrics and citizenship/nationality, noting that 'biometric systems are becoming symptomatic and constitutive of the ongoing mutations that are taking place within the rising forms and practices of citizenship'. The biometric ideal rests on an optimistic view of this relationship between biometrics and belonging, which assumes that integration of identification systems leads to more efficient determination of who can enter or not, or who is entitled to the rights of citizenship. Indeed, the ideal that efficiency is itself a relevant phenomenon to citizenship illustrates the degree to which citizenship is reframed by biometrics as a question of either *access* or *exclusion* (see Muller 2010). Senegal's biometric national ID, launched in 2006, exposes these political limits of biometrics for border control and in particular the failures that come with private sector involvement in biometrics. While the *carte d'identité* is a standard feature in most francophone African states, the move towards biometrics in Senegal's ID card has been significant for what it promises but also what it reveals about the social world of security in the country. In Mauritania's case, the role of committees adjudicating who is enrolled for a national ID or not reveals that even though biometric systems reflect a smooth global security ideal, the nature of determinations of inclusion/exclusion is highly local and sporadic. The relationship between identity and identification, in both countries, is determined new sites of borderwork authority that assemble actors from the world of security and beyond.

The Senegalese national ID card is unable to fulfil the biometric ideal of symbolic modernity through better integrated systems. This system reflects what Martin, Van Brakel, and Bernhard (2010) refer to as resistance from 'artefacts'. They argue that 'apart from the potential to breakdown or fail, the absence of technologies capable of fulfilling a desired surveillance mission is as effective a resistance mode as legislative or executive modifications to the intended scope of surveillance' (224). While the ID card system is housed in the ministry of interior, it is not connected to other systems within the same ministry that exist for the same purpose of making populations legible such as the Senegalese police's $1.15 million criminal fingerprinting programme, provided as a gift by the US Embassy in Dakar on behalf of the US military's Africa Command (AFRICOM). This tool was justified by the regional security context, to be used as a tool to fight against drug trafficking and terrorism (US Embassy Dakar 2011: 3). Even though this AFIS system was provided as a capacity-building tool to improve identification, and is housed within the same ministry, the data do not travel and remain siloed. The claim to a fully integrated 'biometric state' – which is something my interviewees in the Senegalese Police de l'Air et des Frontières tended to support – is held back by the limited coordination of biometrics within the public sector. While there are some highlights of how the ID card has lived up to the ideal of legibility – such as the identification of people admitted to hospital without ID – the ID card is an island of in a system that begs for integration. While there are linkages between the biometric national ID card issued by the police's Direction de l'Automatisation des Fichiers (DAF) and the databases of foreigners at the Direction de la Police des Étrangers et des Titres de Voyage (DPETV), this latter system is not linked to the register of foreigners or to the passport databases at the ministry of foreign affairs. The amount of information in the biometric system is also dwarfed by what is provided and kept on the original paper application forms, which are kept by the ministry of interior. Senegal's paper-based document issuance system – especially in the case of birth registrations – means that the 'breeder' documents that demonstrate eligibility for the biometric national ID are also easy to falsify and difficult to verify. As a result of these disjunctures, the ID card's promise to better 'border' citizen from non-citizen remains tenuous, with the *technical* elements of the assemblage of border security in Senegal failing to link up.

Senegal's national ID system creates a rift between the state's pursuit of integrated biometric systems and private companies' desire to distinguish their products – illustrating the tensions within security assemblages composed of actors with divergent motivations. Securiport, the company which runs the airport security system, including biometric scanning, does not communicate with UK-based DeLaRue even though this company runs the database for the national ID card (which doubles as a travel document within West Africa). This is due to incompatible and proprietary biometric algorithms used to decode and recode the biometrics they collect. The justification for such disjuncture is at first glance a purely technical one: competing algorithms for coding biometric data makes these data incompatible. However, algorithms are also a matter of professional secrecy and a key selling point in the competitive private sector biometrics marketplace. Securiport has tried to decipher DeLaRue's biometric algorithm and failed, something that the latter takes as validation of the strength of its system. This private sector competition is due to the fact that, according to my interviews with high level officials in Senegal, border controls and electoral identification are the two most vibrant private sector markets for biometrics manufacturers.[26] In this context, the profit motivation and the desire to assert expertise (which yields symbolic and economic capital) are

---

[26] Interview with head of data protection authority, Dakar, 25 January 2013.

essential yet they undermine the state's security actors from running a visibly modern, integrated system.

While the public-public and public-private relations in Senegal's bundle of actors involved in biometrics are prone to failure, its ID card does facilitate smooth international-local integration. According to interlocutors in the ministry of interior, information from the database is used by foreign embassies in Dakar, which means the data must be relatively complete and which furthers the culture of verification and authentication around borders.[27] Other users of the ID system include UNHCR, which requests information to check the veracity of refugee requests, and EU election monitors, who audit the ID system in its capacity as the register of electors.[28] Even as it forecloses some relationships, the national identity card also provides points of connection for international actors' own borderwork, thus extending their authority.

In Mauritania, biometrics reflect the social and technical stakes of determining identity. The country's massive biometric enrolment exercise – justified as a comprehensive view of population – has neither been the exclusive privy of security agencies nor as universal as its purposes might suggest. Instead, the determination of eligibility to enrol has been adjudicated by committees composed of local notables and members of the security forces. In this case, committees are an essential part of the story of biometrics in Mauritania because they undermine the pursuit of frictionless governance advanced by the proponents of biometrics. Borderwork is of course the set of practices aiming to answer the question 'who belongs and who does not?', and in Mauritania's biometric census enrolment committees have played a key role in answering it. This structuring of the biometric registration process exposes applicants to a great deal of discretionary power as in each enrolment centre – which are officially called citizen welcome centres (Centres d'Accueil des Citoyens) – enrolment commissions have the final say over who is registered or not. According to ministerial decision 937/MIDEC (Ministère de l'Intérieur 2011), these commissions are composed of a range of officials including the local *hakem* (equivalent to a French prefect) acting as committee president, a committee vice-president representing the *wilaya* (region) administration, a municipal

---

councillor, and representatives from the gendarmerie, national guard, police, and ANRPTS. As such, these commissions have a strong presence from the law enforcement community but also formal (and ad hoc) involvement of local notables, and deliberations of these committees can legally be undertaken behind closed doors. The bundled forms of authority in this particular case represent both the state and customary authorities as well as those from new authorities such as the ANRPTS. This bundling of actors is particularly consequential because it is a formation of authority empowered by the need to make legible but operating in a fraught cultural context.

Mauritania's demographic composition and history have made biometric enrolment, and the determination of who belongs, a fraught process. The country is home to three broadly defined population groups whose boundaries, although obviously fluid and contested, are relatively identifiable. The first is an 'Arabo-Berber' group composed of a variety of light-skinned Arabs, descended from Berber and Arab populations. The second group are the Haratin, a mainly black population of current and former slaves, who have largely been linguistically and culturally 'Arabized' through their roles as domestic workers, or farm workers (and slaves). The third group, mainly in the south of the country, is deemed the 'Negro-Mauritanian' segment of the population, who are less likely to speak Arabic and largely composed of sub-Saharan African ethnic groups such as the Peul (or Fulani), Wolof, Soninké, and Bambara, largely found in either of neighbouring Senegal or Mali. Given the artifices that are colonial borders, like that along the Senegal River that separates Senegal and Mauritania, these populations have been thrust into a multi-ethnic state. The governance of this multiethnic state is highly contested and ethnicity (as well as clan belonging) shapes political decisions in Mauritania to varying degrees, from police promotions to presidential politics to the language of education. While not directly causal to the security sector, a racial construction of authority favouring Arabo-Berber populations has tended to prevail at the intersection of north and sub-Saharan Africa (Hall 2011: 34–69). While colour, ethnicity, caste, and race do not overlap neatly in Mauritania (or anywhere else for that matter), demographic politics a priori make any population enumeration or registration exercise fraught with difficulties. Given these elements of Mauritania's social and political context, the biometric enrolment exercise was bound to be faced with difficulties related to race relations.

Mauritania's enrolment commissions reveal the disaggregation of state power, whereby the orders from the strategy-making heights of the state to enrol everyone (as reflected in the PRSP document) clash with the discretionary power of local recognition influenced by the country's ethnic politics. Put differently, the importance of giving everyone *identification* comes up against the fact that *identity* is locally mediated and recognized. The shadow of November 1989, during which thousands of black Mauritanians were expelled towards Senegal and Mali, looms over the enrolment process along with the country's ever-present demographic concerns. According to my interviews with Mauritanians who have been denied enrolment – all of whom were black Mauritanians – common unofficial tests have included being asked to recite portions of the Quran, quizzed of their knowledge of the Hassaniya language,[29] being asked about specific notables from their area, and being questioned about their knowledge of local geography. Although some of these questions could be justified as asking candidates to prove local knowledge, others testify to the desire to exclude from the enrolment any citizens who are perceived as not performing or embodying national or local belonging. A central paradox in this enrolment process, which was launched to supersede a supposedly unreliable national identity structure, is that paper documents from Mauritania's 1998 census have often been required to show this 'local belonging', and that relatives (rather than one's biometrics alone) are often required to vouch for applicants' local ties.[30] This local approach had been lauded at launch by the Morpho programme head as a way that the France-based contractor had respected the Mauritanian government's wishes by 'adjusting the system to the local culture, which calls on its more senior members to corroborate a citizen's identity' (Morpho 2010). This deference has exacerbated the potential for the type of administrative discretion that facilitates discrimination. The Mauritanian human rights association AMDH identified some key concerns with enrolment in the city of Kaédi, noting that: errors in

---

[29] It is worth noting the similarity between these practices and the policing interview methods used to determine national origin of irregular migrants in the Canary Islands, discussed in Chapter 4. Both operate according to the social determinants of identity, in the absence of a document deemed a final proof of identity.

[30] Interview with professor at the Université de Nouakchott, Nouakchott, 11 June 2013.

peoples' names often prevent enrolment; people from villages around the city are rejected for being 'unknown' even if their parents are already in the biometric system; and some who enrol never receive their confirmation 'receipt' which is crucial for job applications (AMDH 2012). The meeting of a global biometric norm centred on security and efficiency with a local norm based on intersubjective identification undermines the belief held at the high echelons of the security apparatus: that biometric technologies can be both inclusive and a technology of security. Many of the glitches, paradoxes and institutional setups above have been catalysts for popular resistance articulated through the desire to be enrolled in a security technology.

Borderwork of the Uncounted

The state's production of illegibility operates at once as a side effect of its disaggregated nature, but also as a borderwork strategy of inclusion and exclusion. In this vein, the *uncounted* are constitutive of the state's uneven production of legibility. The *assemblage* metaphor remains a useful thinking tool as we are compelled to look beyond the field of security towards the excluded who call for new forms of politics and a break from existing distributions of power.

In Mauritania, controversies over counting have disproportionately fallen on black citizens. This is partly because calls for the biometric census were often founded on the need to 'clean up' the country's system. The view of a Mauritania that is 'too full' is largely attributed to anecdotes about Senegalese people crossing into Mauritania to benefit from the country's supposedly lax 1998 census, and finds assurance in the level of attention given by the government as well as European countries to their country since 2006, which has stressed the country's position as a haven for transit migrants. In a context in which the whole state's ID system is considered to be in need of a 'purge' or a *refonte* (renewal), there is pressure to exclude rather than enrol. In response to the impact of the census, a movement called Touche Pas à Ma Nationalité is actively monitoring and contesting the ongoing process. The group's coordinator, Abdoul Birane Wane, has been featured in a number of local and international publications and the group has used local and national extensively to advance its cause, evoking a racist campaign by the Mauritanian state against its black citizens. With borderwork operating as an order-making practice (see Chapter 2), the borderwork of the uncounted seeks to challenge prevailing orders and reframe the forms of authority that underpin them.

In terms of strategy, TPMN has made extensive use of public sit-ins, many of which have been put down by police for being illegal demonstrations. Clashes between police and protesters – many from TPMN – across the country in September 2011 resulted in one death in the town of Maghama in the south of the country and extensive damage to public buildings and a market (France24 2011). While the TPMN movement has attributed the trouble to reaction against a racist census, figures in the state such as the president of the Senate – himself a black Mauritanian – noted at the time that a lack of information is at the heart of the protests (Magharebia 2011). In the southern city of Kaédi, where TPMN's contestation was most violently put down, one protester was killed and dozens of others injured in clashes with riot police on 25–26 September 2011 (Fédération Internationale des Droits de L'Homme 2011: 15). In October 2011, the Mauritanian government deported seven foreigners who had taken part in demonstrations against the enrolment to Senegal, Mali and Guinea (Bloomberg News 2011). The demand to be counted has not been without risks, and TPMN have relied on a strategy of making demands in public and in as visible a way as possible.

'It depends on the person's mood',[31] TPMN activists told me, whether a Mauritanian can be successfully enrolled into the biometric system or not. TPMN's resistance to the enrolment opposes the method of the enrolment in practice, but it did not seem to oppose biometric enrolment in principle. Rather than radically opposing biometrics or the identification of citizens, the activists call for a more 'objective' assessment of the population.[32] This aspect of the TPMN movement illustrates just how resistance to biometrics need not necessarily challenge the essential functioning of the technology itself, even if it contests the forms of authority that prevail in the national rollout of biometrics. On the contrary, the claims TPMN articulated during interviews were consistent with a view that the enrolment should be *done better* rather than reversed – for everyone to be counted. What is most striking about TPMN is therefore the articulation of state that they

---

[31] Interview with TPMN staff in Nouakchott, 13 June 2013
[32] Interview with TPMN staff in Nouakchott, 13 June 2013.

put forward. Rather than question the very basis of the state's authority to make legible, they question those in whose hands the machinery of state rests, claiming that a fairer distribution of power might restore the procedural justice they deserve as citizens. While at first glance it might seem like TPMN are merely reaffirming the state's power and reconfirming a statist view of identity, they should be seen as radically challenging key tenets of the 'biometric ideal', which holds that biometrics are a technological and technocratic solution. TPMN activists, even when reaffirming many of the tenets of the biometric ideal, are also highlighting the technology's *politics* and its agency as a borderwork 'actant' embedded into a social system they consider unjust.

Conclusion

As Chapter 2 argued, borderwork is the ongoing labour of constructing and performing borders, of determining who is 'inside' and who is 'outside' of the national space and the political community. Biometric technologies at borders focus our attention clearly onto the material factors that make borderwork possible, such as scanners, passports, visas, databases, and cameras. But they also provide an entry point into a broader global security culture that holds such digital technologies in such high, optimistic esteem. Existing approaches to biometric technologies in the global south have not sufficiently addressed the practical elements of their rollout, and more specifically the global and local security politics which animates it. We are witnessing the emergence of a biometric ideal, which represents a form of security expertise (Chapter 3) centred on a vision of digital biometrics as a practical solution to the implementation of polysemic borders and to the buttressing of the state's ability to make populations legible. Using an IPS lens on security politics, we see that key spaces of security such as airports – but also enrolment centres – showcase the implementation of biometrics as a form of connection to global security cultures and systems and represent incubators of new forms of international and local authority in the area of border security. Key objects and technologies such as passports and visas, for their part, reflect the seductive nature of biometrics to border managers, and themselves draw on a broader imperative within the technology towards data-gathering. Such forms of harnessing data are not just points of contention between security actors, but also showcase how forms of identification are put in service of broader national security aims in a Sahel space associated with terrorism and illicit cross-border flows. Borderwork is not only a question for the security actors alone, and the bureaucratic politics underlying the establishment of identification in Mauritania, for instance, contrasts sharply with the claims of universality and efficiency built into the biometric ideal. This, of course, is a source of resistance from those who are excluded by biometric borderwork, who put forward their own politics of how borderwork is to be done. The conclusion of this book, next, sums up the arguments and extends some of the lines of thinking on statebuilding, (de)politicization, and authority developed throughout Parts I and II.

7 | Conclusion

Borders are not just lines demarcating where national territory begins and ends. They are the vibrant social institutions and technical spaces in which decisions about inside and outside, about belonging and exclusion, are made. This book has argued that border security in West Africa is undertaken by a transnational and heterogeneous set of actors whose interactions testify to the competing knowledges about what border security problems are and how to address them. Arguing that borders are heterogeneous order-making devices, the book has provided a critical mapping of actors involved in what it has called *borderwork*: the labour of constructing and performing borders. Building on this idea, the book has sought to find out how this enactment of borders relies on knowledge about how to secure borders, and more specifically how this security knowledge has emerged, been adopted, and moved between different international contexts. This book has drawn on research examining border management practices in West Africa, specifically in Senegal and Mauritania, to give empirical context to claims about the organization and knowledge politics around border security. In doing so, this book has found that key projects – transnational interventions to control migration, the construction of border posts to stop terrorism, and the adoption of digital biometric identification projects – all show the disaggregation of who 'secures' borders but also the circulation of forms of security knowledge across overlapping social and technical worlds of practice.

This book has been focused around three key issues: the construction of borders, the nature and mobility of security knowledge(s), and the relations between diverse security actors and technologies in Senegal, Mauritania, and beyond. The spur for this project has been the observation of a growing importance of 'border management' in the practices and discourses of security actors in the West African context. 'Border management' is not only concerned with the policing of the territorial line, but also with controlling migrant pathways to Europe, confronting a perceived threat of terrorism and smuggling in the Sahel-Sahara zone, and securing national identity documents. This research has emerged from a broader interest in the practices states use to negotiate difference through sovereign practices at borders, as well as an interest in relations that show the disassembly of the state amidst targeted forms of international intervention: international organizations directly targeting sub-state elements of countries in the global south, corporate actors' relationships to arms-length states agencies, or competition between sections of the same country's security services.

The first 'project' of the book, in posing the question of who controls borders in West Africa, has been to theorize the *enactment of borders* and provided the beginnings of an empirical mapping of this practice in the West African context. This has involved grouping and synthesizing the literature on borders, and out of that, adding a novel conception of borderwork foregrounding the role of materiality and the heterogeneity of actors. In order to carry out a mapping of 'who does the borderwork', we need to have the right lens and be attuned to the right factors. The second task this book has set itself has been to provide a theorization of *security knowledge* that takes into account its mobility and its mutability. Building on the idea that security is a knowledge-driven process, rather than just a moment or event, this book has focused on knowledge politics as a means of showing the stakes of border control in West Africa. The third element of this book has been an empirical contribution to our understanding of the security politics of – and by extension global governance in – Senegal and Mauritania. By drawing from interviews and participant observation with security officials from law enforcement and military backgrounds, as well as diplomats, smugglers, and bureaucrats, this book has provided a window into the ways that actors understand their borderwork and their relationships to each other. The research carried for this project has primarily sought to provide an account of the 'everyday' of border control in practice. That is to say that the project sought evidence primarily through the self-understandings and discourses of the actors involved. This, in turn, has provided a window into the relationships that segments of African states have built and maintained with European states and international organizations.

This book has not sought to provide simple answers to the research questions, about borders and security knowledge, and the responses to the questions posed have been answered as much through theory development as through 'evidence' gathered from fieldwork. The conditions and results of my access to interlocutors necessarily mediated the image of borderwork provided in the present work. However, a number of relatively stable assertions can be made, which will be discussed in more detail the sections below. In sum, however, a number of conclusions can be drawn. First, borders in West Africa are not just remnants of the colonial era, but dense institutions in which struggles over how to define borders (and their governance) happen. Second, given the importance of transnational cooperation, the intersection of various sets of practitioners (police, development workers, bureaucrats) is intensified and globalized. Third, these intersections are evidenced by a number of factors, such as technology transfers or workshops, and are spaces in which knowledge contestation occurs. Fourth, these knowledge dynamics, in turn, reflect changes in global governance of security such as the growing role of paramilitary police forces, the internationalization of EU security policy, the privileging of technical expertise, and the emergence of border security as a key site where state security and development meet.

This rest of this chapter *concludes* this book's main arguments and contributions, but also *draws conclusions* about what the politics of securing borders entails. It revisits 'borderwork', assessing how well the concept has withstood the test of empirical examination. The section that follows it assesses the importance of knowledge to security politics and the role of intersecting sets of professionals. The penultimate section assesses the social relations shown in this book, with emphasis on the presence of power disparities and the possibility for agency. The final section of the conclusion describes the avenues for research opened up by this book, on the study of regional information-sharing tools, international organizations, and transnational security politics on the African continent.

Borderwork Redux

This book's use of border-*work* developed a theoretical framework attuned to the spatial, organizational, material, and political dimension of borders. Why 'borderwork'? The term understands the 'border' as an institution as well as a form of repeated performance or process. The -*work* refers to the performances and constructions (material and epistemic) borders require to be sustained. The term is also intended to democratize the way we understand the construction of borders, including actors whose functions go beyond securing (such as the irregular migrants who cross them) and pulling in a range of practices that happen far from the border line which nonetheless shape how inclusion and exclusion are determined (such as the sale of algorithms for biometric screening).

This book has contributed a theorization of borders as *sociotechnical* spaces unmoored from territorial references and increasingly technicalized. Borders are social insofar as they are constructed and performed by actors of various kinds, including professionals of security who bring knowledge and expertise to bear on them. Borders are also technical, however, as their enactment is reliant on non-human materials which interact with social elements. To describe this range of actors, this book has used the term 'assemblage' to capture the heterogeneity and unpredictability of social connections, while still using this language to speak of social relations as competitive, prestige-seeking, or performative. The use of 'assemblage' to has allowed this book to focus on the heterogeneity of who does borderwork, how different functional groupings of practitioners (e.g. law enforcement) overlap, in what ways the state is disassembled, and how different social relations wax and wane. The emphasis on the non-human in the book, while drawn from a Latourian vein, should not imply any rejection of the importance of the social and more specifically human relations that underpin border security. Rather, it is a plea to broaden what we can consider as impactful and active, and expands the evidence that can be deployed to show why social relations are the way they are. This approach has paid dividends throughout the book, which has used key 'actants' as sites of analysis – and as narrative devices – in each of the chapters in Part II.

Rather than look at African borders through the lens of the artificiality of colonial frontiers, or a primordialist focus on ethnic borderlands, this book has mapped the institutional topography, transnational in nature, of the actors that do borderwork in the West African context. Of course, it has not been an exhaustive exposition, but rather the beginnings of one, intended to show the relative 'dimensions' and composition of what happens in the institutional space of the border. The focus on institutions and quotidian practice in African border security has built on contributions such as Chalfin's (2010), but focused on the *patchwork* of different agencies rather than on deep work in a single one. A diverse range of actors and practices has been identified ranging from the IOM's promotion of border management training, the EU's funding for migration control strategies, the ICAO's agenda-setting on identity management, or diplomats' positions as negotiators of quotidian security cooperation. While this has been a novel view of the institutional topography of border management itself, it has also allowed a more complete picture of the approaches to border control that each actor competes for and transmits, which in turn illustrates the politics at play in the buttressing of sovereignty through border control in West Africa.

Understanding Security Knowledge and Intervention

This book has concerned itself with giving an account of the actors involved in shoring up border control in West Africa, but also with the visions of security (and how it is achieved) they bring to the table. Indeed, one of the main 'theses' about borderwork in Chapter 2 related to the cultural nature of border control. This was no attempt to try to reduce borders to some essentialized natural or ethnic culture, but rather a reflection of the fact that security is a practice dependent on and productive of habits, biases, written policies, and shared assumptions. To make these claims, the book has given an account of security as a form of practice, defining it as constituted by the activities and interactions of social and technical actors in assemblages. Chapter 2 defined borderwork as an 'order-making activity', and Chapter 3 defined security as the particular *type* of order-making that reinforces sovereignty and is enacted mainly by security professionals. The question 'what subtends the security practices around borders in West Africa?' is therefore one about the relationship between security as a practice of sovereign power and knowledge as the epistemic basis shaping how and why security happens.

This conception of security as neither a moment nor an event, and not always be aimed to a public audience, has meant focusing attention on the 'micro' factors of how actors go about setting the agenda and shaping practices that define inclusion and exclusion. This focus on the routinization of security practice, in which threats are seen as determined bureaucratically or with reference to actors' histories and career trajectories, has helped to bring new modes of security governance into relief whether these are the importance of memoranda of understanding (Chapter 4), the role of institutional jostling over data ownership (Chapter 5), or the importance of key individual decision-makers' career choices (Chapter 6). Investigating these provides a polyphonic account of the enactment of security, but still locates the urge to 'secure' as firmly on the side of sovereign power.

The concept of assemblage has provided the framework for an analysis of the mobility and mutability of knowledge about security, and for using the movement of knowledge between international spaces to investigate the way security relationships are justified. This book has been based on the assumption that if knowledge is produced in part endogenously from the social interactions and histories of people who carry out security tasks, then it is likely that knowledge transmission is going to be most evidenced in the projects and initiatives that cause them to meet within a particular assemblage. It follows that border knowledge's content, mobility, and mutability is largely determined by the nature and intensity of the connections between these actors. A clear example of this is in the case of police cooperation, which is brought about the increasingly outward-facing role of European security services (as evidenced by the role of the Guardia Civil in Senegal and Mauritania) but also by the internationalized orientation of key security agencies such as gendarmeries in West Africa. In some cases, actors have been receptive to approaches from outside their comfort zone due to institutional similarities with global interveners, while in others knowledge has moved through pedagogical practices such as workshops and the influence of trade publications. This extends, with sociological emphasis, a concern throughout the social science with how expertise travels: we find it in what Gramscians might call the '*nébuleuse*' of social spaces such as workshops in which particular types of subjectivity are reinforced (Cox 1983) or in human geography approaches to transnational governance in which policy moves 'in a number of social forums, including conferences, seminars, meetings and even informal chats over coffee' (Prince 2012: 193). The assemblage concept therefore has helped to grasp not just the social and technical elements of borderwork, but also the material spaces in which these interact.

This book has extended this line of thinking by its openness to material agency afforded by a focus on 'objects', which has allowed us to see the way that knowledge can move across contexts. Objects are crucial due in part to the knowledge relations they either mediate or represent.

As Chapter 5 argued, taking the 'non-human' as serious players in security relations does not mean making them human or watering down the richness of human agency, but rather accounting for their place as objects of struggle, definers of future policy choices, and sites that show us relations around them. Examples of this have arisen throughout the book, such as the analysis of small tokens such as in Chapter 4, in which decorations, pins and certificates show the significance of social relationships of prestige or illustrate differing self-perceptions of the (under)privileged within security agencies. In Chapter 5, the border posts were sites of struggle for self-promotion but also physical infrastructures inculcating a Westphalian approach to defending the border. In Chapter 6, databases and data appeared as points of pride, sources of interlinkage, but also of disconnection and competition. In each of these cases, objects represent a knowledge or actively transmit a whole set of understandings of sovereignty.

This book's approach to knowledge transmission – focusing on exemplars, emulation, and pedagogy – focuses our attention on the ways West African states are (dis)assembled through practices of border security cooperation. These forms of knowledge transmission are dependent on the formation of new clusters of practice which in turn are productive of expertise and authority. For instance, Interpol's role in the WAPIS police database requires practices of communication and coordination between West African police agencies, which effectively produces new bundles of authority in the region as well as generating credibility and expertise for Interpol itself as it positions itself in the crowded institutional space of security cooperation. The capacity-building and technical modernization elements built into such projects raise the thorny issue of the interface between security and development, and how these are increasingly brought together through borderwork in West Africa. Rather than thinking in terms of a fusion of two distinct worlds, the argument has instead been that security practices – whether involving international intervention or not – can be thought of as straddling forms of care and control. Even though security involves the use of sovereign power to draw limits and determine inclusion and exclusion, and the use of coercive force, these are occasionally justified in terms of state capacity (e.g. border posts) or even through humanitarian framings (e.g. joint sea patrols). This raises the question of 'governance', more specifically in relation to international cooperation practices such as mentorship in which the power inequalities between north and south are manifest. This governance question, in turn, brings us to state transformation.

This book has been keen to provide a granular understanding of how security interventions targeting state capacity actually shape the supposedly insecure and low-capacity 'African state'. Rather than use the frequently small-scale nature of these interventions as a means to downplay their importance and impact, this book has instead provided a granular understanding that takes seriously how they function as either transformative, catalytic, or symbolic. Some interventions reshape habits and practices, and form lasting relations – the Spanish efforts described in Chapter 4 have some element of this evidenced in particular by the new forums for cooperation they opened (police conferences) and the ways this has been leveraged into cooperation in new areas (through joint police command posts). On the other hand, many interventions are purely performative and we should treat claims about state transformation with some caution. While the bulk of this book has insisted on African states' desire to pursue greater 'legibility', and enhance their abilities to see and filter, it is crucial to note that many state practices actively undermine this pursuit. Authors such as Keith Breckenridge (2014: 24) provide a counterpoint to work by Torpey (2000) and indeed Scott (1998) by downplaying the existence of a 'compelling desire for comprehensive and universal information' on the part of African states, arguing that governments in Africa have generally tended to be marked by the absence of such as 'will to know'. Herbst (2000: 239) echoes this sentiment, arguing that 'African states, unlike those in Europe, do not face a set of immediate security challenges that make tying the population to the political center a necessity'. This is certainly the case when one thinks of how the notional 'independence' of policing in Western countries (see Deflem 2000) may not apply to cases such as Mauritania where policing is closer to 'high' politics but also to the kinds of racial or clan relationships visible in the enrolment commissions analysed in Chapter 6. Paying attention to these local dynamics helps us show how an African police force might achieve independence precisely because it fulfils a part of the state's strategy of obtaining rents through its integration with international security priorities. In short, participation in international efforts to shore up borders may have nothing to do with legibility and all to do with strategy. This book has devoted attention to two African states, and their components, in particular because they challenge key assumptions taken for granted in the Western CSS literature and show how components of 'rhizomatic' African states participate in new forms of security practice globally and locally.

Politics and Resistance

My research process throughout this book – investigating the social relations that drive borderwork – has continually raised conflicting answers to the question of what the politics of borderwork might be. The answers are, frustratingly, not as straightforward as the north–south encounters described might suggest. Statebuilding practices always contain the seeds of local agency, but global and local are not always what (or where) they seem to be; relations are not colonial but still marked by 'coloniality', and there is always room for resistance even if it comes from unlikely places.

One of the more concerning elements of borderwork interventions is the depoliticizing element of care in border security politics. This is an emerging research theme as evidenced by recent debates about the closening of control and humanitarianism in border security (see Pallister-Wilkins 2015). A recent Frontex annual risk-analysis document explicitly ties deportation to humanitarian concerns, claiming that a 'lack of effective return of persons arriving from West Africa and not eligible for protection is encouraging others to try their chances, leading to unnecessary human suffering as migrants face harassment, exploitation, violence and even death while trying to cross the desert or the Mediterranean Sea' (Frontex 2016: 41). The EEAS's strategy for the Sahel affirms that 'poverty creates inherent instability that can impact on uncontrolled migratory flows' (EEAS 2012). The problem is framed as relational, with poverty *there* causing insecurity *over here*. The politics of care are always imbricated with control is through the interplay of security and mobility, or what Squire (2011) terms the 'politics of control' as set against the 'politics of migration'. By enforcing control mechanisms, justified by the language of care, states actually endanger migrants by forcing them to take new more treacherous routes. Frontex's reports extoll the virtues of its cooperation with Senegal and Mauritania along the 'West African' route. These reports show a sharp downward trend in migrant interceptions in the Atlantic whilst simultaneously showing increases from North Africa. The effect of control is not to stymie the agency of migrants or act as a deterrent. Rather, it shifts trajectories to riskier locales: rather than leave Mali for Spain through Mauritania and Morocco, a migrant might take the riskier trip through Niger and Libya towards Italy or Malta. This, in turn, requires a geographical shift in emphasis for the EU's border management apparatus, rather than an actual diminution in control. Despite this, border security's positioning as a humanitarian activity is essential to the self-perception of many security actors in West Africa, including the Guardia Civil whose 'West Sahel' project in Senegal and Mauritania included an element on migrants' rights and humane forms of readmission. Indeed, care reflects a desire to stave off crises originating in Africa. For instance, the way the Spanish Guardia Civil detachment in Mauritania uses the spectre of potential 'crisis' to justify its presence speaks to the fact that reduction in migrant numbers does not translate to a reduction in the security apparatus. In fact, as Chapter 4 showed, cooperation has ramped up independently of migration levels. Crisis serves to reinforce controls, as one of the first major tests of the EU's external borders agency, Frontex, was alleviating the 'crisis' of migration towards the Canary Islands through its multi-national 'Hera' patrol and readmission operations in 2006. Coming only two years after Frontex's inception, this immediate need to respond to an ostensibly humanitarian situation shaped the agency's later development as a risk-based (see Neal 2009) model of operations, anticipating the movement of migrants.

Chapter 3's discussion of border control as statebuilding laid bare a technicalized worldview that sees border security as a universally generalizable question of state capacity. This view evacuates political discussion over what states should look like, and fundamentally ignores the colonial genealogy of states like Senegal and Mauritania. The term 'statebuilding' has in this book stood in for intervention on a state's ability to see and control, its will to follow specific modes of state behaviour, and its technological modernity. The states considered in this book are not 'failed' or emerging from conflict, but they are considered either 'weak' or having lower capacity to effectively govern their borders. There is, therefore, a state structure in place to accept or resist attempts to impose a particular vision of statehood. As Antil and Touati (2011) argue in Mauritania's case, it is not a failed state but simply one whose material capacity to mimic the sovereign power typical of 'Westphalian' states has not, from the time of independence in 1960, matched its legal sovereignty. This mismatch between de facto sovereignty and its de jure counterpart is precisely the space in which border control intervention operates: such intervention is a transmission of cognitive categories of how a state should function, but also operates within a framework of formal juridical equality. However, the question has not always been about capacity but also of acting on *will*. It is fundamentally through this that ideas about 'mentalities' and the need for 'change in culture' circulate in the world of security. Relations are therefore not colonial, but rather marked by *coloniality*. This mode of relations is defined not by deliberate quests for territorial control or direct political authority, but is exemplified by 'long-standing patterns of power that emerged as a result of colonialism, but that define culture, labor, intersubjective relations, and knowledge production well beyond the strict limits of colonial administrations' (Maldonado-Torres 2007: 243). This is borne out by the continuing dominance of French security cooperation in Senegal and Mauritania and even by the preservation of colonial structures and remit in the police and gendarmeries of francophone Africa.

The pedagogical element of borderwork, theorized in Chapter 3, has been the source of the clearest relations of domination. The language and logics of mentorship (e.g. the workshops discussed in Chapter 5) and the supervisory relationship inherent to joint patrols (in Chapter 4) both bear this out. However, domination is subtle and relies on harnessing the freedom of the intervened actor. A helpful distinction is the one Graham Harrison (2001: 659) makes in the context of donor-recipient relationships in Africa, between the coercive imposition of 'doctrine' on one side, and the collaborative adoption of a common 'ideology' on the other. While his point is made to describe a 'post-conditionality' period in the world of aid, it applies equally to border security 'cooperation' practices where outright coercion is replaced by a shared common agenda. This shared agenda is still largely set by European states, even if African security forces find material and reputational benefits (new gear, or prestigious training) from participation. Ruben Andersson neatly describes this in the context of Spanish-African cooperation on migration management, calling it a 'subcontracting machine' operated by African forces yet claimed as a success by Spanish police (Andersson 2014a: 122). This insight echoes my own research detailed in Chapter 4 and summarizes the illusion of provided by the cover of formal, post-colonial equality.

The structure of the assemblages of security I researched suggested that global and local are difficult too difficult to pinpoint with enough certainty to identify a clear relationship of continual domination, or without risking fetishizing the global and parochializing the local. Participants at the overlap between different national worlds of security may hold different levels of prestige depending on national origin and bureaucratic position, even though they may occupy identical functional roles in their national police structures. Similarly, there may exist within the same security culture two distinct 'worlds' or 'tracks' of the security professionals, where whose authority counts may be dependent on their framing as either global or local. This is akin to what, in the context of peacebuilding interventions, Autesserre (2014) refers to as a continual tension between local knowledge and technical expertise, which sit in a relationship of competition, with the former being in a disadvantaged position of authority. However, in some cases, intervening actors from ostensibly 'global' backgrounds (e.g. EU or IOM) were seemingly more 'local', not least due to their distance from their organization's central control. Similarly, many 'local' actors successfully claimed the mantle of technical expertise in 'global' fora. This impossibility of placing these levels on a hierarchy – a key justification for the assemblage lens – should give pause to any attempt to label border security cooperation as colonial or smoothly dominant.

The politics of borderwork is complicated by the fact that agency arises in unexpected places. In some cases, lack of local interest defeats interventions (such as Mauritanian indifference at the 4×4 donations discussed in Chapters 4 and 5) and we should not underestimate the importance of African agency. More specifically, the mere success of a particular intervention may only be feasible once all sides stand to gain, whether it is as a form of opportunistic rent-seeking behaviour or 'extraversion' (Bayart 2000) in the service of 'extraction' (Tilly 1985) for statebuilding. Put differently, there is always room for agency on all sides in transnational border security practices. Similarly, African security officials willingly partake in their own internationalization through repeated participation in events such as the Euro-African police conferences. Even though this conference's existence is partly due to EU agenda-setting through the Rabat Process, participation in it is a source of some prestige that is freely made. The internationalization of African security relations also has local stakes: during my participation in a counter-terrorism workshop in Mauritania, it became clear to me that far from being some imposed training course, it was also an arena for local security politics in which a litany of high-ranking officials benefited from a relatively captive audience to make their case.

Officials spoke in persuasive style of the primacy of their approaches to terrorism whether it was the role of human intelligence, judicial instruments, or counter-radicalization. In cases like this one, the use of 'local' resources for training workshops acts to subvert the pretences of north–south pedagogy, and facilitates the exercise of local agency which reflects the dynamism of the social relations in security assemblages. Sometimes, local agency manifests as explicit resistance, which appears in forms of refusal and foot-dragging – failures to uphold one side of a bargain of sorts – as evidenced by Senegal's refusal to even participate in negotiating a 'mobility partnership' with the EU in which it felt there was more to lose than to gain. Beyond local resistance, there is local initiative, and this is another major brake on any decision to call this a neo-colonial or entirely dominating form of security relationship. For example, security cooperation takes place south-south (see Chapter 4) and the adoption of biometrics in West African states is very much a function of initiatives on the part of states themselves.

Finally, some of the idiosyncrasies of my research process suggest that the reality is too disorganized and disaggregated to be 'neo-colonial'. The image of the world I engaged with given here was heavily dependent on my own research trajectory, and by definition has exposed the impossibility of calling this a bird's eye view style topography of actors (indeed, the mapping midway through Chapter 2 rested on no such pretense). Even if relations in West Africa's borderwork assemblages *were* neo-colonial, I did not have a totalizing view of the world of practice I sought to enter and neither did most of the actors I spoke to. If there are any imperial effects of statebuilding, they are certainly not the result of a clearly formulated plan. Instead, there are moments of domination that tilt the balance towards a general power imbalance. In other ways, intervention is such a light touch that there are often only one or two representatives of a given organization 'on the ground' to speak to. This closes one door by making the work of triangulating interview accounts difficult, but opens another by highlighting how little investment and attention projects sometimes get.

Further Research Avenues

This book has undertaken theory development and empirical exposition, and in doing so provided the tools for framing new research on borders and security. One of its major contributions has been

developing the view of African borders as institutional spaces of political struggle featuring both global and local actors. This opens up
avenues for research on the organizational and bureaucratic politics
of border security policies. Another contribution in this book has been
a theorization of the mobility of security knowledges with particular
attention to the role of statebuilding logics.

The focus on multi-level governance in this book, and more specifically the assemblage approach to mapping actors and their roles,
has opened up avenues for research on the interplay of international
organizations in the governance of global mobilities. For instance,
the vast majority of border management work remains project-based,
and increasingly brings together a diverse range of international agencies. These agencies in turn bring different framings of expertise and
local knowledge, against which it would be productive to ask how
the global/local split is performed and whether it crosscuts agencies
or individuals. This could be coupled with a deeper examination of
the personal and career trajectories of individuals working in international organizations such as the IOM, ICAO, or UNODC. In the
African context more specifically, there are often few staff assigned to
particular projects, thus making their previous experience and ability to foster local relationships crucial to the tone and success of the
projects they run. This, in turn, might depend on research shining light
on the recruitment practices of organizations such as the ICMPD and
provide a deeper genealogy of the cultures of border control we see in
African border management.

This book's emphasis on the role of information and communication technologies (ICT), afforded by a perspective attuned to 'actants',
opens the door for a more sustained examination of the role of ICTs in
the policies and practices of security officials in West Africa. For example, the West Africa Police Information System (WAPIS) information-
sharing platform has been piloted by the EuropeAid, Interpol, and
ECOWAS in Mauritania, Mali, Niger, Benin, and Ghana. This system
will allow countries in the region to share and analyse criminal information regionally and connect to global databases. Further research
into this system can tell us more about state strategies that emerge in
the pursuit of informational control, but also raise the question of what
the bureaucratic reactions to it have been and might be. As with any
change in the nature of police work, it is likely to be met in similar
ways as biometrics were shown to be in Chapter 6: an enthusiasm for

technological solutions which do not capture the vast unregistered or informal policing interactions. The focus on the normative elements of border-making in this book has also opened up the possibility to ask questions pertaining to the origins of such systems. In the case of WAPIS, it would be fruitful to interrogate commonalities with the EU's Schengen Information System, particularly in light of regional moves in West Africa for a common biometric visa and ID card similar to those in the European integration project. The similarities to the European experience allow us to ask questions about how and why implementations differ, and what it tells us about the international relations of African security agencies.

Finally, this book has opened up lines of inquiry pertinent to an analysis of military relationships in Africa. Much of the work discussed in this project has related to 'policebuilding' (see Cerny 2015) practices, largely leaving out consideration of the emerging international positionings taken on by African military forces. The French role in military-building in West Africa is long-standing, but the consequences of American involvement (through annual regional military exercises and a growing counter-terrorism role) and Spanish training practices (in Niger and Mali) have not been explored in depth. While it is likely that the knowledge politics in these cases might mirror some of what this book found, the different technologies (e.g. drones) and policy structures are likely to lead to outcomes that reveal new insights about the internationalization of security practice in West Africa. This would build productively on some existing cutting edge work on the internal politics of African armies (see Dwyer 2017).

This book has contributed to our understanding of how borders work, and the social and technical relationships that drive them. Coming from an interest in African politics and security, this book has provided a view into the assemblages of security that animate the functioning of borders in Senegal and Mauritania, with particular emphasis on police cooperation practices, the construction of border infrastructure, and the use of digital registration practices. Bringing each of these under the rubric of 'borderwork', this book highlighted the mobility of knowledge about border security as a determining factor in how it unfolds in everyday practice. The stakes of this research have also been critical and explicitly interested in the politics of borderwork, using this concept to highlight actors from outside the world of security practice who nonetheless reframe or challenge security-cantered framings of borders and citizenship. Mapping the epistemic and material topology of actors, practices, and knowledges helps to expose the limits of our ontology of borders, and propose new creative understandings of them, and even their dissolution. This book has demonstrated at once the shoring up of sovereignty at borders, through which terms like 'border management' foreclose possibilities, but also the ways actors of various kinds reframe or challenge border security and open up new ones.

References

Abrahamsen, R. and Williams, M. C. 2011. *Security beyond the State: Private Security in International Politics*. Cambridge: Cambridge University Press.

—— 2016. Tracing Global Assemblages: Bringing Bourdieu to the Field. In: S. Curtis and M. Acuto eds. *Reassembling International Theory: Assemblage Thinking and International Relations*. New York: Palgrave Macmillan, 25–31.

Adey P. 2002. Secured and Sorted Mobilities: Examples from the Airport. *Surveillance and Society* 1(4): 500–519.

Adler, E. and Pouliot, V. 2011. International Practices: Introduction and Framework. In: E. Adler and V. Pouliot eds. *International Practices*. Cambridge: Cambridge University Press, 3–35.

Africa-EU Ministers. 2006. Joint Africa-EU Declaration on Migration and Development. Available at: www.iom.int/jahia/webdav/shared/shared/mainsite/microsites/rcps/igad/african_md_declaration_2006.pdf (Accessed 20 March 2014).

African Union. 2014. Déclaration de Nouakchott du 1er sommet des pays participant au processus de Nouakchott sur le renforcement de la coopération sécuritaire et l'opérationnalisation de l'Architecture Africaine de Paix et de Sécurité dans la région Sahélo-Saharienne. Available at: www.peaceau.org/fr/article/declaration-de-nouakchott-du-1er-sommet-des-pays-participant-au-processus-de-nouakchott-sur-le-renforcement-de-la-cooperation-securitaire-et-l-operationnalisation-de-l-architecture-africaine-de-paix-et-de-securite-dans-la-region-sahelo-saharienne (Accessed 13 November 2016).

Agamben, G. 1998. *Homo Sacer: Sovereign Power and Bare Life*. Stanford, CA: Stanford University Press.

Agnew, J. 1994. The Territorial Trap: The Geographical Assumptions of International Relations Theory. *Review of International Political Economy* 1(1): 53–80.

Ajana, B. 2012. Biometric citizenship. *Citizenship Studies* 16(7): 851–870.

—— 2013. *Governing through Biometrics: The Biopolitics of Identity*. Basingstoke: Palgrave.

AllAfrica. 2013. Sénégal: Un appui en véhicules de la Snedai aux postes frontaliers. 28 March. Available at: http://fr.allafrica.com/stories/201303281533.html (Accessed 28 January 2015).

AMDH. 2012. L'enrôlement. 30 December. Available at: www.facebook.com/notes/amdh-mauritanie/lenr%C3%B4lement/10151254846213283 (Accessed 20 March 2015).

Amoore, L. 2006. Biometric Borders: Governing Mobilities in the War on Terror. *Political Geography* 25: 336–351.

Amoore, L. and De Goede, M. 2008. *Risk and the War on Terror*. London: Routledge.

Andersson, R. 2014a. Hunter and Prey: Patrolling Clandestine Migration in the Euro-African Borderlands. *Anthropological Quarterly* 87(1): 119–149.

2014b. *Illegality, Inc: Clandestine Migration and the Business of Bordering Europe*. Oakland: University of California Press.

Andrijasevic, R. and Walters, W. 2010. The International Organization for Migration and the International Government of Borders. *Environment and Planning D* 28(6): 977–999.

Antil, A. and Touati, S. 2011. Mali et Mauritanie: Pays Sahéliens Fragiles et États Résilients. *Politique Étrangère* 1: 59–69.

Apap, J. and Carrera, S. 2004. Maintaining Security within Borders: Toward a Permanent State of Emergency in the EU? *Alternatives* 29(4): 399–416.

Aradau, C. 2010. Security That Matters: Critical Infrastructure and Objects of Protection. *Security Dialogue* 41(5): 491–514.

Aradau, C. and Van Munster, R. 2007. Governing Terrorism through Risk: Taking Precautions, (Un)knowing the Future. *European Journal of International Relations* 13(1): 89–115.

Arteaga, F. 2007. *Las operaciones de última generación: el Centro de Coordinación Regional de Canarias*. ARI No 54/2007. Madrid: Real Instituto Elcano.

Asiwaju, A. and Adeniyi, P. O. 1989. *Borderlands in Africa: A Multidisciplinary and Comparative Focus on Nigeria and West Africa*. Lagos: University of Lagos Press.

Autesserre, S. 2014. *Peaceland: Conflict Resolution and the Everyday Politics of International Intervention*. Cambridge: Cambridge University Press.

Bachmann, J. and Hönke, J. 2009. 'Peace and Security' as Counterterrorism? The Political Effects of Liberal Interventions in Kenya. *African Affairs* 109(434): 97–114.

Bain, W. 2011. Protectorates New and Old: A Conceptual Critique. In: J. Mayall and R. Soares de Oliveira eds. *The New Protectorates: International Tutelage and the Making of Liberal States*. New York: Columbia University Press, 31–48.

Balibar, É. 1998. The Borders of Europe. In: P. Cheah and B. Robbins eds. *Cosmopolitics: Thinking and Feeling beyond the Nation.* Minneapolis: University of Minnesota Press, 216–233.

    2002. *Politics and the Other Scene.* London: Verso.

Balzacq, T. 2005. The Three Faces of Securitization: Agency, Audience and Context. *European Journal of International Relations* 11(2): 171–201.

    2008. The Policy Tools of Securitization: Information Exchange, EU Foreign and Interior Policies. *Journal of Common Market Studies* 46(1): 75–100.

Bayart, J.-F. 1989. *L'état en Afrique: la politique du ventre.* Paris: Fayard.

    2000. Africa in the World: A History of Extraversion. *African Affairs* 99(395): 217–267.

Belcher, O. and Martin, L. L. 2013. Ethnographies of Closed Doors: Conceptualising Openness and Closure in US Immigration and Military Institutions: Ethnographies of Closed Doors. *Area* 45(4): 403–410.

Bennett, J. 2010. *Vibrant Matter: A Political Ecology of Things.* Durham, NC: Duke University Press.

Bialasiewicz, L. 2012. Off-shoring and Out-sourcing the Borders of EUrope: Libya and EU Border Work in the Mediterranean. *Geopolitics* 17(4): 843–866.

Bigo, D. 1996. *Polices en réseaux.* Paris: Presses de Sciences Po.

    2001. Internal and External Security(ies): The Möbius Ribbon. In: M. Jacobsen, D. Albert, and Y. Lapid, eds. *Identities, Borders, Orders.* Minneapolis: University of Minnesota Press, 91–116.

    2009. Security: A Field Left Fallow. In: M. Dillon and A. W. Neal, eds. *Foucault on Politics, Security and War.* Basingstoke: Palgrave Macmillan, 93–114.

    2012. Security. In: R. Adler-Nissen, ed. *Bourdieu in International Relations.* London: Routledge, 114–130.

Bigo, D., Guild, E. and Walker, R. B. J. 2010. The Changing Landscape of European Liberty and Security. In: D. Bigo, S. Carrera, E. Guild, and R. B. J. Walker, eds. *Europe's 21st Century Challenge: Delivering Liberty.* Farnham: Ashgate, 1–30.

Bigo, D. and Tsoukala, A. 2008. *Terror, Insecurity, and Liberty: Illiberal Practices of Liberal Regimes after 9/11.* London: Routledge.

Bigo, D. and Walker, R. B. J. 2007. International, Political, Sociology. *International Political Sociology* 1(1): 1–5.

Bloomberg News. 2011. Mauritania Court Deports 7 after Anti-Census Protest, Group Says. 11 October. Available at: www.bloomberg.com/news/articles/2011-10-11/mauritania-court-deports-7-after-anti-census-protest-group-says (Accessed 28 January 2015).

Bonditti, P. 2004. From Territorial Space to Networks: A Foucauldian Approach to the Implementation of Biometry. *Alternatives* 29: 465–482.

Bonelli, L. and Ragazzi, F. 2014. Low-Tech Security: Files, Notes, and Memos as Technologies of Anticipation. *Security Dialogue* 45(5): 476–493.

Booth, K. 2007. *Theory of World Security*. Cambridge: Cambridge University Press.

Boswell, C. 2003. The 'External Dimension' of EU Immigration and Asylum Policy. *International Affairs* 79(3): 619–638.

Bourbeau, P. 2011. *The Securitization of Migration: A Study of Movement and Order*. Abingdon: Routledge.

Bourdieu, P. 1977. *Outline of a Theory of Practice*. Cambridge: Cambridge University Press.

    1994. Rethinking the State: Genesis and Structure of the Bureaucratic Field. Trans. L. Wacquant and S. Farage. *Sociological Theory* 12(1): 1–18.

Bourdieu, P. and Wacquant, L. 1992. *An Invitation to Reflexive Sociology*. Cambridge: Polity.

Brachet, J., Choplin, A. and Pliez, O. 2011. Le Sahara entre espace de circulation et frontière migratoire de l'Europe. *Hérodote* 142: 163–182.

Breckenridge, K. 2014. *Biometric State: The Global Politics of Identification and Surveillance in South Africa: 1850 to the Present*. Cambridge: Cambridge University Press.

Broeders, D. 2007. The New Digital Borders of Europe: EU Databases and the Surveillance of Irregular Migrants. *International Sociology* 22(1): 71–92.

    2011. A European 'Border' surveillance system under construction. In: H. Dijstelbloem & A. Meijer eds. *Migration and the New Technological Borders of Europe*. Houndsmills: Palgrave, 40–67.

Buur, L., Jensen, S. and Stepputat, F., eds. 2007. *The Security-Development Nexus: Expressions of Sovereignty and Securitization in Southern Africa*. Uppsala: Nordiska Afrikainstitutet.

Buzan, B., Waever, O. and De Wilde, J. 1998. *Security: A New Framework for Analysis*. Boulder, CO: Lynne Rienner.

CAERT. 2016. About Us. African Centre for the Study & Research on Terrorism. Available at: http://caert.org.dz/About%20us.pdf (Accessed 13 November 2016).

Callon, M. 1986. Some Elements of a Sociology of Translation: Domestication of the Scallops and the Fishermen of St Brieuc Bay. In: J. Law, ed. *Power, Action and Belief: A New Sociology of Knowledge*. London: Routledge and Kegan Paul, 196–223.

Campbell, D. 1998. *Writing Security: United States Foreign Policy and the Politics of Identity*. Minneapolis: University of Minnesota Press.

Canada Newswire. 2011. Ten Years after 9/11, ICAO Meeting Considers New Options for Countering Terrorism and Trans-border Crime. 12 September. Available at: www.newswire.ca/en/story/839431/-for-terrorists-travel-documents-are-as-important-as-weapons (Accessed 20 March 2015).

Carling, J. and Hernández-Carretero, M. 2011. Protecting Europe and Protecting Migrants? Strategies for Managing Unauthorised Migration from Africa. *The British Journal of Politics and International Relations* 13(1): 42–58.

Carrera, S. 2007. *The EU Border Management Strategy: FRONTEX and the Challenges of Irregular Immigration in the Canary Islands.* Working Document No. 261/March 2007. Brussels: Centre for European Policy Studies.

CASE Collective. 2006. Critical Approaches to Security in Europe: A Networked Manifesto. *Security Dialogue* 37(4): 443–487.

Cassarino, J.-P. 2005. Migration and Border Management in the Euro-Mediterranean Area: Heading towards New Forms of Interconnectedness. CADMUS: European University Institute Mediterranean Yearbook 2005, 226–231.

Cerny, P. G. 2015. From Warriors to Police? The Civilianisation of Security in a Globalising World. *International Politics* 52(4): 389–407.

Chalfin, B. 2010. *Neoliberal Frontiers: An Ethnography of Sovereignty in West Africa.* Chicago: University of Chicago Press.

Choplin, A. 2008. L'immigré, le migrant, l'allochtone: circulations migratoires et figures de l'étranger en Mauritanie. *Politique africaine* 109: 73–90.

Choplin, A. and Lombard, J. 2010. 'Suivre la route': Mobilités et échanges entre Mali, Mauritanie et Sénégal. EchoGéo 14. Available at: http://echogeo.revues.org/12127?lang=fr (Accessed 20 March 2015).

Cole, S. A. 2002. *Suspect Identities: A History of Fingerprinting and Criminal Identification.* Cambridge, MA: Harvard University Press.

Collyer, M. 2008. Euro-African Relations in the Field of Migration, 2008. CADMUS: European University Institute Mediterranean Yearbook 2009, 281–285.

Coole, D. and Frost, S. 2010. *New Materialisms: Ontology, Agency, and Politics.* Durham, NC: Duke University Press.

Coplan, D. 2010. Introduction: From Empiricism to Theory in African Border Studies. *Journal of Borderlands Studies* 25(2): 1–5.

Cox, R. 1983. Gramsci, Hegemony and International Relations: An Essay in Method. *Millennium* 12(2): 162–175.

Curzon, (Lord) G. 1908. *Frontiers* (Romanes Lecture 1907). Clarendon, Oxford University.

Datacard Group. 2012. Guinea Bissau Opts for Secure National ID Card to Combat Fraud. Available at: www.datacard.com/id/knowledge_center/knowledge_center_detail.jhtml?id=repositories/downloads/xml/GOV_CS_GuineaBissau.xml (Accessed 20 March 2015).

Dean, M. 1996. Putting the Technological into Government. *History of the Human Sciences* 9(3): 47–68.

Deflem, M. 2000. Bureaucratization and Social Control: Historical Foundations of International Police Cooperation. *Law and Society Review* 34(3): 739–778.

De Haas, H. 2008. The Myth of Invasion: The Inconvenient Realities of African Migration to Europe. *Third World Quarterly* 29(7): 1305–1322.

Dezalay, Y. and Garth, B. G. 2002. *The Internationalization of Palace Wars: Lawyers, Economists, and the Contest to Transform Latin American States*. Chicago: University of Chicago Press.

Doty, R. L. 2009. *The Law into Their Own Hands: Immigration and the Politics of Exceptionalism*. Tucson: University of Arizona Press.

Doucet, M. G. 2016. Global Assemblages of Security Governance and Contemporary International Intervention. *Journal of Intervention and Statebuilding* 10(1): 116–132.

Dwyer, M. 2017. *Soldiers in Revolt: Army Mutinies in Africa*. London: Hurst.

Epstein, C. 2007. Guilty Bodies, Productive Bodies, Destructive Bodies: Crossing the Biometric Borders. *International Political Sociology* 1(2): 149–164.

EuropeAid. 2013. *Thematic Global Evaluation of the European Union's Support to Integrated Border Management and Fight against Organised Crime*. Brussels: DEVCO Evaluation Unit.

European Commission. 2016a. Commission Announces New Migration Partnership Framework: Reinforced Cooperation with Third Countries to Better Manage Migration. European Commission Press Release Database. Available at: http://europa.eu/rapid/press-release_IP-16-2072_en.htm (Accessed 14 November 2016).

 2016b. COM/2016/700, First Progress Report on the Partnership Framework with Third Countries under the European Agenda on Migration. Available at: https://eeas.europa.eu/sites/eeas/files/com_2016_700_f1_communication_from_commission_to_inst_en_v8_p1_english.pdf (Accessed 14 November 2016).

European Delegation Nouakchott. 2011. Projet West Sahel: Inauguration des premières activités. Available at: http://eeas.europa.eu/delegations/mauritania/documents/press_corner/discours_west_sahel_amende_fr.pdf (Accessed 20 March 2015).

European External Action Service. 2012. Strategy for Security and Development in the Sahel. Brussels: European Union. Available at: www.eeas.europa.eu/africa/docs/sahel_strategy_en.pdf (Accessed 20 March 2015).

European Parliament. 2006. Regulation (EC) No 562/2006 of the European Parliament and of the Council of 15 March 2006 Establishing a Community Code on the Rules Governing the Movement of Persons across Borders (Schengen Borders Code). Brussels: European Union.

European Union. 2006. Schengen Borders Code. Available at: http://eur-lex.europa.eu/legal-content/EN/TXT/PDF/?uri=CELEX:32006R0562&from=EN (Accessed 27 February 2018).

Fédération Internationale des Droits de L'Homme. 2011. Mauritanie: Critiquer la gouvernance, un exercise risqué. Available at: www.fidh.org/IMG/pdf/rapport_mauritanie_vf.pdf (Accessed 28 January 2015).

Ferrer-Gallardo, X. 2008. The Spanish-Moroccan Border Complex: Processes of Geopolitical, Functional and Symbolic Rebordering. *Political Geography* 27(4): 301–321.

Fitz-Gerald, A. M. 2004. Addressing the Security-Development Nexus: Implications for Joined-up Government. *Policy Matters* 5(5): 1–24.

Foster, N. 2010. *Mauritania: The Struggle for Democracy*. Boulder, CO: Lynne Rienner.

Foucault, M. 1990. *The History of Sexuality, Vol. 1: An Introduction*. New York: Vintage.

France24. 2011. Le recensement, jugé 'raciste', déchire les Mauritaniens. Available at: http://observers.france24.com/fr/content/20110928-recensement-juge-raciste-dechire-mauritaniens-negro-africains-discrimination-nationalite (Accessed 20 March 2015).

Frontex. 2011. Programme of Work 2011. Available at: http://frontex.europa.eu/assets/About_Frontex/Governance_documents/Work_programme/2011/fx_pow_2011.pdf (Accessed 20 March 2015).

2013. Programme of Work 2013. Available at: http://frontex.europa.eu/assets/About_Frontex/Governance_documents/Work_programme/2013/PoW_2013.pdf (Accessed 20 March 2015).

2015. AFIC report. Available at: http://frontex.europa.eu/assets/Publications/Risk_Analysis/AFIC/AFIC_report_2015.pdf (Accessed 20 March 2015).

2016. Risk Analysis for 2016. Available at: http://frontex.europa.eu/assets/Publications/Risk_Analysis/Annula_Risk_Analysis_2016.pdf (Accessed 14 November 2016).

Gaibazzi, P., Bellagamba, A. and Dünnwald, S. 2017. *EurAfrican Borders and Migration Management: Political Cultures, Contested Spaces, and Ordinary Lives*. New York: Palgrave Macmillan.

Geiger, M. 2010. Mobility, Development, Protection, EU-Integration! The IOM's National Migration Strategy for Albania. In: M. Geiger and A. Pécoud, eds. *The Politics of International Migration Management*. Basingstoke: Palgrave, 141–159.

Gelb, A. and Clark, J. 2013. *Identification for Development: The Biometrics Revolution*. Working Paper 315. Washington, DC: Center for Global Development.

Gerspacher, N. and Dupont, B. 2007. The Nodal Structure of International Police Cooperation: An Exploration of Transnational Security Networks. *Global Governance* 13(3): 347–364.

Godenau, D. and López-Sala, A. 2016. Multi-layered Migration Deterrence and Technology in Spanish Maritime Border Management. *Journal of Borderlands Studies* 31(2): 1–19.

Guardia Civil. 2013. Spanish NCC: National Coordination Centre – 'Perspective from an European Union Country'. Available at: www .processusderabat.net/web/uploads/cms/2013Nov_EN_Spain-Vicente-Guardia-Civil.pdf (Accessed 20 March 2015).

2014. Nuevo proyecto de colaboración de la Guardia Civil con Mauritania para reducir la inmigración irregular. Available at: www.guardiacivil .es/es/prensa/noticias/4806.html (Accessed 4 June 2014).

Guittet, E.-P. and Jeandesboz, J. 2010. Security Technologies. In: J. P. Burgess, ed. *The Routledge Handbook of New Security Studies*. London: Routledge, 229–239.

Haggerty, K. D. and Ericson, R. 2000. The Surveillant Assemblage. *British Journal of Sociology* 51(4): 605–622.

Hall, B. S. 2011. *A History of Race in Muslim West Africa: 1600–1960*. Cambridge: Cambridge University Press.

Hameiri, S. 2010. *Regulating Statehood: State Building and the Transformation of the Global Order*. Basingstoke: Palgrave.

Hameiri, S. and Jones, L. 2013. The Politics and Governance of Non-traditional Security. *International Studies Quarterly* 57(3): 462–473.

2015. *Governing Borderless Threats: Non-traditional Security and the Politics of State Transformation*. Cambridge: Cambridge University Press.

Hansen, L. 2000. The Little Mermaid's Silent Security Dilemma and the Absence of Gender in the Copenhagen School. *Millennium* 29(2): 285–306.

2006. *Security as Practice: Discourse Analysis and the Bosnian War*. Abingdon: Routledge.

Harrison, G. 2001. Post-conditionality Politics and Administrative Reform: Reflections on the Cases of Uganda and Tanzania. *Development and Change* 32(4): 657–679.

Help Net Security. 2011. Interpol Chief Calls for Global Electronic Identity Card System. 6 April. Available at: www.net-security.org/secworld .php?id=10860 (Accessed 20 March 2015).

Herbst, J. 1989. The Creation and Maintenance of National Boundaries in Africa. *International Organization* 43(4): 673–692.

2000. *States and Power in Africa: Comparatives Lessons in Authority and Control*. Princeton, NJ: Princeton University Press.

Hernández i Sagrera, R. 2013. Exporting EU Integrated Border Management beyond EU Borders: Modernization and Institutional Transformation in Exchange for More Mobility? *Cambridge Review of International Affairs* 27(1): 167–183.

Hollstegge, J. and Doevenspeck, M. 2017. 'Sovereignty Entrepreneurs' and the Production of State Power in Two Central African Borderlands. *Geopolitics* 22(4): 815–836.

Hosein, I. 2004. The Sources of Laws: Policy Dynamics in a Digital and Terrorized World. *The Information Society* 20(3): 187–199.

Hüsken, T. and Klute, G. 2010. Emerging Forms of Power in Two African Borderlands a Theoretical and Empirical Research Outline. *Journal of Borderlands Studies* 25(2): 107–121.

Huysmans, J. 2007. *The Politics of Insecurity: Fear, Migration and Asylum in the EU*. Abingdon: Routledge.

ICAO. 2006. *MRTD Report*. Vol. 1, Issue 1. Montreal: International Civil Aviation Organization.

2007. *MRTD Report*. Vol. 2, Issue 1. Montreal: International Civil Aviation Organization.

2010. Benefits to Governments. Available at: www.icao.int/Security/mrtd/ Pages/BenefitstoGovernments.aspx (Accessed 28 January 2015).

2011. ICAO Regional Aviation Security Conference in Dakar, Senegal, 17–18 October 2011. Available at: www.icao.int/Security/Pages/ RegionalAviationSecurityConferenceDakar.aspx (Accessed 25 April 2016).

2013. Resolutions Adopted by the Assembly: 38th Session, Montréal 24 September–8 October 2013. Available at: www.icao.int/Meetings/ a38/Documents/Resolutions/a38_res_prov_en.pdf (Accessed 28 January 2015).

2014. *MRTD Report*. Vol. 2, Issue 2. Montreal: International Civil Aviation Organization.

2015a. *MRTD Report*. Vol. 10, Issue 3. Montreal: International Civil Aviation Organization.

2015b. ICAO Public Key Directory (PKD). Available from: www.icao.int/ security/mrtd/pages/ICAOPKD.aspx (Accessed 2 March 2015).

Interpol. 2016. Border Management: Stolen and Lost Travel Documents Database. Available at: www.interpol.int/INTERPOL-expertise/Border-management/SLTD-Database(Accessed 14 November 2016).

IOM. 2010. Summary of Activities: African Capacity Building Center. Available at: http://acbc.iom.int/documents/pdfs/ACBC_annual_report_2010_FINAL.pdf (Accessed 20 March 2015).

———. 2011. PIRS, the International Organization for Migration's Personal Identification and Registration System. Available at: www.iom.int/jahia/webdav/shared/shared/mainsite/activities/ibm/09-IOM-IBM-FACT-SHEET-Personal-Identification-and-Registration-System-PIRS.pdf (Accessed 20 March 2015).

———. 2012. Workshop on the Threats and Risks of Integrated Border Management. Available at: www.iom.int/cms/en/sites/iom/home/news-and-views/events/events-listing/workshop-on-the-threats-and-risk.html (Accessed 20 March 2015).

———. 2013. IOM Tanzania Facilitates Identity Management Workshop. 26 February. Available at: www.iom.int/cms/en/sites/iom/home/news-and-views/press-briefing-notes/pbn-2013/pbn-listing/iom-tanzania-facilitates-identit.html (Accessed 20 March 2015).

Islamic Republic of Mauritania. 2011. *Document de stratégie nationale pour une meilleure gestion de la migration en République Islamique de Mauritanie* [National Strategy Document for Better Management of Migration in the Islamic Republic of Mauritania]. Nouakchott: Government of Mauritania.

Jackson, R. H. 1993. *Quasi-States: Sovereignty, International Relations and the Third World*. Cambridge: Cambridge University Press.

Jackson, R. H. and Rosberg, C. G. 1982. Why Africa's Weak States Persist: The Empirical and Juridical in Statehood. *World Politics* 35(1): 1–24.

Jacobsen, E. K. U. 2012. Unique Identification: Inclusion and Surveillance in the Indian Biometric Assemblage. *Security Dialogue* 43(5): 457–474.

Jeandesboz, Julien. 2016. Smartening Border Security in the European Union: An Associational Inquiry. *Security Dialogue*, 0967010616650226.

Jeune Afrique. 2015. Sénégal: La Filière Touristique Salue la Suppression du Visa d'entrée Annoncée Par Macky Sall. 7 April. Available at: www.jeuneafrique.com/228428/economie/senegal-la-filiere-touristique-salue-la-suppression-du-visa-dentree-annoncee-par-macky-sall/ (Accessed 14 November 2016).

Johnson, H. L. 2013. The Other Side of the Fence: Reconceptualizing the 'Camp' and Migration Zones at the Borders of Spain. *International Political Sociology* 7(1): 75–91.

Jourde, C. 2007. Constructing Representations of the 'Global War on Terror' in the Islamic Republic of Mauritania. *Journal of Contemporary African Studies* 25(1): 77–100.

Kaldor, M. and Selchow, S. 2015. From Military to 'Security Interventions': An Alternative Approach to Contemporary Interventions. *Stability: International Journal of Security & Development* 4(1).

Kendall, G. 2004. Global Networks, International Networks, Actor Networks. In: W. Larner and W. Walters, eds. *Global Governmentality: Governing International Spaces*. London: Routledge, 59–75.

Khadiagala, G. M. 2010. Boundaries in Eastern Africa. *Journal of Eastern African Studies* 4(2): 266–278.

Klüfers, P. 2014. Security Repertoires: Towards a Sociopragmatist Framing of Securitization Processes. *Critical Studies on Security* 2(3): 278–292.

Koch, N. 2013. Introduction – Field Methods in 'Closed Contexts': Undertaking Research in Authoritarian States and Places. *Area* 45(4): 390–395.

Kopytoff, I. 1987. *The African Frontier: The Reproduction of Traditional African Societies*. Indianapolis: Indiana University Press.

Kornprobst, M. 2002. The Management of Border Disputes in African Regional Sub-systems: Comparing West Africa and the Horn of Africa. *Journal of Modern African Studies* 40(3): 369–393.

Krause, K. and Williams, M. C. 1997. Preface: Toward Critical Security Studies. In: K. Krause and M. C. Williams, eds. *Critical Security Studies: Concepts and Cases*. Minneapolis: University of Minnesota Press, vii–xxi.

Krogstad, E. G. 2012. Security, Development, and Force: Revisiting Police Reform in Sierra Leone. *African Affairs* 111(443): 261–280.

Kunz, R., Lavenex, S. and Panizzon, M., eds. 2011. *Multilayered Migration Governance*. Abingdon: Routledge.

Latour, B. 1992. Where Are the Missing Masses? The Sociology of a Few Mundane Artifacts. In: W. Bijker and J. Law, eds. *Shaping Technology/Building Society: Studies in Sociotechnical Change*. Cambridge, MA: MIT Press, 225–259.

1999. *Pandora's Hope: Essays on the Reality of Science Studies*. Cambridge, MA: Harvard University Press.

2004. Why Has Critique Run Out of Steam? *Critical Inquiry* 30: 225–248.

2005. *Reassembling the Social: An Introduction to Actor-Network-Theory*. Oxford: Oxford University Press.

Law, J. 1986. On the Methods of Long Distance Control: Vessels, Navigation, and the Portuguese Route to India. In: J. Law, ed. *Power, Action and Belief: A New Sociology of Knowledge?* Sociological Review Monograph 32. Henley, UK: Routledge, 234–263.

1992. Notes on the Theory of the Actor Network: Ordering, Strategy and Heterogeneity. *Systems Practice* 5: 379–393.

1999. Traduction/Trahison: Notes on ANT. Centre for Science Studies, Lancaster University. Available at: www.lancaster.ac.uk/sociology/research/publications/papers/law-traduction-trahison.pdf (Accessed 20 March 2015).

2003. Materialities, Spatialities, Globalities. Centre for Science Studies, Lancaster University. Available at: www.lancaster.ac.uk/sociology/research/publications/papers/law-hetherington-materialities-spatialities-globalities.pdf (Accessed 20 March 2015).

2004. *After Method: Mess in Social Science Research.* Abingdon: Routledge.

2007. Actor Network Theory and Material Semiotics (version of 25 April 2007). John Law's STS Web Page. Available at: www.heterogeneities.net/publications/Law2007ANTandMaterialSemiotics.pdf (Accessed 20 March 2015).

Leese, M. 2016. Governing Airport Security between the Market and the Public Good. *Criminology and Criminal Justice* 16(2): 158–175.

Leonard, D. K. 2010. 'Pockets' of effective agencies in weak governance states: Where are they likely and why does it matter? *Public Administration and Development* 30(2): 91–101.

Léonard, S. 2010. EU Border Security and Migration into the European Union: Frontex and Securitisation through Practices. *European Security* 19(2): 231–254.

Lutterbeck, D. 2004. Between Police and Military: The New Security Agenda and the Rise of Gendarmeries. *Cooperation and Conflict* 39(1): 45–68.

Lyon, D. 2009. *Identifying Citizens: ID Cards as Surveillance.* Oxford: Polity.

Magharebia. 2011. Census Riots Hit Southern Mauritania. 3 October. Available at: http://magharebia.com/en_GB/articles/awi/features/2011/10/03/feature-02 (Accessed 28 January 2015).

Magnet, S. A. 2011. *When Biometrics Fail: Gender, Race, and the Technology of Identity.* Durham, NC: Duke University Press.

Maldonado-Torres, N. 2007. On the Coloniality of Being: Contributions to the Development of a Concept. *Cultural Studies* 21(2): 240–270.

Mann, M. 1984. The autonomous power of the state: its origins, mechanisms and results. *European Journal of Sociology* 25(2): 185–213.

Marcus, G. E. 1995. Ethnography in/of the World System: The Emergence of Multi-sited Ethnography. *Annual Review of Anthropology* 24: 95–117.

Martin, A. K., Van Brakel, R. E. and Bernhard, D. J. 2010. Understanding Resistance to Digital Surveillance: Towards a Multi-disciplinary, Multi-actor Framework. *Surveillance and Society* 6(3): 214–232.

Mbembe, J.-A. and Rendall, S. 2000. At the Edge of the World: Boundaries, Territoriality, and Sovereignty in Africa. *Public Culture* 12(1): 259–284.

Ministère de l'Intérieur. 2010. *Contribution au Processus de Révision du CSLP et l'Élaboration de son Plan d'Actions 2011–2015*. Nouakchott: Islamic Republic of Mauritania.

——— 2011. *Arrêté n°937/MIDEC portant création, organisation et fonctionnement des instances départementales d'enrôlement*. Nouakchott: Islamic Republic of Mauritania.

Ministère des Affaires Étrangères et de la Coopération. 2012. *La Mauritanie face au défi terroriste: De la Stratégie Nationale de Lutte contre le Terrorisme et la Criminalité Transnationale*. Nouakchott: Islamic Republic of Mauritania.

Morpho. 2010. Mauritania: A Single Integrated System. Available at: www.morpho.com/references/identite-125/mauritania-a-single-integrated-system (Accessed 20 March 2015).

Muller, B. J. 2010. *Security, Risk and the Biometric State: Governing Borders and Bodies*. Abingdon: Routledge.

Mutlu, C. E. 2013. The Material Turn: Introduction. In: M. B. Salter and C. E. Mutlu, eds. *Research Methods in Critical Security Studies: An Introduction*. Abingdon: Routledge, 173–179.

Neal, A. 2009. Securitization and Risk at the EU Border: The Origins of Frontex. *Journal of Common Market Studies* 47(2): 333–356.

Nugent, P. and Asiwaju, A. 1996. *African Boundaries: Barriers, Conduits and Opportunities*. London: Pinter.

Nyers, P. 2012. The Politics of Dirt. *Radical Philosophy* 174 (July/August).

Paasi, A. 1998. Boundaries as Social Processes: Territoriality in the World of Flows. *Geopolitics* 3(1): 69–88.

Pallister-Wilkins, P. 2015. The Humanitarian Politics of European Border Policing: Frontex and Border Police in Evros. *International Political Sociology* 9(1): 53–69.

Paris, R. 2004. *At War's End: Building Peace after Civil Conflict*. Cambridge: Cambridge University Press.

Parker, N., Vaughan-Williams, N., et al. 2009. Lines in the Sand? Towards an Agenda for Critical Border Studies. *Geopolitics* 14(3): 582–587.

Phillips, J. 2006. Agencement/Assemblage. *Theory, Culture, and Society* 23(2–3): 108–109.

Porter, T. 2012. Making Serious Measures: Numerical Indices, Peer Review, and Transnational Actor-networks. *Journal of International Relations and Development* 15(4): 532–557.

Poutignat, P. and Streiff-Fénart, J. 2010. Migration Policy Development in Mauritania: Process, Issues and Actors. In: M. Geiger and A. Pécoud, eds. *The Politics of International Migration Management*. Basingstoke: Palgrave, 202–219.

Prescott, J. R. V. 1965. *The Geography of Frontiers and Boundaries*. Chicago: Aldine.

Prince, R. 2012. Policy Transfer, Consultants and the Geographies of Governance. *Progress in Human Geography* 36(2): 188–203.

Prokkola, E. 2013. Technologies of Border Management: Performances and Calculation of Finnish/Schengen Border Security. *Geopolitics* 18(1): 77–94.

Pugliese, J. 2010. *Biometrics: Bodies, Technologies, Biopolitics*. Oxford: Routledge.

Raeymaekers, T. 2012. Reshaping the State in Its Margins: The State, the Market and the Subaltern on a Central African Frontier. *Critique of Anthropology* 32(3): 334–350.

Reeves, M. 2014. *Border Work: Spatial Lives of the State in Central Asia*. Ithaca, NY: Cornell University Press.

Reid-Henry, S. M. 2012. An Incorporating Geopolitics: Frontex and the Geopolitical Rationalities of the European Border. *Geopolitics* 18(1): 198–224.

RFI. 2017a. Paris et Dakar signent de nouvelles conventions de cooperation. 19 October. Available at: www.rfi.fr/afrique/20171019-paris-dakar-signent-nouvelles-conventions-cooperation?ref=tw_i (Accessed 8 November 2017).

2017b. Sénégal: inquiétude après plusieurs arrestations au poste frontière de Rosso. 23 October. Available at: www.rfi.fr/afrique/20171023-senegal-terrorisme-rumeurs-presse-jihadiste-turquie-mauritanie-mali-algerie-etat-is?ref=tw (Accessed 8 November 2017).

Richey, M. 2013. The North African Revolutions: A Chance to Rethink European Externalization of the Handling of Non-EU Migrant Inflows. *Foreign Policy Analysis* 9(4): 409–431.

Robin, N. 2009. La CEDEAO, un espace de libre circulation, poste frontière avancé de l'espace Schengen. In: M. Trémolières, ed. *Les enjeux régionaux des migrations ouest-africaines: perspectives africaines et européennes*. Paris: OECD, 149–165.

Roll, M. 2014. The State That Works: A 'Pockets of Effectiveness' Perspective on Nigeria and Beyond. In: T. Bierschenk and J.-P. Olivier de Sardan, eds. *States at Work: Dynamics of African Bureaucracies*. Leiden: Brill, 365–398.

Rumford, C. 2006. Theorizing Borders. *European Journal of Social Theory* 9(2): 155–169.

2008. Introduction: Citizens and Borderwork in Europe. *Space and Polity* 12(1): 1–12.

Salter, M. B. 2004. Passports, Mobility, and Security: How Smart Can the Border Be? *International Studies Perspectives* 5(1): 71–91.

2006. The Global Visa Regime and the Political Technologies of the International Self: Borders, Bodies, Biopolitics. *Alternatives* 31: 167–189.

2007. Governmentalities of an Airport: Heterotopia and Confession. *International Political Sociology* 1(1): 49–66.

2008a. Securitization and Desecuritization: A Dramaturgical Analysis of the Canadian Air Transport Security Authority. *Journal of International Relations and Development* 11(4): 321–349.

ed. 2008b. *Politics at the Airport*. Minneapolis: University of Minnesota Press.

2013. To Make Move and Let Stop: Mobility and the Assemblage of Circulation. *Mobilities* 8(1): 7–19.

Sandor, A. 2016. Tightly Packed: Disciplinary Power, the UNODC, and the Container Control Programme in Dakar. *African Studies Review* 59(2): 133–160.

Sassen, S. 2006. *Territory, Authority, Rights: From Medieval to Global Assemblages*. Princeton, NJ: Princeton University Press.

Scheel, S. 2013. Autonomy of Migration Despite Its Securitisation? Facing the Terms and Conditions of Biometric Rebordering. *Millennium* 41(3): 575–600.

Scheele, J. 2012. *Smugglers and Saints of the Sahara: Regional Connectivity in the Twentieth Century*. Cambridge: Cambridge University Press.

Schomerus, M. and De Vries, L. 2014. Improvising Border Security: 'A Situation of Security Pluralism' along South Sudan's Borders with the Democratic Republic of the Congo. *Security Dialogue* 45(3): 279–294.

Scott, J. S. 1998. *Seeing Like a State: How Certain Schemes to Improve the Human Condition Have Failed*. New Haven, CT: Yale University Press.

Seabilla. 2013. Main Menu. Available at: www.seabilla.eu/cms/ (Accessed 20 March 2015).

Securiport. 2014. The Fund for Philanthropy (TFFP) and Securiport LLC Formalize Strategic Partnership and Launch $75 Million (US) 'Campaign to Help Contain Ebola'. 19 November. Available at: www.securiport.com/fund-philanthropy-tffp-securiport-llc-formalize-strategic-partnership-launch-75-million-us-campaign-help-contain-ebola/ (Accessed 28 January 2015).

Security Dialogue. 2010. The Security-Development Nexus Revisited [special issue]. 41(1).

Seymour, L. J. M. 2013. Sovereignty, Territory and Authority: Boundary Maintenance in Contemporary Africa. *Critical African Studies* 5(1): 17–31.

Shamir, R. 2005. Without Borders? Notes on Globalization as a Mobility Regime. *Sociological Theory* 23(2): 197–217.

Shore, C. and Wright, S. 1997. *Anthropology of Policy: Perspectives on Governance and Power*. New York: Routledge.

Smirl, L. 2013. *Spaces of Aid: How Cars, Compounds and Hotels Shape Humanitarianism*. London: Zed.

Squire, V. 2011. *The Contested Politics of Mobility: Borderzones and Irregularity*. Abingdon: Routledge.

Swiss Federal Office for Migration. 2012. Integrated Border Management Strategy Switzerland. 14 October. Available at: www.bfm.admin.ch/content/bfm/en/home/themen/einreise/ibm.html (Accessed 20 March 2015).

Thomas, O. D. 2014. Foucaultian Dispositifs as Methodology: The Case of Anonymous Exclusions by Unique Identification in India. *International Political Sociology* 8(2): 164–181.

Tiedge, D. 2012. MRTD Assistance to States: Building on the Success of Aviation Security Technical Cooperation. Remarks at ICAO 8th Symposium and Exhibition on MRTDs, Biometrics, and Security Standards, Montreal, 10–12 October. Available at: www.icao.int/Meetings/mrtd-symposium-2012/Documents/10_pm_Tiedge.pdf (Accessed 20 March 2015).

Tilly, C. 1985. War-Making and State-Making as Organized Crime. In: P. Evans, D. Rueschmeyer, and T. Skocpol, eds. *Bringing the State Back In*. Cambridge: Cambridge University Press, 169–187.

Torpey, J. 2000. *The Invention of the Passport: Surveillance, Citizenship and the State*. Cambridge: Cambridge University Press.

Trauner, F. and Deimel, S. 2013. The Impact of EU Migration Policies on African Countries: The Case of Mali. *International Migration* 51(4): 20–32.

UNHCR. 2012. UNHCR Distributes Biometric ID Cards to Refugees in Senegal. 22 October. Available at: www.unhcr.org/508536389.html (Accessed 20 March 2015).

United Nations. 2013. United National Integrated Strategy for the Sahel. Available at: https://oses.unmissions.org/sites/default/files/united_nations_integrated_strategy_for_the_sahel_s-2013-354.pdf (Accessed 14 November 2016).

UNODC. 2010. *The Globalization of Crime: A Transnational Organized Crime Threat Assessment*. Vienna: United Nations Office on Drugs and

Crime. Available at: www.unodc.org/documents/data-and-analysis/tocta/TOCTA_Report_2010_low_res.pdf (Accessed 4 June 2014).

2013. *Transnational Organized Crime in West Africa: A Threat Assessment*. Vienna: United Nations Office on Drugs and Crime. Available at: www.unodc.org/documents/data-and-analysis/tocta/West_Africa_TOCTA_2013_EN.pdf (Accessed 20 March 2015).

US Embassy Dakar. 2011. L'Ambassade offre au Sénégal un système automatisé d'identification d'empreintes. *Panorama*, July–August.

Uvin, P. 2002. The Development/Peacebuilding Nexus: A Typology and History of Changing Paradigms. *Journal of Peacebuilding and Development* 1(1): 5–24.

Van der Ploeg, I. 1999. The illegal body: 'Eurodac' and the politics of biometric identification. *Ethics and Information Technology* 1(4): 295–302.

Van Houtum, H. 2010. Human Blacklisting: The Global Apartheid of the EU's External Border Regime. *Environment and Planning D* 28(6): 957–976.

Vaughan-Williams, N. 2009. *Border Politics*. Edinburgh: Edinburgh University Press.

Villumsen, T. 2012. Knowledges. In: R. Adler-Nissen, ed. *Bourdieu in International Relations*. London: Routledge, 59–77.

Vives, L. 2017. Unwanted Sea Migrants across the EU Border: The Canary Islands. *Political Geography* 61: 181–192.

Voelkner, N. 2011. Managing Pathogenic Circulation: Human Security and the Migrant Health Assemblage in Thailand. *Security Dialogue* 42(3): 239–259.

Waever, O. 1988. *Security, the Speech Act*. Unpublished manuscript.

1995. Securitization and Desecuritization. In: R. D. Lipschutz, ed. *On Security*. New York: Columbia University Press, 46–86.

Walker, R. B. J. 1993. *Inside/Outside: International Relations as Political Theory*. Cambridge: Cambridge University Press.

Walters, W. 2002. Mapping Schengenland: Denaturalizing the Border. *Environment and Planning D* 20(2): 561–580.

2008. Putting the Migration-Security Nexus in Its Place. In: L. Amoore and M. De Goede. eds. *Risk and the War on Terror*. New York: Routledge, 158–177.

Watkins, S. C., Swindler, A. and Biruk, C. 2009. Hearsay Ethnography: A Method for Learning about Responses to Health Interventions. In: B. A. Pescosolido et al., eds. *Handbook of the Sociology of Health, Illness, and Healing: A Blueprint for the 21st Century*. New York: Springer, 431–445.

Wedeen, L. 2009. *Political Ethnography: What Immersion Contributes to the Study of Power*. Chicago: University of Chicago Press.

Willems, R. 2007. 'Barcelona or the Hereafter': Senegalese struggling with perilous journeys and perilous livelihoods. *In Kolor: Journal on Moving Communities* 7(1): 23–47.

Williams, M. C. 2003. Words, Images, Enemies: Securitization and International Politics. *International Studies Quarterly* 47(4): 511–531.

World Bank. 2014. *Digital Identity Toolkit: A Guide for Stakeholders in Africa*. Washington, DC: World Bank Group.

Zaiotti, R. 2011. *Cultures of Border Control: Schengen and the Evolution of European Frontiers*. Chicago: University of Chicago Press.

Zampagni, F. 2016. Unpacking the Schengen Visa Regime: A Study on Bureaucrats and Discretion in an Italian Consulate. *Journal of Borderlands Studies* 31(2): 251–266.

Zartman, I. W. ed. 1995. *Collapsed States: The Disintegration and Restoration of Legitimate Authority*. Boulder, CO: Lynne Rienner.

Zetes. 2013. Zetes Produces Senegalese Biometric Visa and Delivers 66 Fixed Enrolment Stations. Available at: www.zetes.com/en/press-and-events/press-releases/2013/130523-peopleid-senegal (Accessed 28 January 2015).

Zielonka, J. 2001. How New Enlarged Borders Will Reshape the European Union. *Journal of Common Market Studies* 39(3): 507–536.

Zoellick, R. B. 2008. Fragile States: Securing Development. *Survival* 50(6): 67–84.

Index

For EU product safety concerns, contact us at Calle de José Abascal, 56–1°,
28003 Madrid, Spain or eugpsr@cambridge.org.

www.ingramcontent.com/pod-product-compliance
Ingram Content Group UK Ltd.
Pitfield, Milton Keynes, MK11 3LW, UK
UKHW020328140625
459647UK00018B/2061

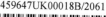